THE
DHAMMAPADA
FOR AWAKENING

THE
DHAMMAPADA
FOR AWAKENING

A commentary on Buddha's Practical Wisdom

SWAMI NIRMALANANDA GIRI
(ABBOT GEORGE BURKE)

LIGHT ᴼᶠ ᴛʜᴇ SPIRIT
PRESS

CEDAR CREST, NEW MEXICO

Published by
Light of the Spirit Press
LightoftheSpiritPress.com

Light of the Spirit Monastery
P. O. Box 1370
Cedar Crest, NM 87008

OCOY.org

ISBN 13: 978-1-7331643-3-7
Library of Congress Control Number: 2014908826

08012023

TABLE OF CONTENTS

PREFACE

History of the Dhammapada

The Dhammapada is not a transcription of a single talk by Gautama the Buddha. Rather, it is a collection of his words on the most important subjects for those seeking Nirvana. It was compiled only three months after his passing away by his enlightened disciples (arhats), who gave it the name Dhammapada, which means "Portions of the Dharma" or "The Way of Dharma." The Dhammapada consists of four hundred twenty-three Pali verses that were gleaned from about three hundred discourses of the Buddha. It is a distillation of forty-five years of teaching. The translation mostly used will be that of John Richards.

In this commentary you will encounter the word "Aryan" which Buddha used extensively in his teachings. Aryan literally means "one who strives upward." It is an exclusively psychological term having nothing whatsoever to do with birth, race, or nationality. In his teachings Buddha habitually referred to spiritually qualified people as "the Aryas." Although in English translations we find the expressions "The Four Noble Truths" and "The Noble Eightfold Path" Buddha actually said: "The Four Aryan Truths," and "The Eightfold Aryan Path." I have followed his example.

Also in this commentary there is a great deal of reference to the Bhagavad Gita. This is for two reasons: the Gita expresses the truths so well and expands on them, and I want to demonstrate that Buddha was a classical Sankhya Yogi whose philosophy was identical with that of the Gita.

The Dhammapada is traditionally divided into twenty-six sections, and so this commentary is divided accordingly.

Chapter 1

THE TWIN VERSES

What is the mind?

Mind precedes its objects. They are mind-governed and mind-made (Dhammpapada 1).

What is the mind? The language of Buddha as well as Pali, in which his complete teachings are set down, was based on Sanskrit, so we can get some understanding by looking at the Sanskrit terms from which the Pali was derived. Sanskrit and Pali have the same word for mind: *mana*. Mana comes from the root verb *man*, which means "to think." However, mind takes in more territory than the intellect; it includes the senses and the emotions, because it is in response to feelings and sensory impressions that thoughts arise to label and understand them.

Evolved minds have the capacity to think abstractly and to determine what shall be experienced by the senses or the feelings. In lesser evolved minds these impressions precede thought, but in higher evolved minds thought becomes dominant and not only often precedes those impressions but also determines them. Undoubtedly this is progress, but like everything in relative existence it has a down side, and that is the capacity of the mind to "create reality" rather than simply respond to it or classify it.

Perception is not a matter of exact and undistorted experience. Perception itself is learned, and is therefore extremely subjective. People born blind who later gained their sight have said that it took them weeks to tell the difference between circles, squares, triangles, and other geometric shapes, as well as the difference between many other kinds of visual impressions. This tells us that we do not just perceive spontaneously through the senses. We *learn* perception, it is not just a faculty. In other words, the senses do not perceive; it is the mind alone that perceives even though it uses the impressions of the senses as its raw material for those perceptions. Objectivity in human beings is virtually impossible. We might even hazard the speculation that objectivity is impossible outside of enlightenment.

The understanding to be gained from this is that our life experiences are a training film, an exercise in the development of consciousness with the mind as its main instrument. We are to look and learn. The question "Is it real?" is almost irrelevant, "Is it comprehensible?" being more vital. There is a sense in which the individual alone exists and all that he experiences is but the shifting patterns of the movies of the mind, but for a purpose: insight that leads to freedom from the need of any more movies. Then the liberated can rest in the truth of his own self.

The problem is that those who have only an intellectual idea about the relation of experience to reality will come to erroneous conclusions that may result in very self-destructive thought and behavior. Only right experience garnered from right meditation and right thought (which is based on meditation) can clear away the clouds of non-perception and misperception and free us. The demarcation between "out there" and "in here" must become clear to us in a practical sense, as must "me" and "not me." We must also come to understand that "real" and "unreal" have both correct and mistaken definitions, that all our perceptions are *interpretations* of the mind and never the objects themselves.

Our perceptions may be more or less correct as to the nature of an outside object, but how can we know? The enlightened of all ages have told us that a stage of evolution can be reached in which the mind is no longer necessary, a state in which we can go beyond the mind and enter into direct contact and communication with "out there" through a state of unity with "in here" and then perceive objects as they truly are, or at least as they momentarily are. The knowledge of temporality or eternality is inseparable from that state, so confusion cannot arise regarding them.

In our childish way we always think of perfection as consisting of all our good traits greatly increased and our bad traits eradicated. In the same way we think of eternity as time without end rather than a state that transcends time. Our ideas of eternal life are pathetic since we have no idea what life is, much less eternity. It only follows, then, that our ideas about enlightenment and liberation are equally puerile and valueless. This is why the wise center their attention on spiritual practice rather than theology and philosophy. Experience, Right Experience, will make all things clear or else enable us to see that they do not exist.

At the moment we can say that we do not know just what the mind is, but we are working on knowing it. So let us again set forth the opening words of the Dhammapada.

Mind, the source

Mind precedes its objects. They are mind-governed and mind-made. First there is the mind. It is possible to view "mind" as both the machinery of perception we have been talking about and the consciousness which perceives the perception, the consciousness that is unconditioned and permanent–in other words, the spirit, the eternal Self. "The Self is ear of the ear, mind of the mind, speech of speech. He is also breath of the breath, and eye of the eye" (Kena Upanishad 2). From this higher aspect of mind all things proceed, in both the macrocosmic and the microcosmic sense. From the Mind of God all things are projected that are found in the cosmos; and from the mind of the individual are projected all that are distinctive to his life. We are all co-creators with God, even though we have long ago forgotten that and consider everything that goes on in our life as acts of God. From this delusion erroneous religion has arisen, religion that thinks it necessary to pray to and propitiate God in order for the "good" to come to us and the "bad" to be eliminated from our life. It is this religion and its false God that Buddha adamantly rejected and from which we must be freed if we are to gain any true understanding of what is really happening to us from life to life.

On the other hand, we need true religion, the conviction and aspiration for the uniting of the finite consciousness with the Infinite Consciousness in eternal Being. The call of the self to the Self is the essence of true religion, and in that sense those who would turn from death to life must be thoroughly religious. Any god that is separate from us is a false god; the true God is the very Self of our self. Though distinct from us, he is not separate. We are eternally one with Him. But we have to realize that, not just intellectually, but through direct experience. And that experience is only possible in meditation.

All right: mind precedes its objects, which are themselves governed and made by the mind. This has profound implications.

1)   Karma is the creation of the mind, is simply the mind in extension. Karma need not be worked out or fulfilled; the mind need only be changed, or better yet brought into complete abeyance. Then karma is no more and its attendant compulsions, including birth and death, no longer exist. "You dream that action is done, you dream that action bears fruit. It is your ignorance, it is the world's delusion that gives you these dreams" (Bhagavad Gita 5:14).

2)   Our entire life experience is but a mirroring of the mind. If something is not already within our mind it cannot be projected outward as a (seemingly) external factor or experience of our life. So our life is our mind in motion. By observing it we can come to know what is in our mind, just as by running a film through a projector we come to know what is in it. If we do not like what is happening in our life, the solution is to alter our mind. People who like to tell of how cruel, selfish, dishonest, and disloyal others habitually are to them are merely telling us how cruel, selfish, dishonest, and disloyal *they* are, potentially if not actually. Victims are only victimizers in a down cycle. The moment the upswing comes in their life rhythms they will go back to victimizing others.

Action and reaction are purely psychological matters, the film in the projector, the light and sound on the screen being only its projection. Change the film and you change the experience. Since objects come from the mind they can only be compatible with the mind and therefore express and reveal its character.

3) All the factors of life are really only thought, attitude, and outlook in manifestation.

4) Study your life and thereby know your mind.

5) You are always in control, even though that control may be on an unconscious level.

6) Change your mind and you change your life. (Do not forget that mind includes consciousness.)

7) Mary Baker Eddy was right: All is Mind and Mind is All.

Action and reaction

To speak or act with a defiled mind is to draw pain after oneself, like a wheel behind the feet of the animal drawing it (Dhammapada 1).

Suffering is inevitable for the person with a defiled mind, for it is impossible not to act or think (which is speaking inwardly, even if not outwardly). "Good" or meritorious acts done by a person with a defiled mind will bring suffering–perhaps not as much as evil acts, but still the suffering will not be avoided. This is imperative for us to comprehend: *Action is not the determining factor in our life–mind is.* And mind alone. This is why in the seventeenth chapter of the Bhagavad Gita Krishna describes how bad people do good in a bad way and thus accrue more misery to themselves.

It is very important to understand this fact, since we tend to mistakenly assume that "good" acts produce "good" karma, etc., when in reality the actions mean nothing–it is the condition of the mind that determines their character and therefore their consequences. (Buddha was very insistent on this.) Selfish people do "unselfish" deeds to either cover up their selfishness or to get merit for themselves so they can enjoy this or a future life. Their intentions defile the actions and so little good (if any) accrues to them. Instead their selfishness and pettiness is compounded. This is the plain truth. False religion gets rich on such persons through promises of merit and remission of sins. Even after death the deception goes on as their relatives and friends offer prayers and almsdeeds that supposedly will mitigate their negative karmas and alleviate, or even eliminate, the after-death consequences of their defiled thoughts and deeds. It is common to hear patently evil people excused on the grounds of "all the good" they do along with their evil actions. The truth is plain: evil minds can only produce evil actions that produce evil results. That is why Jesus, a student of Buddha's teaching, said: "A good tree cannot bring forth evil fruit, neither can a corrupt tree bring forth good fruit" (Matthew 7:18).

How then can a negative person break the pattern of negativity and escape it? By thinking and acting with the intention to change from negative to positive. The admission of negativity and the resolution to turn from it can produce positive thoughts and deeds when the intention is to change the consciousness, not just the consequences. Without the desire for real change nothing worthwhile can take place in life.

Unavoidable good

Buddha repeats his statement about the nature of objects and then continues:

To speak or act with a pure mind is to draw happiness after oneself, like an inseparable shadow (Dhammapada 2).

What is defiled and what is pure? Buddha is speaking of something much more than good and bad thoughts and deeds in the ordinary sense. Instead, he is speaking of defiled and pure minds. What is a defiled mind? One that is smudged and clogged with egotism and its demon attendants: selfishness, greed, jealousy, spite, hatred, and materiality. A pure mind is free from all these things, including their root, egotism. Further, a defiled mind is outward-turned and a pure mind is inward-turned. One roves through the jungle of illusion and delusion that is the world of man's making, and the other rests in the truth and perfection of its immortal Self. A person who is spirit-oriented cannot but produce peace and happiness for himself. It is as inevitable as the suffering of the matter-oriented person. It is a matter of polarity of consciousness.

Again we see that suffering and happiness are matters of the mind alone.

Thinking makes it so—the indignant "injured"

I have been insulted! I have been hurt! I have been beaten! I have been robbed! Anger does not cease in those who harbor this sort of thought.

I have been insulted! I have been hurt! I have been beaten! I have been robbed! Anger ceases in those who do not harbor this sort of thought (Dhammapada 3, 4).

Earlier I spoke about people who like to tell of how cruel, selfish, dishonest, and disloyal others habitually are to them, and that they are merely telling us how cruel, selfish, dishonest, and disloyal *they* are. As Jesus said: "A good man out of the good treasure of his heart bringeth forth that which is good; and an evil man out of the evil treasure of his heart bringeth forth that which is evil: for of the abundance of the heart his mouth speaketh" (Luke 6:45). So those who speak habitually of evil, especially in an emotional or angry way, are harboring that very evil in their hearts. We have all known people who love to foster resentment, brooding on "wrongs" of various sorts, both personal, social, and religious. These miserable souls continually stir themselves up to negative emotions, seeking justifications for their anger, hatred, and all-round discontent. Wishing to feel and spew out anger and hostility, they work themselves up into a state of "righteous indignation" to cover up the evil that resides in them. Many hope that by pointing the finger at others their own evil will remain undetected.

The truth of things

The main idea of this quotation from the Dhammapada is that by such thinking people consciously perpetuate their anger, and therefore their delusion. From them we see that all delusion is not only self-caused, it is self-maintained and even self-defended. Such a state is classically pathological–sociopathic, actually, as it is used to manipulate others as well as one's self. Modern society trains its members to be sociopaths. We are never to blame for anything. Criminals have been "failed" by society. Laws make people criminals(!). Others have been failed or harmed by their family, religion, or close associates (including spouse). Others are failures because they did not have the support of family, friends, or society. A great deal of government programs are based on sociopathic thinking. The moving finger points everywhere but to the source: the individual himself. Psychiatry in many instances is a major factor in the creation of a sociopathic attitude.

Buddha shows us how to free ourselves from this vicious cycle. This is not easy, but Buddha is speaking to those who want to strive for enlightenment, not to those who want an easy path. The first step in weaning ourselves–or guarding ourselves–from falling into the muck trap of self-pity is the facing and accepting of some basic facts such as karma and the source of all things being in the mind.

Nothing that occurs in the world is an entity unto itself. Rather, all things are reactions to previous actions: karma. I am stolen from because I stole; I am lied about because I lied; I am harmed because I harmed. My actions may have been in previous lives, but the reaction is no less a revelation of my present life. And it is much more a revelation of my mind as it is right now.

In the nineteenth century children were often told the story about a little boy who visited his aunt that lived in a valley where sounds were echoed. One day he came into the house and told her: "There is a bad little boy who lives up on the hill." "Really? And how do you know he is bad?" inquired the aunt. "Because he called me bad names." The aunt understood the situation. The little boy had called out something while playing and heard an echo of his voice. Thinking it was another child, he began calling out and became frustrated by the "bad boy" just repeating everything he said. So he started calling out insults, and got them back, so he went to "tell on" the bad boy to his aunt, who sat him down and told him the facts, showing him that he was only getting back what he had first projected. Karma is like an echo. What we shout will be shouted back at us.

Our life is a continuous stream of karmic echoes. Yes, others become instruments for the manifestation of the karma, but we are the origin of it all. So who shall we blame? As Pogo said: "We have met the enemy and they are us." The answer is to get busy and change ourselves. Then our lives will change automatically.

Ending hate

Occasions of hatred are certainly never settled by hatred. They are settled by freedom from hatred. This is the eternal law (Dhammapada 5).

Let us not waste our time trying to apply this to world peace or strife among nations. Certainly the principle enunciated by Buddha would bring peace, but vast numbers of people are simply not going to follow spiritual wisdom. That is the nature of the world. It is the violent ward of the lunatic asylum we call the universe. Everyone here is either an active or a recovering homicidal maniac. This is the truth. Recovery is never in a group; it is entirely an individual matter. The intelligent recognize this and work toward their own recovery so they can be released from the cosmic booby hatch. They may encourage and even assist other individuals who wish to further their own cure, but they can accomplish nothing on a mass level.

Also, we need to cure ourselves of addiction to "others." We are individuals and have to live as individuals. What others think or do should not influence us at all. Whether we are supported or opposed it should make no difference at all. We should do the needful and get off the revolving wheel of birth and death. And it is only done one by one, not in batches or multitudes. Buddha's wisdom must be applied personally to our own lives. Even if millions do so it will still be absolutely individual. A vast forest is green because each tree in the forest is green. There is no group-green in the forest, it is all individual.

So, what shall we do? Well, first of all, negativity is never counteracted by like negativity. So we do not react with hatred, anger, or suchlike. But neither do we mistakenly think that "positive" reaction is the answer either. Yes, I know, we have been told from Day One that love overcomes hatred, generosity overcomes selfishness, and gentleness overcomes violence. THEY DO NOT. Since negativity directed toward us comes from within us, our overt response effects nothing. Buddha does not say that love cancels out hatred. He says something far more profound (and practical): *freedom from hatred within ourselves eliminates hatred directed toward us.* Nothing else. Oh, indeed, we can shame others by our positive reaction, and even make them conclude (selfishly) that "nice" is more advantageous than "nasty." But in the long-term nothing will change, just be delayed.

Until we are freed from negativity, consciously and subconsciously, negativity will occur in our life. That is the fact. Buddha says: "This is the eternal law." Until we become incapable of evil our lives will be riddled with evil.

Peace with others

Others may not understand that we must practice self-control, but quarreling dies away in those who understand this fact (Dhammapada 6).

What? Buddha is advocating *repression*? Horror! We all know how destructive repression is, don't we? No, we do not. We only hope it is destructive so we can run amok in our life-sphere and rejoice in our "healthy self-expression." Buddha is not so sophisticated; he prefers the truth: Self-mastery is essential for peace with ourselves and with others. It is definitely true that (most) others will not understand "that we must practice self-control," but that should not matter at all to us. We should just go ahead and do it and let them eat our dust.

Quarreling should not just not take place; it must die. That is, the root of ego that produces quarreling must be dissolved like the root of a baby tooth. Self-control does the dissolving to a great extent.

In such a few sentences Buddha has told us the way to both inner and outer peace. May we follow that way and demonstrate their truth.

The Tempter masters

The Tempter [Mara] masters the lazy and irresolute man who dwells on the attractive side of things, ungoverned in his senses, and unrestrained in his food, like the wind overcomes a rotten tree (Dhammapada 7).

There is a cosmic force of negativity that is the sum total of all the negativity, past and present, that has arisen in the history of creation. This force operates efficiently and therefore may be considered intelligent. This we may call Mara, as does Buddha, or Ahriman or Satan as do the Zoroastrians and Christians. Besides this there are intelligent beings who either consciously or unconsciously ally themselves with this force, merging themselves in it and becoming its instruments. Such beings may be in a body or disembodied. They may consider themselves evil, neutral, or even good, depending on the degree of their capacity for self-deceit. Put all together we have a league for evil that can collectively be called Mara. Since it is domination by evil that is being considered here, it matters little which aspect of Mara is doing the dominating, the result will be the same.

It is the nature of evil to coerce, cajole, tempt, entrap, dominate, weaken, and control. The nature of goodness is exactly the opposite. Its purpose is to provide freedom, encourage reason, strengthen, and make us independent–even of itself. Evil works through threats and the instilling of fear; goodness works through wisdom and freedom from fear. (From this we can see that virtually all religion is part of Mara, is Satanic. In their pure form most religions are free of Mara's ways, but their degenerate forms are just as Satanic as any other.)

Mara, then, wishes to master men, whereas God wishes to make men masters–gods. ("I have said, Ye are gods; and all of you are children of the most High" Psalms 82:6.)

But man has free will, so who is subject to Mara's domination?

The lazy and irresolute man

The one who acts not, whether from laziness or from lack of resolution, is overcome by Mara. Why? Because no one can stand still–we

11

are either moving forward or backward. Those who are doing nothing, standing idle, are swept by Mara into the current of anti-evolution and become increasingly degenerate.

Spiritual laziness is a terrible curse, for it is not actively evil and therefore does not seem so bad. After all, tomorrow is another day, and perhaps then we will set out on the journey to higher consciousness.... Laziness plunges us into spiritual sleep that often becomes the sleep of death (see Psalms 13:3, 4). Solomon wrote: "I went by the field of the slothful, and by the vineyard of the man void of understanding; and, lo, it was all grown over with thorns, and nettles had covered the face thereof, and the stone wall thereof was broken down. Then I saw, and considered it well: I looked upon it, and received instruction. Yet a little sleep, a little slumber, a little folding of the hands to sleep: So shall thy poverty come as one that travelleth; and thy want as an armed man" (Proverbs 24:30-34). Yes indeed: "a little sleep, a little slumber, a little folding of the hands to sleep" and all is lost, at least for that lifetime. Spiritual sleep becomes a habit, even from life to life. Often only intense suffering wakes us up, and then we often blame God or cite it as proof that there is no God.

Irresolution is as much a curse as laziness for the result is the same, though the irresolute person often suffers from his constant vacillation. Irresolution arises from ignorance, fear, and confusion—torments all. Which way should I go? How can I know the right thing? Will I be safe from harm? What will happen to me if I go in that direction? These and many other agonies torture the irresolute. Seeing this weakness Mara strikes him down and tramples him mercilessly underfoot. Here, too, the slavery can last for ages.

Who dwells on the attractive side of things

Those who are always looking for pleasure, enjoyment, and gratification in all things are specially vulnerable to Mara's ways, for they have no standards but "I like" and "I want." Selfish to the core, they have no interest in the consequences of the actions that may be needed to get the things they want, considering that even wrongdoing is justified if that obtains their desires. Nor do they care about the real nature of the desired things. Addicts of all kinds embody this foolish disregard of reality, refusing to acknowledge the destructive effects of their actions on themselves and others and classically blind to the dangers and defects of the objects of their addiction. So inveterate can addiction to objects become that the addict in time may even admit their harmful consequences but boldly declare that he simply does not care. Spiritual suicide is the end result of all continued addiction.

Ungoverned in his senses

The slave of Mara is dragged along the road of life by the wild horses of the senses, horses he has himself whipped into mad frenzy. "Everyone knows repression and suppression are bad for you!" they trumpet as they plunge on down the path of willful self-destruction. The chariot race of their life gives them no pause for reflection or good sense—they are too busy "living life to the full" and know not that they are sinking into dullness and death. Such persons often (if not usually) become earthbound after death, obsessing others like them and urging them to like addiction in anticipation of some kind of vicarious experience. Only exorcism can free them from this baleful cycle, for they have truly become demons.

Unrestrained in his food

The importance of diet in the context of spiritual life can hardly be overestimated. What we eat and how much we eat is important for two reasons: the effect of food on the mind and its effect on the body.

Everything is vibrating energy, including the mind. What we eat is absorbed in the form of energy into the various levels of our being. Some energies are life-sustaining, some are life-inhibiting and some are even life-destroying. Animal flesh, alcohol, nicotine, and mind-altering drugs consist of destructive energies, and so do other forms of food and drink, including sugar, coffee, tea (non-herbal) and junk food. If we take them into our body we not only harm our body, we distort our mind and greatly hinder any attempts at increased and clear-sighted awareness. We are already too body-conscious, and if we make ourselves ill we only compound the problem. Overeating does not directly harm the mind, but the motives for it, such as greed and desire for sensory distraction from inner discontent, are evil habits to cultivate. Overeating, however, does greatly harm the body, which in turn distracts the mind. Buddha gave an entire discourse on the importance of eating only once a day, and that before midday. By observing this discipline he claimed to eliminate nearly all disease and functional problems from the body. (Section 2 of the Kitagiri Sutra, Majjhima Nikaya 70. See also the sixth section of the Latukikopama Sutra, Majjhima Nikaya 66.) In the Jivaka Sutra (Majjhima Nikaya 55) he also spoke of the necessity to avoid the eating of meat.

Gandhi discovered that mastery of greed and taste brought about mastery of the other senses as well. "I eat everything" and "I eat what I want, when I want, and as much as I want" are self-imposed death warrants.

Like the wind overcomes a rotten tree

Those who have spent much time in forests know the frustration of sitting or stepping on a fallen tree only to have it collapse into a spongy ruin. The tree looks fine, but a little pressure reveals its thoroughly decayed condition. A rotten tree standing upright can be toppled by the slightest of breezes because its fibers are no longer strong or even intact. The same is true of those who are lazy, irresolute, addicted to pleasure, undisciplined in their senses and their indulgence: they have no moral fiber, no strength of will, no inner integrity. Just a puff from Mara and over they go, because spiritually they are already fallen to the ground. Being self-centered they are neither the friends of God or man, or even of themselves, really.

The unmastered

But the Tempter cannot master a man who dwells on the distasteful side of things, self-controlled in his senses, moderate in eating, resolute and full of faith, like the wind cannot move a mountain crag (Dhammapada 8).

14

Buddha did not advocate a hating of life or self-loathing, but he did advocate a realistic view of the perishable world and all within it, including our body. He also urged his hearers to look beyond the attractive surface appearance of harmful things and see the poison and ugliness hidden therein. It works the other way, too: we should look at what seems unattractive or miserable and see the benefits and healing they may bring. Buddha did not recommend either total acceptance or total rejection, but a clear-sighted understanding of all we encounter in earthly life. When we see the defects inherent in a thing we will not become addicted or unreasonably attached to it, nor will we loathe or avoid that which is essentially positive and helpful to us in our ascent to higher life. And at all times we should have a calm attitude to everything. This is the true Middle Way.

The other traits listed by Buddha as belonging to the Mara-resistant are just the opposite of the negative ones previously set forth, with one exception. He speaks of the wise man as being "full of faith." The seeker has not yet come to the goal, so how can he know he does not waste his time in pursuing it? If an enlightened person is at hand, he can see a living demonstration of the goal's reality, but what if he cannot? By practice, which includes purification of heart, faith—which is not blind trust or hope but intuition that arises as the veils that cover the inner light are dissolved—arises and becomes established in him, giving him the perseverance needed to press on and attain the goal himself.

Such a person is likened by the Buddha to a mountain crag. Just as the crag cannot be moved because it is made of the very stone of the mountain and is organically united to the mountain, so the wise is anchored in spirit, is himself spirit irrevocably united to infinite Spirit. Knowing this, Emily Bronte wrote shortly before her death:

> No coward soul is mine,
> No trembler in the world's storm-troubled sphere:
> I see Heaven's glories shine,
> And Faith shines equal, arming me from Fear.

O God within my breast,
Almighty, ever-present Deity!
Life, that in me has rest,
As I, undying Life, have power in Thee!

Vain are the thousand creeds
That move men's hearts: unutterably vain;
Worthless as withered weeds,
Or idlest froth amid the boundless main,

To waken doubt in one
Holding so fast by Thy infinity,
So surely anchored on
The steadfast rock of Immortality.

With wide-embracing love
Thy Spirit animates eternal years,
Pervades and broods above,
Changes, sustains, dissolves, creates, and rears.

Though earth and moon were gone,
And suns and universes ceased to be,
And Thou wert left alone,
Every existence would exist in Thee.

There is not room for Death,
Nor atom that his might could render void:
Thou–Thou art Being and Breath,
And what Thou art may never be destroyed.

This is the status of those who follow the Buddha Way. Already they begin to experience to a limited degree the limitless life of Buddhahood.

The unworthy and the worthy

The following relates to any who claim to be spiritual and even teach others, not just monastics.

The man who wears the yellow-dyed robe but is not free from stains himself, without self-restraint and integrity, is unworthy of the robe.

But the man who has freed himself of stains and has found peace of mind in an upright life, possessing self-restraint and integrity, he is indeed worthy of the dyed robe (Dhammapada 9, 10).

Buddha is making a play on words. The word for robe and stain (of passion) are very similar in Pali, the only difference being in the pronunciation of a single vowel.

Free from stain

Although the bhikkhu (monk) may wear cloth that is dyed, his mind should be free from the stains of anything external. "When the heart is made pure by that yoga, when the body is obedient, when the senses are mastered, when man knows that his Atman is the Atman in all creatures, then let him act, untainted by action. The illumined soul whose heart is Brahman's heart thinks always: 'I am doing nothing.' No matter what he sees, hears, touches, smells, eats; no matter whether he is moving, sleeping, breathing, speaking, excreting, or grasping something with his hand, or opening his eyes, or closing his eyes: this he knows always: 'I am not seeing, I am not hearing: it is the senses that see and hear and touch the things of the senses.'…The lotus leaf rests unwetted on water: he rests on action, untouched by action" (Bhagavad Gita 5:7-10).

There are two ways to be in the stainless condition: to always keep our consciousness immersed in the Transcendent through yoga, and to become incapable of being stained by any thing. This latter is the state of the liberated being, but those of us struggling toward liberation can manage the former if we really try. Of course we also have to work at ridding ourselves of the stains (samskaras, past life conditionings) accumulated in the past. And always we must remain aware that, however pure we may make ourselves, we are "stainable" until fully liberated.

Self-restrained

Unworthy is he that is "without self-restraint." Animals, infants and children are instinctual rather than rational. Unworthy men and women, however intelligent they may be, and capable in other areas of life, do not restrain themselves—usually because they do not wish to. Others, approaching worthiness, would like to restrain the instinctual impulses that lead them back into pre-human patterns of behavior, but do not know how. For a while they struggle against the forces of their lower nature and then fail, falling into despair, denial, or hypocrisy. These unhappy souls are especially victimized by two vicious kinds of people:

1) the libertines who assure them that repression is negative and harmful, and urge them to indulge their chaotic instincts and even expand and elaborate on them, and

2) the "righteous" who attempt to show them how "bad" they are and how "displeasing to God" are their impulses and actions, instilling fear and self-disgust in them, but offering no real practical solution to their dilemma and frustration. Both of these types are degraders and destroyers of their victims. It is rare indeed to encounter a third type: those who, like Buddha, can not only reveal the cause of their problems, but can also show the means to eliminate both cause and effect. They can show the practical way out of the labyrinth of confusion, not relying on the whimsy of any force external to the seeker, but on his innate nature which he can awaken and unfold according to an exact and verifiable methodology.

This latter point is essential, because Buddha says the worthy are *self*-restrained, not ruled by another. Trading the bondage of our lower nature for the ideas and demands of an "authority" is merely trading one form of enslavement for another. Right Meditation enables us to awake, arise, and free ourselves.

One thing our reluctant egos like to do is torment us with ideals so high that they cannot be attained. "You should not need to... Only once should be sufficient...If it was real...Well, if it was...If you were..." etc., etc., etc. Buddha is speaking to people who are not perfect and who should accept that and work onward. The ego likes to condemn us for even needing discipline or restraint ("What kind of a person...?"), but that is a ploy to maintain its hold over us.

By telling us that self-restraint is needed, Buddha is acknowledging that he is not speaking to bodiless beings of perfect knowledge. He does not condemn us for needing his teaching, and neither should we. It is easy to think a worthy person is one who cannot be touched by the impulses or desires of lower nature, but Buddha sees it differently. He who masters himself must have something to master. He who is purified must have once been impure. Krishna tells us: "Desire flows into the mind of the seer but he is never disturbed. The seer knows peace" (Bhagavad Gita 2:70). There we have it. Even the sage may experience the impulse of negativity, but he is unmoved by it. So being tempted or hard pressed by evil or folly is no fault in itself. Yes, we shall grow beyond these impulses in time, but until then we can remain untouched. Regarding this Swami Yukteswar Giri, the guru of Paramhansa Yogananda, wrote a song in which he says: "Desire, my great enemy, with his soldiers surrounding me, is giving me lots of trouble.... That enemy I will defeat, remaining in the castle of peace." Here, again, the simile of the lotus leaf unwetted, afloat on the water, is apt.

Integrity

Integrity is the third necessary trait of the worthy. In an era where the drive for getting ahead and for material gain and personal power are so prevalent—even obsessive—the idea of integrity as more important than any of them is not only shunted aside, it is mocked and despised. I cannot think how long it has been since I even heard the word self-respect come up in a conversation, book, or lecture. Egotism and arrogance under the label of self-esteem are tacitly considered virtues, whereas self-effacement and humility are looked upon as marks of either weakness, stupidity, or Oriental craftiness.

Frankly, although I do not hesitate to write on metaphysical subjects of cosmic significance or of mystical and esoteric arcana, I find myself stymied when confronted with a need to expound the simple virtue of integrity. I just do not know where to begin in addressing those who, like myself, live in a society that has been stripped of nearly all virtue in every aspect of public and personal life. Those once-cited historical models of virtue are busily being "debunked" and besmirched by the fabrications of revisionist historians who are frantic to prove that virtue is not only non-existent but impossible except in the minds of fools who live in fantasy. The "real world" they present to us is not only devoid of divinity, it is also devoid of genuine humanity. Is there anything more inhuman than contemporary humanism?

Some translators use "truthfulness" or "truth" rather than integrity to underline the ideal of living true to our true nature. But rather than expound at great length on what integrity means, I will tell you how to get it: turn within and evoke it from your own essential being. It will put you out of step with much of life but that is the idea, is it not? At least it is Buddha's idea and, I hope, it is yours.

Peace of mind

According to Buddha, those who possess purity, self-restraint, and integrity will find "peace of mind in a upright life." There is no other way for individuals, associations, nations, and the world. And peace does exist only in the mind, not in the uneasy cease-fires or political apathy that the world means by peace. Those who speak or act for world peace do good, but those who become *peaceful* do best. For peace, like unrest, is contagious, and is an inward state. The meditator does more for peace and world order than any other. If we look at the great peacemakers and world teachers we will see that every one of them without exception was firmly rooted in the consciousness of spirit. This is why Gandhi was called Mahatma: Great Soul. He was manifesting his spirit through his life. And we can do the same. I lived for some time with Sri Kaka Sahib Kalellkar, who was Gandhi's personal secretary and his personal attendant in jail. He told me that Gandhi spent his nights in meditation so intense that each morning he could see the change that had been produced in him by the previous night's meditation. Meditation was the secret of Gandhi's personal holiness and power for social transformation. Setting the inner life right, he perfected the outer life, seeing God in all, even in his murderer. Longfellow was right: "Lives of great men all remind us we may make our lives sublime, and in passing leave behind us footprints on the sands of time." If we follow in the footsteps of Buddha and Gandhi we shall do the same.

Seeing wrong

There are a lot of jokes about people who cannot see correctly, the Mr. Magoo films and television programs are a prime example, and before Mr. Magoo the readers of the newspaper comics were treated to the vagaries of Weakeyes Yokum in the Li'l Abner comic strip. But in real life it is no joke, and in the more real life of the spirit it is even less so. Wherefore Buddha assures us:

To see the essence in the unessential and to see the essence as unessential means one can never get to the essence, wandering as one is in the road of wrong intentions (Dhammapada 11).

Instead of "essence/unessential" Max Muller and Sanderson Beck render it "truth/untruth," T. Byrom: "true/false" and the Venerable Thanissaro Bhikkhu: "essence/non-essence." This latter is perhaps preferable to the rendering of John Richards that I am using for this commentary, but the ideas are basically the same: mistaking the real for the unreal and the unreal for the real. Since Buddha avoided abstract metaphysical speculation as much as possible, I think we can be safe in assuming that his words are a focus on our minds and their function and the consequences they incur.

Literal negativity

The word "negative" is tossed about a lot, often to mean some-thing we do not like, whatever its real character. Its essential charac-ter, though, is best revealed by a photographic negative. Everything is backwards: what is light is seen as dark, and what is dark is seen as light. So to be truly negative is to see things exactly opposite to what they really are. This is an essential point, for the most common frailty of the egocentric mind is to pretend to see things as of a character different from their actual quality, or to try to make others see them in a manner opposite to how they really are. But in those cases the truth is known, only being ignored or denied. Buddha, however, is speaking of truly seeing things completely opposite to their reality and believing it fully. This is the situation for all human beings, though in varying degrees, otherwise we would not be human beings, but be living in a higher world than this.

To mistake the unreal for the real and the real for the unreal is a terrible condition that distorts our perception and response to every-thing we encounter, both inwardly and outwardly, including our own self. Such a condition is absolutely hopeless in and of itself. It is not something that can be turned back on itself for alleviation or extrica-tion. It will lead to nothing but increasing distortion. It must be either destroyed or thoroughly cast off.

As the individual consciousness evolves and becomes further entan-gled in this mess, there are moments when it is put into total or partial abeyance through outer influences such as the holy atmosphere of a sacred place, person, or object. Words sometimes momentarily shock the individual out of the grip of this dynamic ignorance. Whatever the nature of the outer force or the length of its duration, this clearing away of the mist of delusion cannot be permanent. Consequently such events are almost always completely useless, and many times are taken up by the deluded mind and distorted for further involvement in illusions. In time, however, the *memory* of those moments persists and becomes a stimulus from which arises the desire to escape the nets of delusion. For a while that, too, is of little meaning, for the deluded person begins wandering about seeking external factors to free him from his darkness. This is understandable since his moments of temporary sanity have usually come from external contact of some kind. After a while he either gives up or intuits that freedom must occur from within. Then the hope of freedom dawns. Once the understanding that meditation is the key to the prison is established in his consciousness, then his escape is assured, though he will no doubt have to wander down the byways of worthless (or even destructive) meditation teachers and practices before hitting on the real road out of the tangle. But once he does start on the road it is only a matter of...not time, but eternity.

False experience

To see the essence in the unessential and to see the essence as unessential. These words are frightening, for they express an actual experience on the part of the wanderer, not just some crack-brain ideas or concepts held only in the intellect. All of us consider that we know something when we have experienced it. So many firmly-binding illusions have arisen from our own wrong-seeing. "I know it for myself" is often nothing more than the raving of the strait-jacketed ego. And things can get worse. Illusions of truth and enlightenment abound in the world of the "awakened" unawakened. And as Buddha points out, we cannot get to the perception of reality as long as these errors exist.

Wrong intent

It is not just our mistaken perceptions that prevent our escape from bondage. Rather, they give rise to another ingredient in the stew of our samsaric misery: *wrong intention*. Our whole purpose is wrong. Our goals are themselves delusive. We want "things" or power, or exalted positions, even in heaven-worlds. In other words, we want some more chains to wind around us rather than to slip out of the bonds and be free, free not only from such stuff, but free from even the capacity to desire them or be bound by them.

In the seventh chapter of the Bhagavad Gita Krishna lists four kinds of spiritual seekers: "The world-weary, the seeker for knowledge, the seeker for happiness and the man of spiritual discrimination." The first he calls *artas*: one who is aware of a sense of loss or emptiness, who is aware of oppressions inner and outer, and who is suffering from it all. The second is *jijnasus*: one who desires to know, to gain knowledge. The third he calls *artharthi*: one who wishes to attain the *summun bonum* of life in the form of Highest Truth. The fourth is the pure *jnani*: one who is a man of wisdom, who seeks not to either gain something or be divested of something, who is not motivated by desire or aversion, but aims for the entrance into his essential nature. He seeks for What IS for Itself alone.

Now if we look closely we will see that these four types embody the Four Aryan Truths enunciated by Buddha. The first is aware of suffering; the second knows that suffering has a cause and wants to know what to do about it; the third knows that the cessation of suffering is possible and is the *paramartha*—the highest aim and attainment—for all beings; and the fourth has known the way to end suffering and looks to that goal alone, knowing that knowledge (*jnana*) alone is the way to the goal.

"The man of discrimination [*jnani*] is the highest of these. He is continually united with me. He devotes himself to me always, and to no other. For I am very dear to that man, and he is dear to me.

"Certainly, all these are noble: but the man of discrimination I see as my very Self. For he alone loves me because I am myself: the last and only goal of his devoted heart. Through many a long life his discrimination ripens: he makes me his refuge, knows that Brahman is all. How rare are such great ones!" (Bhagavad Gita 7:18, 19).

Getting the right idea

But to see the essence in the essential and the unessential as the unessential means one does get to the essence, being on the road of right intentions (Dhammapada 12).

Through Right Meditation—one of the factors of the Aryan Eightfold Path—a complete change-around is accomplished, and the seeker comes to see the real as real and the false as false. What a pity that fake religion sends its adherents running about frantically—literally out of their minds—in search for everything but this one necessary thing: Right Seeing, for it "means one does get to the essence, being on the road of right intentions" as Buddha points out. To possess *viveka*, the ability to tell the difference between the true and the false, is itself a foretaste of the ultimate Freedom.

Rainproofing our mind

In the last century (!) millions of people listened to a vinyl Beatle croon:

> I'm fixing a hole where the rain gets in,
> And stop my mind from wandering....
> I'm filling the cracks that ran through the door
> And keep my mind from wandering....

As a friend of mine listened to it with vacuous admiration, I asked her: "Do you know what that song is about?" What a sour note to intrude into her beatific coma! It did not need to mean anything, and she told me so. "But it does," I crudely insisted. "It is about meditation. If you analyze the words, they are describing the way meditation repairs the inner consciousness and makes it fit for 'living in.'" Something clicked, even though I had not really expected it to, and it was not long until she, too, was stopping up the holes and filling the cracks through daily meditation. Long before that inane little ditty with the profound message, Buddha had said:

In the same way that rain breaks into a house with a bad roof, desire breaks into the mind that has not been practicing meditation (Dhammapada 13).

What is wrong with desire? I have been reading oriental philosophy for over forty years, and the books unanimously point to desire as one of the major symptoms of ignorance and sources of suffering. But usually this is not explained, merely accepted without question. Blind acceptance of even the truth can bear no positive or lasting fruit, so we need to know: what *is* wrong with desire?

Desire as an effect

Desire springs from the root illusion that we are not complete, that we need something we presently lack to be a whole being. Even more, there is the illusion that "things" can satisfy and bring fulfillment and produce happiness, that "things" can make us more than we are, that without "things" we are minimal or nothing. Being addicted to "things" we naturally assert vehemently that "things" are "necessities" which all sensible people will pursue with their whole strength. Desire is the denial of our own essential being and the affirmation of the non-existent value of "things." This two-edged sword cuts off the head of our discrimination and renders us truly senseless. Desire is the deadly fruit of ignorance and delusion.

Desire sensitizes us to the objects of the physical senses and desensitizes us to the presence and the call of the spirit. Consequently Krishna says: "Restless man's mind is, so strongly shaken in the grip of the senses: gross and grown hard with stubborn desire for what is worldly. How shall he tame it? Truly, I think the wind is no wilder" (Bhagavad Gita 6:34).

Desire as a cause

As a cause, desire is immeasurably destructive. Here are a few things about desire revealed in the Bhagavad Gita.

One of the first things a spiritually awakening person sees with painful clarity is his inability to do the right and avoid the wrong. Religion usually posits a "devil" of some form who is responsible for this. Consequently nothing lasting is accomplished in the struggle to do the right and avoid the wrong. Only when the real devil is discovered can we intelligently deal with the impulse to wrong action. Krishna states the fact: "the chains of desire bind you to your actions" (2:39). End of case. Desire is the culprit that we are nourishing in our own breast while demanding that God "deliver us from evil." It is not God, but we ourselves who need to act, for Krishna assures Arjuna that when a man is "free from the things of desire, I call him a seer, and illumined" (2:56). And: "He knows peace who has forgotten desire. He lives without craving: free from ego, free from pride" (2:71). For ego and egoism are the source of desire, which is a symptom of their dominance. Desire binds, but "when a man can act without desire,...no bonds can bind him" (4:41). Otherwise: "Man is a prisoner, enslaved by action, dragged onward by desire" (5:12).

"Self-controlled, cut free from desire, curbing the heart and knowing the Atman, man finds Nirvana that is in Brahman, here and hereafter.... Holding the senses, holding the intellect, holding the mind fast, he who seeks freedom, thrusts fear aside, thrusts aside anger and puts off desire: truly that man is made free for ever" (Bhagavad Gita 5:26, 28).

"When can a man be said to have achieved union with Brahman? When his mind is under perfect control and freed from all desires, so that he becomes absorbed in the Atman, and nothing else" (6:18). "Devotees enter into Him when the bonds of their desire are broken" (8:11). Otherwise: "They are addicts of sensual pleasure, made restless by their many desires, and caught in the net of delusion. They fall into the filthy hell of their own evil minds" (16:16). For: "He who...acts on the impulse of his desires, cannot reach perfection, or happiness, or the highest goal" (16:23).

Desire as religion

When negativity begins to experience the pressure of scrutiny and attempts at its eradication, its most common trick—like other germs, bacteria, and viruses—is to mutate into an unrecognizable form, the most unrecognizable of which is externalized religion. Krishna unmasks this, telling Arjuna: "Men whose discrimination has been blunted by worldly desires, establish this or that ritual or cult and resort to various deities, according to the impulse of their inborn natures" (7:20), and get what they desire (righteously!) and thus remain bound and in darkness. Nor is Krishna pointing the finger at religions outside India; he is speaking of Vedic religion itself: "Thus go the righteous who follow the road of the triple Veda in formal observance; hungry still for the food of the senses, drawn by desire to endless returning" (Bhagavad Gita 9:21).

Such desire-based religion binds its adherents to the wheel of birth and death. Wherefore: "When the whole country is flooded, the reservoir becomes superfluous. So, to the illumined seer, the Vedas are all superfluous" (2:46). Instead: "When a man has achieved non-attachment, self-mastery and freedom from desire through renunciation, he reaches union with Brahman, who is beyond all action" (18:49).

Ridding ourselves of desire

We need to free ourselves from the destructive curse of desire. How? Buddha tells us plainly:

While in the same way that rain cannot break into a well-roofed house, desire cannot break into a mind that has been practicing meditation well (Dhammapada 14).

Many people claim to be practicing meditation, but Buddha spoke of *Right* Meditation when enumerating the components of the Aryan Eightfold Path. When desire remains on the rampage in the mind of the meditator he should realize that: 1) his meditation method is defective; 2) his practice of the method is defective; or 3) some elements in his inner and outer life are preventing success in meditation. If, after checking carefully, he finds that his practice is not incorrect and his way of living and thinking is not wrong, he must face up to the unhappy truth that the methodology itself and association with the one who taught it to him should be abandoned and a right form of meditation adopted. For when the meditation practice is correct, *and is being engaged in for the necessary amount of time*, desire becomes increasingly attenuated and finally annihilated altogether. This is verifiable through our own practice and experience.

Jesus expounded it this way: "Whosoever cometh to me, and heareth my sayings, and doeth them, I will shew you to whom he is like: He is like a man which built an house, *and digged deep, and laid the foundation on a rock*: and when the flood arose, the stream beat vehemently upon that house, and could not shake it: for it was founded upon a rock" (Luke 6:47, 48), the rock of meditative gnosis. Those who go deep in meditation and make the consciousness of the spirit gained thereby the foundation of their life will know peace of mind and heart–none other.

In summation: "Make a habit of practicing meditation, and do not let your mind be distracted. In this way you will come finally to the Lord, who is the light-giver, the highest of the high" (Bhagavad Gita 8:8).

The two ways of life and death

"There are two ways, one of life and one of death; but a great difference between the two ways." So opens the *Didache: The Teaching of the Twelve Apostles*, perhaps the only authentic document we possess authored by the apostles of Jesus assembled in Jerusalem a few years after his death and resurrection. They were no doubt echoing words spoken to them by Jesus, and he was no doubt recalling the fifteenth and sixteenth verses of the Dhammapada which he would have either read or heard during the years he lived in the Buddhist monasteries of Northern India. In those verses Buddha set forth the two ways of life.

When Buddha first spoke to others the knowledge gained through his enlightenment, the first principle he gave was: "There is suffering." This is the fundamental fact of relative existence. It is nonsense to accuse Buddha of being pessimistic or negative for saying this, for he continued with three other facts that give hope to anyone who ponders them: "Suffering has a cause. Suffering can be ended. There is a way to end suffering." Everything else spoken by Buddha was the practical way to demonstrate the truth of these Four Aryan Truths by attaining Nirvana, the ending of all possibility of suffering. Now in the Dhammapada Buddha is going to put it very succinctly:

Here and beyond he suffers. The wrong-doer suffers both ways. He suffers and is tormented to see his own depraved behavior.

Here and beyond he is glad. The doer of good is glad both ways. He is glad and rejoices to see his own good deeds (Dhammapada 15, 16).

The "Big Catch"

Since duality is necessary for relative existence, there is no thing that does not have both advantages and drawbacks. Countless people in the West have hoped to escape the truth about their wrongdoing and its attendant guilt and retribution by seeking spiritual asylum in Oriental religions, notably Hinduism and Buddhism. "No hell here!" they exult, unaware that the popular scriptures of both Hinduism and Buddhism contain far more material on hell and threats of hell (often for incredibly petty offenses) than the Bible. "No talk about sin!" they shrill, perhaps not so unaware that both religions contain virtual libraries of material on those unescaped bugaboos. "No guilt!" they shout, not realizing that their desperation proves just the opposite. It is definitely true that Hinduism and Buddhism have a far more accurate and optimistic definition and outlook regarding these things, but that is because they greatly emphasize the two things those refugees have most been seeking to escape: *personal responsibility for wrongdoing and the inevitability of retribution for it.* For those seeking a higher consciousness through the adoption of a higher (i.e., sin-free) life, hope and confidence are abundantly proffered: "Though a man be soiled with the sins of a lifetime, let him but love me, rightly resolved, in utter devotion: I see no sinner, that man is holy. Holiness soon shall refashion his nature to peace eternal; O son of Kunti, of this be certain: the man that loves me, he shall not perish" (Bhagavad Gita 9:30, 31).

But there is no optimism for those who intend to stay in the hog-wallow mud of ignorance and evil: "Men of demonic nature know neither what they ought to do, nor what they should refrain from doing. There is no truth in them, or purity, or right conduct. They maintain that the scriptures are a lie, and that the universe is not based upon a moral law, but godless, conceived in lust and created by copulation, without any other cause. Because they believe this in the darkness of their little minds, these degraded creatures do horrible deeds, attempting to destroy the world. They are enemies of mankind.

"Their lust can never be appeased. They are arrogant, and vain, and drunk with pride. They run blindly after what is evil. The ends they work for are unclean. They are sure that life has only one purpose: gratification of the senses. And so they are plagued by innumerable cares, from which death alone can release them. Anxiety binds them with a hundred chains, delivering them over to lust and wrath. They are ceaselessly busy, piling up dishonest gains to satisfy their cravings.

"'I wanted this and today I got it. I want that: I shall get it tomorrow. All these riches are now mine: soon I shall have more. I have killed this enemy. I will kill all the rest. I am a ruler of men. I enjoy the things of this world. I am successful, strong and happy. Who is my equal? I am so wealthy and so nobly born. I will sacrifice to the gods. I will give alms. I will make merry.' That is what they say to themselves, in the blindness of their ignorance.

"They are addicts of sensual pleasure, made restless by their many desires, and caught in the net of delusion. They fall into the filthy hell of their own evil minds. Conceited, haughty, foolishly proud, and intoxicated by their wealth, they offer sacrifice to God in name only, for outward show, without following the sacred rituals. These malignant creatures are full of egoism, vanity, lust, wrath, and consciousness of power. They loathe me, and deny my presence both in themselves and in others. They are enemies of all men and of myself; cruel, despicable and vile. I cast them back, again and again, into the wombs of degraded parents, subjecting them to the wheel of birth and death. And so they are constantly reborn, in degradation and delusion. They do not reach me, but sink down to the lowest possible condition of the soul" (Bhagavad Gita 16:7-20).

That is how Krishna put the matter before Buddha did; the sum of both are the same.

"Wrong" and "right"

Suffering is the lot of the wrong-doers and happiness is the lot of the right-doers. But what is "wrong" and what is "right"? Here, too, a lot of moral slackers take up Buddhism and Hinduism with the idea that they will escape "Judeo-Christian morality." And they do, being neither Buddhist nor Hindu in any viable sense. On the other hand, those who investigate either religion to any significant degree will encounter a moral code that extends far beyond the simplistic "good doggie, bad doggie" code of externalized Judaism or Christianity.

First of all, the concepts, of sin, wrong, good, right, and virtue are completely different from their seeming equivalents in Western religion. In Western religion a thing is good because God commands it, and bad because God forbids it. The inherent nature of the thing is irrelevant. Do what God wants and you will be good and rewarded accordingly; do what God hates and you will be evil and punished accordingly. It is all a matter of divine law. The flaw in this should be obvious: everyone under the constraints of law seeks to get around it and yet be considered law-abiding. All kinds of stretches and concessions are sought and obtained. (Just consider the Jesuitical contortions of Roman Catholic moral theology.) If one church will not make concessions, just go find one that will, or start your own. I knew a man who did just that. He belonged to a fundamentalist church that said those who divorced and remarried would go to hell, and so would those they married. He preached it fervently, and once when rebuking a man for having married a divorced woman, was astounded when the man countered that the preacher's own sister had married a divorcee! He investigated and found that to be so. So "God" led him to start his own church that held to all his original principles, except for the allowance of divorce and remarriage.

In the East the criterion is very different. If a thing spiritually harms the individual then it is wrong; if something spiritually benefits the individual then it is right. What else need be said? Naturally addicts and ignoramuses loudly insist that harmful things are not harmful and protest that beneficial things are burdensome and hurtful. But that does not matter to Eastern religion, because unlike Western religion there is no compulsion to coerce people into doing the good and avoiding the bad. If someone wants to harm himself, calling it good, that is his business. For such a person religion is irrelevant anyway, and he is irrelevant to religion.

Here again we see a profound difference between East and West. In the Western religions God as an almighty monarch is the center of attention, the adherents have no value or relevance except in relation to His ideas about them. In Eastern religions, the spiritual liberation of the individual is the center of concern, and the truth about his spiritual status is all-important (whether he or others accept or deny it). Since liberation is the result of union with God, Eastern religions make Him truly the center of things, the center of life itself, in contrast to the basically political centrism of Western religions that insistently maintains an infinite gulf between God and us. In the West the question is: "Are you obeying and pleasing God?" and in the East it is: "Are you moving toward union with God?" As I say, it is politics versus states of being. One reduces us to nothing, the other makes spirit, both finite and Infinite, everything.

Here and beyond

Wherever we may be, we experience the effect of our deeds, whether we are physically incarnate in the material plane of existence or out of the body in an astral or causal world. Our presence in those worlds as well as our situation in them is determined solely by our own deeds. As a well-known Buddhist sutra affirms, we have nothing but our own actions and we never shall have anything but our own actions in the form of their results. As Saint Paul wrote to Saint Timothy: "Some men's sins are open beforehand, going before to judgment; and some men they follow after" (I Timothy 5:24). They may be either actualized or potential, but they are there.

"He suffers....He is glad"

It is the results that reveal the character of our actions, not the excuse-making or rationalization of ourselves or others. Consequently: "The wrong-doer suffers both ways. He suffers and is tormented to see his own depraved behavior....The doer of good is glad both ways.

He is glad and rejoices to see his own good deeds." Anyone who wants can try to weasel out of it by claiming that God favors and purifi es us by making us suffer to make us more pleasing to him and curses those He detests by damning them through prosperity and ease, and therefore misery is proof of virtue. Such a view makes God a fool and a monster, but reveals that the view-holder is the fool, the monster–and is suffering accordingly.

Why does Buddha not explain to us about those bad, even horribly evil people, who live in high style and seem to have all they want, and those good people who have hardship and misfortune? The answer is twofold, external and internal. Externally, the good fortune of the bad is the result of good deeds done in the past, and the misfortune of the good is the result of bad deeds done in the past. There is nothing more to it. Internally, the truth is that no matter what advantages a person may have, how easy their outer life may be, the evil suffer constantly in their hearts and minds–that is why they are so addicted to alcohol, drugs, and frantic pleasure, especially sex. Conversely, however unfortunate the external situation of the good may be, they experience peace and contentment and even rejoice in heart and mind. So there is no need to comment on them; Buddha is speaking of internal suffering and rejoicing, not prosperity, poverty, or other external conditions.

The heart of the matter

Here and beyond he is punished. The wrong-doer is punished both ways. He is punished by the thought, "I have done evil," and is even more punished when he comes to a bad state.

Here and beyond he rejoices. The doer of good rejoices both way. He rejoices at the thought, "I have done good," and rejoices even more when he comes to a happy state (Dhammapada 17, 18).

Now we come to the major message of these two Dhammapada verses in relation to both good and bad: "He suffers and is tormented to *see* his own depraved behavior....He is glad and rejoices to *see* his own good deeds." When we look at our life, both internal and external, and intelligently perceive it, we SEE the nature of our past (and often present) deeds. Our external life reveals our inner life; our life as it unfolds before us is an objectification of our mind, and nothing else. Study your life and you will come to know your mind. When we suffer we are seeing our negativity, and when we rejoice we are seeing our positivity. Our life is a revelation/reflection of our inner life. The effect reveals the nature of the cause.

Actually, Buddha's words apply mostly to the wise, for only the wise grieve or rejoice over their wrong or right behavior–others only grieve or rejoice over their *results*. The ignorant says: "How miserable I am: look at my poverty and illness." The wise says: "How wrong have been my past actions: look at my poverty and illness." It is the difference between the person who repents because he understands his deeds are evil and the one who repents because he is going to be caught and punished.

The ignorant only look at their outer condition, whereas the wise look at their inner condition as revealed by the outer. So, as is usual with the words of all the wise, only those already substantially wise will understand and heed them, and the foolish will either not even see them or will disdain them altogether.

Words are not wisdom

Even if he is fond of quoting appropriate texts, the thoughtless man who does not put them into practice himself is like a cowherd counting other people's cows, not a partner in the Holy Life (Dhammapada 19).

These pungent words of Buddha immediately bring to mind a part of Chapter Twelve of *Autobiography of a Yogi*. Swami Yukteswar, the guru of Paramhansa Yogananda, was the very embodiment of jnana, divine wisdom. He often encountered the braying of jackasses–donkeys carrying the scriptures and words of the wise while dinning them into others' ears like overbearing parrots. One of these squawkers received a real jolt from him in this way:

"With ostentatious zeal, the scholar shook the ashram rafters with scriptural lore. Resounding passages poured from the *Mahabharata*, the *Upanishads*, the *bhasyas* [commentaries] of Shankara.

"'I am waiting to hear you.' Sri Yukteswar's tone was inquiring, as though utter silence had reigned. The pundit was puzzled.

"'Quotations there have been, in superabundance.' Master's words convulsed me with mirth, as I squatted in my corner, at a respectful distance from the visitor. 'But what original commentary can you supply, from the uniqueness of your particular life? What holy text have you absorbed and made your own? In what ways have these timeless truths renovated your nature? Are you content to be a hollow victrola, mechanically repeating the words of other men?'

"'I give up!' The scholar's chagrin was comical. 'I have no inner realization.'

"For the first time, perhaps, he understood that discerning placement of the comma does not atone for a spiritual coma.

"'These bloodless pedants smell unduly of the lamp,' my guru remarked after the departure of the chastened one. 'They prefer philosophy to be a gentle intellectual setting-up exercise. Their elevated thoughts are carefully unrelated either to the crudity of outward action or to any scourging inner discipline!'"

In spiritual matters, theory is vastly preferred to practical experience, perhaps because experience entails change and responsibility. In religion many experts on externals are completely ignorant of spiritual matters, including many experts on mysticism. Hilda Graf, for example, who wrote volumes on mysticism and mystical theology only met one actual mystic in her life, Teresa Neuman the stigmatist, and hated her virulently and wrote slanderous denunciations of her. One of the more tragic figures of the American stage and screen–alcoholic, drug addict and sexual addict–was perhaps the foremost expert in this country on the lives of Christian saints. I knew an Eastern Orthodox priest who was considered the world's expert on the mystical theology of Saint Gregory Palamas, one of the major figures in Orthodox mysticism. When questioned as to whether he practiced Hesychia (the main subject of Saint Gregory's writings), he indignantly avowed that he certainly did not(!). Fr. Herbert Thurston, the twentieth century's self-elected expert on mystical phenomena, had neither experience of mystical phenomena nor even much belief in it, often discounting or deriding it in the lives of saints and blesseds.

Mark Twain said that the difference between the right word and the almost-right word was the difference between lightning and lightning-bug. The same may be said about those who know spiritual principles and those who put them into practice.

Spiritual busybodies

Closely related to the mental librarians, though vastly inferior to them intellectually, are the movers and shakers that invade virtually every spiritual institution that shows promise of growth and influence. These people neither study nor practice the principles and disciplines of those groups, yet they insinuate themselves into administrative positions and eventually control everything, turning it into an opportunity for both profit and power. They are always busy in the work of the institution (which they often refer to as "the Work" or "this Work"), darting here and there and hurling directives everywhere. The dupes of the organization stand aside in awe at their supposed dedication and practical abilities, not knowing they are being sheared like sheep in body (pocketbook), mind, and spirit.

The Venerable Ming Zhen Shakya, in *The Seventh World of Chan Buddhism*, discusses these people who turn Zendos into Zen-do's. They are "practical people who excel in improving earthly existence. [In the spiritual organization they] are always involved in non-spiritual activities, doing jobs which they perform with exemplary efficiency. Their strategy is simply to become indispensable and it succeeds admirably since, invariably, they are fearless and proficient in all tasks which scare the wits out of Chan masters and other spiritual persons. They know how to fill out forms, handle media, arrange excursions, regulate crowds, collect fees, profitably manufacture and peddle religious articles and other souvenir items, compile mailing lists, and operate restaurants, bakeries, retreats, hostelries, etc. When it comes to developing monastery real estate and putting the bite on tourists, pilgrims and congregation members to pay for the improvements, [they] have no peers." But meanwhile they are a deadweight on the spiritual dimension of the organization and often stifle it altogether, while making it well-known and very profitable. "[They] simply do not understand that Chan is Buddhism and Buddhism is a religion, a religion of salvation. Though Buddhism may well provide for such ancillary functions, it is not a health club or a social center, a guild, an arts and crafts studio, a sanitarium, a study group, a philanthropical society, a boarding house or a profit making enterprise. The aim of Buddhism is not to cope with earthly existence but to transcend it, not to gain material comfort but to dispense with the notion of it, not to enhance or to rehabilitate reputations, but to be born anew without earthly identity in the glorious anonymity of Buddha Nature. Being a good fund raiser is a little off the mark." So is being a good preacher, teacher, author and debater when there is no inner realization. For example, one highly-renowned American teacher, lecturer, and writer on Buddhist meditation never meditates except in his classes, when he can hardly do otherwise. The motto seems to be: Monkey talk, monkey write, monkey teach; but monkey not do.

The thoughtless

The problem with the "thoughtless man" is that he is completely heedless of the spiritual life, confusing intellectual activity with spirituality. The heart of the problem is his incomprehension of the need to take it personally and apply the principles and practices in his life and change himself. This malady afflicts all, both East and West, but it is particularly pernicious and persistent in the West. Knowing about something is not the same as being or possessing it, yet people avidly read books and attend lectures and seminars on spiritual life (including meditation) without the slightest intention of engaging in serious, dedicated practice. Just a few days ago I received a letter from someone telling me that she had given a lecture on the need for spiritual study.

Afterward the attendees were rhapsodizing about how inspiring and wonderful it had been. But not a single one of them took her advice and opened a book.

Quite some time back I gave a talk at a Christian monastery on meditation. Everyone was thrilled and uplifted–they said. Not only did they say, "At last we know the way!" they even claimed that some time before in a vision one of them had been told that this teaching would be coming to them as fulfillment of their spiritual aspiration. (I modestly omit that in the vision the monk was told that "a master" would be giving them the teaching.) Two days later, when I asked them how they were managing in meditation, as per my talk, they looked utterly blank and then unanimously said that they had not even tried to do so. When I asked why not? one of them replied: "It just didn't seem so important." I went home.

My chagrin was uncalled for, really, because a few years before that I had been invited to a contemplative Catholic monastery to talk with the members on meditation. The first thing I did was ask who had read *The Way of a Pilgrim*, a Russian Orthodox book about constant prayer and meditation in the Holy Name of Jesus. Every one of them had not only read it, they all expressed great enthusiasm and admiration for it. It was their favorite spiritual book. "Have you tried to pray always and meditate as the book says?" was my innocent query. Silence. They looked at me as though I had asked if they had considered burying themselves alive, or something equally outrageous. I went home, then, too.

Multitudes want to hear about enlightenment, meditation, the Self, and the Buddha Nature, but hardly any want to do anything about it. As Saint Paul lamented: "Many sleep" (I Corinthians 11:30). And many talk in their sleep.

Counting cows

Most religion is worthless cow-counting, obsession with the glories, powers, and even divinity of one or more superior beings, whether called avatars, buddhas, bodhisattwas, prophets, or saints.

Religious people believe in, hope in, take refuge in, surrender to them, in exchange for great rewards here or hereafter. How they trumpet the praises of these goody-vendors to the skies and decry those not so praising. They even tot up lists of glories and benefits of various divinities and produce a religious consumer report that establishes the superiority of their particular cult. They write sermons, poems, hymns, and even shed tears of devotion and faith. *But they do not live the Holy Life* exemplified by the objects of their devotion. They do not need to–they have faith! I well remember a church full of people desperately singing over and over: "I can, I will, I do believe; I can, I will, I do believe; I can, I will, I do believe, that Jesus saves me now." But in their hearts they knew it was bunkum. That is why they "believed" it so insistently. And like all delusionals they became emotional and violent when their delusion was challenged. (Just try it.)

Partners in the Holy Life

Buddha lets us know quite clearly that the Holy Life is what matters, and that it is a matter of *living*–that is, *doing*. "Doing, doing, done!" is a common statement in India regarding spiritual life. In Buddhism, the mantra beginning *"Gate, gate,"* conveys the same idea: Going, going,… gone. *"Partner* in the Holy Life" may not be the best translation. Some translators render it "sharer," but that can be misunderstood as someone spreading it around or having it handed to them. "Partaker in the Holy Life" is better, for it implies activity on the part of the aspirant, activity that results in his *participation* in the Holy Life. No part of the idea is then passive, but thoroughly active. The idea is also there that the Holy Life is an ever-present thing, that it need not be produced, but only entered into for it is a matter of our eternal nature. It has always been there, we have just not accessed it. It is there for everyone; we need have no one else give it to us, nor does it depend on the whimsy of some deity. Rather we must learn how to access it and then do so. End of story.

The holy life defined

Even if he does not quote appropriate texts much, if he follows the principles of the Teaching by getting rid of greed, hatred and delusion, deep of insight and with a mind free from attachment, not clinging to anything in this world or the next— that man is a partner in the Holy Life (Dhammapada 20).

Better than "Teaching" is the original term, "Dharma," for that is not mere philosophy or theology, but the way of life that leads to the true wisdom of enlightenment, to Nirvana. And Buddha Dharma, the dharma that leads to Buddhahood, consists of "getting rid of greed, hatred and delusion," being "deep of insight" and having "a mind free from attachment, not clinging to anything in this world or the next."

Raga and dwesha

Two of the most important words in analyzing the dilemma of the human condition are raga and dwesha, the powerful duo that motivate virtually all human endeavor. Buddha, in common with all philosophers of India, continually refers to them, so an understanding of their import is essential to us. Unfortunately, both Hindu and Buddhist translators are prone to do just that (translate them) and thus obscure or distort their meaning. There may be exact equivalents in other languages, but not in English, and translators do us a real disservice by not retaining them and explaining them somewhere in the text by a footnote or by a glossary. Here is my preferred definition of them:

Raga: Attachment/affinity for something, implying a desire for that. This can be emotional (instinctual) or intellectual. It may range from simple liking or preference to intense desire and attraction.

Dwesha: Aversion/avoidance for something, implying a dislike for that. This can be emotional (instinctual) or intellectual. It may range from simple nonpreference to intense repulsion, antipathy and even hatred.

They are commonly referred to as "rag-dwesh"—as a duality, for they are the alternating currents or poles that keep us spinning in relativity, reaching out and pushing away, accepting and rejecting, running toward and running away from. The horror of them is that they not only alternate, spinning us around, they also mutate into one another. What we like at one time we dislike at another, and vice versa. For they, like everything else, are essentially one, a double-headed monster. "When he has no lust, no hatred, a man walks safely among the things of lust and hatred. To obey the Atman is his peaceful joy; sorrow melts into that clear peace: his quiet mind is soon established in peace" (Bhagavad Gita 2:64, 65).

Buddha lists ridding ourselves of raga and dwesha as the first step in the Holy Life. But what a gigantic step! It will not be made overnight, we may be sure, for raga and dwesha have driven us along from the moment we were plants, what to say of animals and human beings.

Moha

In his teachings Buddha frequently listed the Unholy Trinity: Raga, Dwesha, and Moha. Here is my preferred definition of moha that I feel covers all aspects: *Moha:* Delusion in relation to something, usually producing delusive attachment or infatuation based on a completely false perception and evaluation of the object.

It is bad enough to be pulled toward or pushed away from just about everything we encounter in external and internal life, but to top it off we are totally wrong most of the time about the character or nature of those things. This is moha. Although in Hindu usage there is always an implied attachment or desire resulting from moha, that is not an absolute, and Buddha used it to indicate confusion and misperception in general.

Is there significance in his listing of raga-dwesha before moha? Is he indicating that raga and dwesha produce moha—at least at the beginning, although later on they combine to make a rolling wheel of general confusion?

Deep of insight

Buddha has told us what to jettison from our minds, and now he tells us what is to be established in their place: deep insight. The

Venerable Thanissaro Bhikkhu renders it "alert" in the sense of keen awareness. Sanderson Beck prefers "possessed of true knowledge," as does Max Muller. "Firmly established in liberated thought" is Harischandra Kaviratna's choice. All convey the right idea, whichever may be the most exact. We need *profound knowing*, not intellectual theorizing and mind-gaming, but direct knowledge, which is possible only to those free from raga, dwesha, and moha. No small order, as we Americans are wont to say.

With a mind free from attachment

Obviously when we have no delusion about things and neither attraction nor repulsion for them, our minds will be free from attachment/involvement. Again: "When he has no lust [raga], no hatred [dwesha], a man walks safely among the things of lust and hatred" for they do not touch him, nor does he touch them. "The world is crucified unto me, and I unto the world," said Saint Paul (Galatians 6:14).

The Venerable Thanissaro Bhikkhu translates the expression: "his mind well-released, not clinging." This is most significant, for it is not enough to merely be unattached at the moment; rather, we must be in that condition of release (genuine separation) in which attachment is no longer a possibility.

Not clinging to anything in this world or the next

That being the case, Buddha says that the final component of the Holy Life is a mind "not clinging to anything in this world or the next," underscoring what I have just said. Those who have either not correctly pursued enlightenment or have not had the time needed to become perfectly established in it, may in a subsequent birth lapse back into attachment and clinging and begin the awful cycle of rag-dwesh and moha over again, wiping out the former attainment, perhaps sinking even lower than before. This is almost guaranteed in the case of those of incorrect pursuit. This is the cruel fate of those whose practice is not "right," as Buddha knew well from his own pursuit and observation.

A final consideration

It is relatively easy to become detached from the defective and pain-producing elements of this material world, but the beauties and seeming perfections of the subtle worlds are not so easy to be indifferent to. And this includes their equivalents in our own private inner world of the mind. A person can break all chains of this world and yet remain completely bound to other worlds. In the same way we can turn away from the gross allurements of the earth plane while remaining thoroughly bound by the psychological and "spiritual" elements of our creative and "higher" natures.

To be a total renouncer is a rare thing indeed. Many may become weaned from the outer sense-life, but what about the inner senses and the conceptualizing "wisdom" of the intellect? Saint Silouan of Athos stated that delight in philosophical and theological niceties is the false mysticism of the ego.

"For when a man's heart has reached fulfillment through knowledge and personal experience of the truth of Brahman, he is never again moved by the things of the senses. Earth, stone and gold seem all alike to one who has mastered his senses. Such a yogi is said to have achieved union with Brahman" (Bhagavad Gita 6:8).

The Holy Life leads to The Holy.

Chapter 2
ATTENTION

Attention leads to immortality. Carelessness leads to death. Those who pay attention will not die, while the careless are as good as dead already (Dhammapada 21).

"Attention"–*appamada* in Pali–literally means "non-infatuation," but is usually interpreted as the result of such freedom from infatuation. Narada Thera says it has the connotations of "ever-present mindfulness, watchfulness, or earnestness in doing good."

If loose lips sink ships, then lax and unaware minds sink lives. This is important for us to comprehend, since we often think that spiritual life is charging ahead in some kind of inspired enthusiasm that precludes any intellectual application or plain good sense, that somehow our sincerity and aspiration will ensure success and safety. It is as silly as that terrible and criminal debacle known as the Children's Crusade. At this time in history we are appalled and astounded that any sane human being could possibly believe that the sight of little barefoot children coming in innocence and trust would conquer the minds and hearts of murderous plunderers, who were actually no worse than those who engineered such a monstrous folly as a kind of "spiritual" trick on them. As Will Cuppy pointed out, it is useless to appeal to the higher nature of those who have none.

(If you do not know about the Children's Crusade, see http://www.historyguide.org/ancient/children.html, online, or read about it in Steven Runciman's *A History of the Crusades,* Volume III, pp. 139-144.)

Tarzans of the Light

For those of us who have wandered through the tangled jungle of world scriptures–each one usually claiming to be the sole truth– that are compounded of revelations, exhortation, cajolings, threats, mind-boggling assertions, and supposed profundities that can never be either proved or disproved, the rational and practical teachings of Buddha found in the Pali scriptures come as a shock. So much so that, conditioned by prior study, we may disregard them. After all, where is the esoteric wisdom, the secrets meant for only the select few? Where are the symbols and the mysteries? Above all, where are the irrational formulas of "truth" that demonstrate how ignorant and limited we are in our inability to make any sense of them because they are above all sense? And where are the mystic techniques that will open the universe to us and reveal all mysteries and bestow all knowledge and power?

We are so used to religion being either a magic shop or a launching pad to higher worlds, that Buddha's uncompromising good sense and insistence on freedom from all that binds us right here and now disorients us. And his assertion that we must look at all things and see their truth (or untruth) and act honestly regarding them is a real comedown for us who prefer to leap and swing from tree to tree in life's jungle, happy carefree Tarzans of the White Light to whom "Everything Is God, So Why Worry?" "What is there to do, and where is there to go?" is our way of saying: "I won't" in response to Buddha's urging to real happiness and freedom from care. But eventually we begin to get the idea, and then every word of Buddha is a key to liberation.

Immortality

Attention leads to immortality. The Pali word translated "immortality" is *amata*, which literally means "deathlessness." Venerable Narada Thera says that amata is a synonym for Nirvana, and comments: "As this positive term clearly indicates, Nirvana is not annihilation or a state of nothingness as some are apt to believe. It is the permanent, immortal, supramundane state which cannot be expressed by mundane terms." It must be noted, though, that immortality is a *state*, not eternal embodiment, in this or some other realm, and consequently identified with "I am this, I am that." To transcend both birth and death is immortality, is eternity.

Since it leads to immortality, attention is definitely more than simple awareness or even insight. It is "earnestness in doing good," in pursuing the sole good: liberation. Naturally, a great deal more than attention is needed, but Buddha mentions it because without its dynamic all the other requisites are worthless, like machines without the energy to run them.

Death
Again, death is not divestment of a body, but immersion in the relative world of samsara and its bonds. It, too, is a state, even though external conditions necessarily follow and mirror its presence. "Life" in any relative condition is really death, because it shrouds the truth of our essential being. "Carelessness" is the opposite of attention, and is the way we all lead our lives, physical and psychological. If that were not so, none of us would be here. We neither see nor deal with anything in a realistic manner. Frankly, we are profoundly delusional, and our only hope is the correct pursuit of ultimate reality, which is ultimate freedom. Consequently we pray: "Lead me from death to immortality."

Cultivation
Attention cannot be produced immediately, it requires constant and vigilant cultivation, meditation being the prime implement of such cultivation. For "those who pay attention will not die, while the careless are as good as dead already." Keeping this perspective in mind daily, there is hope for our ascent to life and immortality.

So having clearly understood the value of attention, wise men take pleasure in it, rejoicing in what the saints have practiced (Dhammapada 22).

Unworthy aspirants
There are two kinds of unworthy aspirants in spiritual life: those that when they learn what is required of the successful seeker honestly

refuse and turn away, and those who sigh, mope, carp, and whine, grudging the slightest discipline or denial, dragging their feet every step of the way. The first kind are not so bad–they go away and leave the path of dharma (and those who are traveling it) in peace. The second type, however, are much worse. They both disrupt and exasperate the sincere and worthy who take delight in meeting the requirements of dharma, and they keep hanging on like deadly parasites, doing their utmost to compromise and degrade the dharma to their level of laziness and corruption. These are enemies both to themselves and to those that come after, for if there are enough of them and they get into some position of authority, they often succeed in completely destroying the dharma for many, and sometimes for ages. Of them Saint Jude wrote: "These are spots in your feasts of charity, when they feast with you, feeding themselves without fear: clouds they are without water, carried about of winds; trees whose fruit withereth, without fruit, twice dead, plucked up by the roots; raging waves of the sea, foaming out their own shame; wandering stars, to whom is reserved the blackness of darkness for ever" (Jude 12,13) until they change direction completely. They are always getting "confused," "worried," "bothered," "disturbed," and depressed–usually over everybody else but themselves. They spread gloom and discontent. As Yogananda said, they are spiritual skunks, stinking up wherever they go, but all the time blaming it on others. "I don't understand" and "I don't see why" are the javelins they are forever hurling, acting the part of the injured, the neglected, the misunderstood, and the despised.

On the other hand...

By contrast, "wise men take pleasure in" the way of truth, and gladly meet the requirements. Since they really want freedom, for them no price is too high. Knowing that you really do get only what you pay for, even in the abstract realms of consciousness, they "rejoice in what the saints have practiced." Yes, they rejoice! For they *practice* that which the saints, the true Aryas, have practiced, and get the same results.

The way of the wise

Those who meditate with perseverance, constantly working hard at it, are the wise who experience Nirvana, the ultimate freedom from chains (Dhammapada 23).

Guru Nanak, founder of the Sikh religion, frequently used the expression "godwards" for those who were moving toward Divine Consciousness. We might coin the ungainly word "Nirvanics" for those Buddha is describing in this twenty-third verse of the Dhammapada. They are the wise. As Yogananda said, the world is divided into two types of human beings: the wise who are seeking God and the foolish who are not.

Whatever the terms we may use for "the ultimate freedom from chains," the idea is the same: right now we are bound, but we can become unbound. How? Buddha is telling us how.

Meditation

One time a man asked me if he could speak with me about some problems and questions he had. "Why bother?" brayed an eavesdropper standing nearby, "All he will do is tell you to meditate!" Yes, it is true: meditation is the only solution. Many things are needed to support our meditation and ensure its success, but meditation is the prime means for those seeking real freedom of being. Paramhansa Yogananda, writing about Yogiraj Shyama Charan Lahiri, one of nineteenth-century India's greatest yogis, said: "The great guru taught his disciples to avoid theoretical discussion of the scriptures. 'He only is wise who devotes himself to realizing, not reading only, the ancient revelations,' he said. 'Solve all your problems through meditation. Exchange unprofitable religious speculations for actual God-contact. Clear your mind of dogmatic theological debris; let in the fresh, healing waters of direct perception. Attune yourself to the active inner Guidance; the Divine Voice has the answer to every dilemma of life. Though man's ingenuity for getting himself into trouble appears to be endless, the Infinite Succor is no less resourceful.'"

Long before these wise words of Lahiri Mahasaya, Buddha made clear to his students again and again that meditation was the way to freedom.

Perseverance

Wonderful as it is, meditation is no magic trick. Only those gain its benefit who "meditate with perseverance, constantly working hard at it." So two things must characterize our meditation practice: constancy and effective effort. We keep on and keep on, never stopping for a moment in the endeavor to continually direct our awareness toward Reality. And that endeavor cannot be done in a lackadaisical manner. The Path is walked, or even run, along, not shuffled or moseyed along.

The great twentieth-century Roman Catholic philosopher, Dietrich van Hildebrand, wrote in his masterful study of spiritual evolution, *Transformation in Christ*, that the majority of people suffer from what he calls "discontinuity." That is, most people simply cannot sustain either effort or thought unless driven by the base passions. In other words, they have no real freedom of mind and will, though they think they do. Addiction impels us, but wisdom does not, for freedom is both its goal and its requisite. Hence, our sustained effort at meditation must come directly from within us as a fully conscious and willful choice. Every day this is true: each step on the path is a conscious choice, clear to the end. This is not a path for the timid or the lazy or the merely curious.

Intent on meditation

Perhaps Richard's translation: "constantly working hard at it," is not the best, for meditation is certainly a matter of effort, but not one of stress or strain. The Venerable Thanissaro Bhikkhu renders it "firm in their effort." We must be focussed, intent, on our practice, certainly exerting will and strength, but in a judicial and cool-headed manner. Constant and steady is the way.

The chains

We are bound by millions (if not billions) of chains, yet meditation pursued rightly will dissolve them all. In the meantime we have to make sure we are not binding more chains on us, like the washed dog that immediately runs out and rolls in the filth to counteract the cleanliness. Here, too, meditation is the answer, for the insight born of meditation enables us to see the folly of bondage and the understanding to turn away from more involvement in chaining ourselves.

Nirvana

The purpose of all this is Nirvana. Just as a child cannot comprehend adulthood, so we cannot really understand just what Nirvana is. But one thing we can know: it is the opposite of where we now find ourselves! Attempts at definition are risky. Some time back I saw a television show on which a reputed "authority" on Buddhism was asked by an interviewer to describe Nirvana. He proceeded to give a checklist of the characteristics of Nirvana, *every one of which is listed by Buddha in the Pali sutras as NOT Nirvana*, though many mistake them for Nirvana. It was sort of like hearing a Christian recite the opposite qualities listed by Jesus in the Beatitudes or a Jew reciting the exact opposites to the Ten Commandments.

But let us give ourselves at least an approximation, a whiff, of what Nirvana surely entails: "It is a supramundane state that can be attained in this life itself. It is also explained as extinction of passions, but not a state of nothingness. It is an eternal blissful state of relief that results from the complete eradication of the passions." So says the Venerable Narada Thera.

And so seek all of us.

Expanding Glory

When a man is resolute and recollected, pure of deed and persevering, when he is attentive and self-controlled and lives according to the Teaching, his reputation is bound to grow (Dhammapada 24).

The last words of this verse comprise the key idea. The word which Richards renders "reputation" is *yasha* which in Sanskrit and Pali can mean reputation, but usually means success, fame, or glory. Most translators prefer "glory," but we should keep the other meanings in mind as well.

Glory

Most religions, in order to impose their authority and convince people of their need for religion, put out a single main message: "You are nothing without me." And usually compound it with: "You are evil, and without me you deserve pain and death." Interestingly enough, *with* them there never seems to be much of a difference between the believers and the unbelievers, the faithful and the unfaithful, as regards their states of mind and conditions of life. But "true believers" are so busy believing, hoping, and obeying that they almost never follow the sage wisdom of Dr. Bronner of peppermint soap fame and "judge only by the results."

Even Hinduism and Buddhism, that have such an optimism for the eventual condition of their adherents, insist that at the present their adherents are ignorant, degraded, and basically crazy or idiots—so much so that in most people's mind the Divine Atma and the Buddha Nature are so far over the horizon that for all practical purposes they suffer under the same condemnations as those of other religions, adding bad karma and the certainty of rebirth to their burdens. But if we look we shall see that Buddha does not say the virtuous and wise attain or are given glory. The implication is that each human being already has some degree of glory by his very nature, and that sadhana (spiritual practice) is intended to expand that glory or, more rightly put, to extend his awareness of his own glory to infinity, to Nirvana.

If we have no idea who or what we are, then how can we formulate any intelligent goals for ourselves or rightly estimate our ability to attain those goals? It is therefore absolutely necessary for us to understand our innate worth, for that is the foundation on which we can build our future advancement or self-discovery. Then our rallying cry can be with David: "Awake up, my glory;…I myself will awake early" (Psalms 57:8). Motivated by both hope and assurance, we can then sculpt ourselves into the image Buddha presents to us as that of one whose glory is ever-increasing.

Resolute

We have previously spoken about the problem of "discontinuity," that so many of us suffer from a seeming incapacity to sustain a course of thought or action unless we are impelled to it by the force of addiction, desire, aversion, or fear. Making a sustained effort of will in the sphere of our personal life is a far too rare matter, indeed. Yet, we can see from Buddha's checklist that the capacity for active resolve is the first step, not some far-off target in our development.

As said, the requisite resolve is active, not merely intellectual. "I have to quit smoking," "Some day I must get to around to that," and "As soon as I have the time…" are phrases we use like the ticking of a clock that counts the passing away of our very lives. Buddha, however, is not speaking of wishful thinking but of active doing. The path to rebirth is paved with good intentions; the path to Nirvana is paved with right resolve and right action—*sustained* right resolve and action. For only the end result counts. To go full steam down the road for a while and then fizzle out means nothing.

One time a young woman, seized with momentary spiritual aspiration, insisted on leaving home and traveling with Sri Anandamayi Ma. Her father accordingly brought her to where Ma was currently staying. After a few days he accompanied Ma to the railway station as she was leaving that place. Seeing his daughter firmly ensconced among the group of women that usually travelled with Ma, he happily remarked: "I see she has passed the test and been accepted." "Baba," replied Mother with emphasis, "the only test that matters is the *last* test." In a few weeks the daughter was back home, having lost interest.

We, too, often congratulate ourselves on the fact that we are trying, but in time we get bored with the spiritual dressing up and play-acting, tired of looking at ourselves in the mirror of our egos, or the mirror of other people's egos as they observe us, and we get "disillusioned" or realize we Don't Really Need To Do All That. It is a great marvel that Buddha was able to resist and conquer Mara, but it may be an even greater marvel that he got to the point of development where Mara needed to appear.

Instead of "resolute" some other translations are: "energetic," "with initiative," "with great perseverance," "has roused himself," and "exerts himself." The idea is clear.

Recollected

Yet, Buddha does not want us to be charging along heedlessly, mistaking sheer energy output as the desideratum. Stephen Leacock, the Canadian humorist, wrote in one of his satires about a man who "jumped on his horse and rode off wildly in all four directions." This is not the way. As a workplace sign says: "Would you rather work harder— or smarter?" Intelligence must prevail, and that is only in a calm and balanced mind. So "recollected" is the second item of Buddha's list. It can also be translated: "mindful," "aware," and "thoughtful." "Self-possessed" is a very good Victorian term that is rarely heard nowadays and even more rarely seen.

Through meditation alone can the mind be put into shape and kept there. It is the meditational mind that is able to see how to act and how to gauge the status of the present moment in the context of the intended future. The second chapter of the Bhagavad Gita gives a very full description of exactly the state of mind needed to successfully navigate our way across the sea of samsara.

Keeping the goal in mind is no small thing. The greatest of all Christian monks, Saint Arsenius the Great, wrote in large letters on the wall of his hut in the Egyptian desert: "Arsenius, why did you come here?" Each day he considered that challenge in order to maintain the original intention and perspective which had brought him to that place. It is very easy to get so caught up in the journeying that we forget or ignore our purpose in starting out and wander into byways and even regress. "I have been on the Path for many years" is usually an admission of just such forgetfulness and wandering.

Pure of deed

We simply have to face the facts: in spiritual life as in every other endeavor there are thoughts and deeds that hinder and thoughts and deeds that help. The idea that anyone can at any time in any condition live The Life is inexcusably foolish. Those who refuse to believe that right and wrong, good and bad, exist, or that those classifications apply to their personal life, should take up hobbies and forget Nirvana. Otherwise they simply make a mess of things and insult the Dharma. Those who wish may pretend that purity of intention or "heart" are sufficient, but Buddha does not think so. He does not talk about theory, but says a seeker must be *pure of deed*. Words and feelings are not the issue.

Right away the impure and the unqualified will demand a definition of purity so they can argue about it, knowing full well what they are and what they are not—and consequently are not going to be. So Buddha enunciated five precepts that will cover everything pretty well for those who want it covered. (Those who want a cover-up will of course supply their own in the form of misinterpretation of what one or more of the precepts really mean.) Here they are: 1) Abstinence from speaking untruth; 2) abstinence from intoxication; 3) abstinence from sexual immorality; 4) abstinence from theft; and 5) abstinence from taking life. These obviously have very wide scopes, especially since the Pali terms and their Sanskrit equivalents have broad meanings. For example, lying can take many forms, even silence. A serious student of dharma will thoughtfully consider each precept in turn and honestly figure out all their forms and applications. I will make only this observation: Although many years ago I was told by a junior high school librarian that Buddha taught "moderation," even I could see that moderation does not come in here at all. Total abstinence is the intent. Anything less is not the dharma.

Those who follow the precepts will thereby always be pure of deed.

Persevering

Perseverance is included in "resolute." Just why Richards uses that term here I have no idea, but four other translators understand it as meaning someone who acts with careful consideration, with due analysis before acting. In his teachings Buddha insists on the need for appropriate reflection before acting or speaking, a counsel we transgress untold times each day. But our folly increases rather than diminishes the relevance of Buddha's admonition.

Attentive

We have just considered what is meant by "attentive," needing only to add that heedfulness should become continuous in our thoughts and deeds, "Watch yourself" being very good advice.

Self-controlled

Many of us suffer from—and suffer because of—what I call the Pinocchio Complex. Pinocchio lived in the continual hope that one day he would wake up and find himself a real boy instead of a puppet. We think that if we just wait long enough and lounge around the vestibule of spiritual life (reading the magazines in the Dharma Waiting Room) we will one day find ourselves out on the track and on our way—and soon at the goal. We are not really lazy, otherwise we could not even sustain our life on earth, yet effortlessness appeals to us endlessly, especially in spiritual matters. Any yogi who adopts the soap-commercial line about how quick and easy—"just like magic"—it is to meditate and attain enlightenment will sell his "product" very easily. His customers will not get anything in the long run, but maybe they did not want to, anyway.

Before we can know our true, inmost self, we must first gain control over our untrue, outer self. It is this control that is meant by "self-controlled." And when we attain that control we restrain the false self in all its aspects. Moderation is not the purpose here, either, but eventual effacement so the true self can resurrect, ascend, and reign (the real meaning behind the same events in the life of Christ).

Living according to the Teaching

"Living the Dharma" is a better translation of *dhammajivino*. This indicates a life based fully on the precepts and extending to all the details that make up the Holy Life. It is much easier to believe, accept, discuss and even teach dharma, but Buddha tells us to *live* it. Excessive involvement in philosophy, theology, and scriptural (textual) study is an evasion of dharma in its only meaningful form: as a way of life.

Putting it all together, Buddha still says it best: "When a man is resolute and recollected, pure of deed and persevering, when he is attentive and self-controlled and lives according to the Teaching, his reputation [glory] is bound to grow."

Each man must make an island

By resolution and attention, by discipline and self-control, a clever [wise] man may build himself an island that no flood can overthrow (Dhammapada 25).

The factors listed in this verse–resolution, attention, discipline and self-control–have been analyzed already, so the new idea here is the nature of who we are and what we are doing. Hopefully we are a *medhaav*, a wise man, as the Pali text indicates. So what does the wise do? He makes for himself an island that no flood, no tides or waves, can overwhelm and submerge, not even momentarily.

The sea of samsara

We are adrift in–not just upon–the sea of samsara, the cycle of repeated births and deaths, the whole process of earthly life. We flounder in its waves, rising and falling, alternately getting breath and nearly drowning. At the same time we are in the grip of fevered illusion and rarely have even a glimpse of the utter horror of our situation. It takes many lives for us to awaken to the awesome possibilities of either remaining tossed about in the waters or the rising out of them altogether and attaining peace. We must choose. The wise choose getting out of the waves, but the moment they make that choice they are confronted with the fact that they are going to have to build their own "island" of liberation, that all the talk of "the other shore" both is and is not true and that no one is going to "save" us and bring us "safely home" however appealing that nursery-tale may be.

Implications

Creating our island implies two major facts:

1) It is a matter of complete self-effort on our part; no outside help or moving toward association or "community." (The Sanskrit word is *kaivalya*, total self-sufficiency and total self-containment.) This may daunt us at first hearing, but reflection reveals that it is a remarkable statement of our capacity to do all the needful for ourself. We can do it! Another facet of this is that there is just no such thing as making our island in conjunction with other people. Yes, we may labor on our island at the same time others do, and we may even encourage one another in the project, but the doing is ours alone. Looking outward is useless and even delusive; the inward orientation alone succeeds.

2) The idea is to get out of the water, to separate ourselves utterly from it, never again to experience even a drop of samsara. I think we all know people who complain about something or someone while clinging to them with thorough determination. This cannot be our way. Many want to be like those in the caucus race described in *Alice in Wonderland*. They run around in a circle on the beach and every so often waves wash over them and soak them through. The stated purpose of the race is to dry off, but it is impossible. Most people prefer that—to have their samsara and beat it, too. But it is a matter of either/or: wet or dry. Complete separation is necessary, because that is the whole idea, not just a side effect. This is not for weekenders and dabblers. Think of the scope: we aim to escape and transcend that which has kept numberless sentient beings in its thrall for numberless creation cycles, not just "ages." We intend to move from relative being to absolute being all on our own. And we can.

The Foolish and the Wise: Vigilance

Foolish, ignorant people indulge in careless lives, whereas a clever man guards his attention as his most precious possession (Dhammapada 26).

Thomas Jefferson spoke more truly than he knew when he stated that eternal vigilance is the price of liberty. For those who seek the ultimate liberation, constant awareness is a prime necessity. On the other hand, "Foolish, ignorant people indulge in careless [heedless] lives." Interestingly, the Venerable Thanissaro Bhikkhu renders it: "They're addicted to heedlessness." This is certainly so. There is a persistent urge toward self-destruction that habitually grips most people, impelling them to negligence, carelessness, and outright blindness to what little reality they are able to perceive if they will to do so.

It is astounding to see how feckless most "spiritual" people really are in relation to their inner development. Over and over they endanger themselves and incur great risk, particularly psychically (mentally), either doing things that can only rebound to their detriment or failing to do that which will protect and strengthen them. They simply do not take seriously the fact that this entire world is a maelstrom calculated to whirl them around and around by continual birth and death, drowning their consciousness from life to life. They take no account of their daily lifestyle or their environment, physical or metaphysical. And the field of their personal relationships is the most chaotic and destructive of all.

There is such a thing as healthy fear, the force that sends us indoors in a hailstorm and up a tree when a dangerous animal is around. This is completely lacking in the foolish. I heard of a school board that interviewed prospective drivers of their school bus. To each one they asked a single question: If you were driving a bus full of children and came to an ice-covered bridge without any railings on the side, how close could you drive to the edge without being afraid of mishap? The estimates were various, but one man replied: "I would drive straight down the middle as far from the edges as I could get, and even then

I would be terrified every second until I got across." He was the one they hired, for they did not want any driver who could feel confident in endangering their children. We need the same grave caution regarding our own lives and aspirations to higher awareness.

The wise prize clearsightedness—and clear thought and action—above all treasures of earth and heaven, aware that not for a moment do they dare to fold their hands and sleep the sleep of inner death. Their vigilance will be their liberty. For them is the admonition of Buddha:

Do not indulge in careless behavior. Do not be the friend of sensual pleasures. He who meditates attentively attains abundant joy (Dhammapada 27).

Indulgence in careless behavior has been already covered, but the next clause brings us to a new subject.

A friend of sensual pleasure

Do not be the friend of sensual pleasures. There are many ways to be a "friend" of sensual pleasure: indulgence, thought, speech, and deliberate proximity as well as association with other "friends" of sensuality. Why go into detailed explanation of these? Anyone with good sense and right intention can figure it out for himself.

There is one form of "friendship" that should be mentioned: the friendship of pretended enmity. Many addicts to sensuality (as well as other toxicities) often express their affinities and desires through "hating," "feeling disgust," and fulminations against what they secretly desire. A friend keeps company with his friends; he seeks them out. Many people keep company with sensuality under the guise of denunciation and opposition. They constantly think about "sin" and "sinners" and even seek them out for the titillation of confrontation and conflict. One of the dirtiest-minded men I ever met specialized in reforming (?) prostitutes. At least he said he did. Many seek out the various tentacles of sensuality and sensual expression "to know the enemy" and be up on what they have to fight against. So they say. In this as in other matters, behind a big front there is always a big back.

Joy

He who meditates attentively attains abundant joy. One of the great defects of half-informed and outward-turned religion is its incapacity to offer something better than "sin." An abstract threat of going to hell at the end of life (which most people think will never end, anyway) is not much of a substitute for enjoyment. Nor is a future heaven of dubious assurance. Authentic religion, however, offers the seeker the means to obtain what he really wants in all his external pursuits: inner joy.

All that we pursue, thinking that happiness lies in its possession, is only valued by us because it imparts but a fraction of a fragment of that happiness which is found abundantly in our own Self (atma). In the Brihadaranyaka Upanishad (2.4.5), the sage Yajnavalkya says:

"It is not for the sake of the husband, that the husband is dear, but for the sake of the Self.

"It is not for the sake of the wife, that the wife is dear, but for the sake of the Self.

"It is not for the sake of the children, that the children are dear, but for the sake of the Self.

"It is not for the sake of wealth, that wealth is dear, but for the sake of the Self.

"It is not for the sake of the Brahmins, that the Brahmins are held in reverence, but for the sake of the Self.

"It is not for the sake of the Kshatriyas, that the Kshatriyas are held in honor, but for the sake of the Self.

"It is not for the sake of the higher worlds, that the higher worlds are desired, but for the sake of the Self.

"It is not for the sake of the gods, that the gods are worshiped, but for the sake of the Self.

"It is not for the sake of the creatures, that the creatures are prized, but for the sake of the Self.

"It is not for the sake of itself, that anything whatever is esteemed, but for the sake of the Self."

The Taittiriya Upanishad (2.8.1-4) took up this theme, saying:

"Who could live, who could breathe, if that blissful Self dwelt not within the lotus of the heart? He it is that gives joy.

"Of what nature is this joy?

"Consider the lot of a young man, noble, well-read, intelligent, strong, healthy, with all the wealth of the world at his command. Assume that he is happy, and measure his joy as one unit.

"One hundred times that joy is one unit of the joy of Gandharvas: but no less joy than Gandharvas has the seer to whom the Self has been revealed, and who is without craving.

"One hundred times the joy of Gandharvas is one unit of the joy of celestial Gandharvas: but no less joy than celestial Gandharvas has the sage to whom the Self has been revealed, and who is without craving.

"One hundred times the joy of celestial Gandharvas is one unit of the joy of the Pitris in their paradise: but no less joy than the Pitris in their paradise has the sage to whom the Self has been revealed, and who is without craving.

"One hundred times the joy of the Pitris in their paradise is one unit of the joy of the Devas: but no less joy than the Devas has the sage to whom the Self has been revealed, and who is without craving.

"One hundred times the joy of the Devas is one unit of the joy of the karma Devas: but no less joy than the karma Devas has the sage to whom the Self has been revealed, and who is without craving.

"One hundred times the joy of the karma Devas is one unit of the joy of the ruling Devas: but no less joy than the ruling Devas has the sage to whom the Self has been revealed, and who is without craving.

"One hundred times the joy of the ruling Devas is one unit of the joy of Indra: but no less joy than Indra has the sage to whom the Self has been revealed, and who is without craving.

"One hundred times the joy of Indra is one unit of the joy of Brihaspati: but no less joy than Brihaspati has the sage to whom the Self has been revealed, and who is without craving.

"One hundred times the joy of Brihaspati is one unit of the joy of Prajapati: but no less joy than Prajapati has the sage to whom the Self has been revealed, and who is without craving.

"One hundred times the joy of Prajapati is one unit of the joy of Brahma: but no less joy than Brahma has the seer to whom the Self has been revealed, and who is without craving."

Meditation

The way to abundant joy is meditation. For the one who meditates attentively: "His mind is dead to the touch of the external: it is alive to the bliss of the Atman. Because his heart knows Brahman his happiness is for ever" (Bhagavad Gita 5:21).

In Limitless Consciousness is Limitless Joy.

The View From On High

When a wise man has carefully rid himself of carelessness and climbed the High Castle of Wisdom, sorrowless he observes sorrowing people, like a clear-sighted man on a mountain top looking down on the people with limited vision on the ground below (Dhammapada 28).

When, through constant awareness or heedfulness, the wise one has dispelled heedlessness, a great thing has been accomplished. But that is far from the end of the matter. Now he must climb the high tower of wisdom (discernment). Being high, it will take both time and intense effort, for there is no elevator to the top. The Short Path and the Quick Path simply do not exist. There are, indeed, shorter and quicker paths, comparatively speaking, but frankly our distance from the goal is so long that to bother with such comparisons is laughable and a waste of time.

Once that height has been attained, sorrow is over for him. As Swami Yukteswar Giri pointed out: "Finding God will mean the funeral of all sorrows." For Wisdom is God. Everything else is ignorance.

Once that state has been established in the consciousness, then the sorrowing state of others is clearly seen and–contradictory as it may seem for a sorrowless person–keenly felt. Although he perceives, even feels, the sorrows of the sorrowing, yet he does so from such a distance that his mind is in no way seized or agitated by that suffering. The same factor that renders him incapable of suffering enables him to objectively observe the miseries of those he would help. He can see both where they came from (what caused the suffering) and where they should be going (to remove and avoid the suffering), a perspective completely impossible to most of them. Does such a person intellectually decide to help suffering humanity? No. Having arisen to such a level, it becomes a matter of spontaneous volition on his part. "Who burns with the bliss and suffers the sorrow of every creature within his own heart, making his own each bliss and each sorrow: him I hold highest of all the yogis" (Bhagavad Gita 6:32).

The Way To Excellence

Careful amidst the careless, amongst the sleeping wide-awake, the intelligent man leaves them all behind, like a race-horse does a mere hack (Dhammapada 29).

However repulsive the memory of the Nazis may be, it is a grave mistake to jettison a word from our vocabulary just because those spoilers sought to pervert it. Such a word is arya(n). Having nothing whatsoever to do with birth, race, or nationality, arya is often translated "noble" or "worthy," but it literally means "the striving upward," from the root *ri*, which means "to rise upward." Anyone who seeks to genuinely better himself in any way (not just spiritually) is an arya. We really do not have an English equivalent, so it is best to use it while blocking out the image of goose-stepping killers.

Now Buddha, formulator of the Four aryan Truths and the Aryan Eightfold Path, is describing how an arya manifests and increases his upward-moving nature, how he excels as a human being. This is important, for until we realize our full human potential, how can we hope to rise to divine potential? That is why Arya Dharma (Sanatana Dharma) is also called Manava Dharma, Human Dharma.

Aware

It is incredible but true that most human beings need to be told: Be Conscious. Many years ago a brilliant physician told me in relation to maintaining health: "Always be aware." It took me decades to figure out the meaning and value of those three words. Buddha explains to us that the intelligent human being is "aware among the unaware." The Venerable Thanissaro Bhikkhu renders it: "Heedful among the heedless."

A renowned French esotericist of the nineteenth century, Sar Hieronymous, observed that human beings are of two basic types: intellectual and instinctual. By "intellectual" he did not mean academic or scholarly, but centered in their intellects rather than in their senses, emotions, or physical bodies. Most people live in an instinctual, reactive manner, rarely letting their intelligence take the lead, and often only use their intelligence to fake up justifications for their irrational (instinctual) behavior.

Terrible as the picture is, humanity rushes headlong into pain, destruction, and death. And this is habitual, utterly reflexive. Once I visited a yoga center and had a satsang (informal spiritual discussion) with the members, all of them deeply sincere and quite intelligent. Yet, after about twenty minutes I realized that the answers to their questions did not need my special qualifications of having lived in India with Masters and having gained experience in meditation. Only good, practical sense was needed. Often through the years I have marveled at the way very good people seek answers to questions that any thoughtful person could easily answer. They themselves should have been able to answer their questions, but they simply were not used to doing so. They did not even realize they could.

Use your mind

"Use your mind" (intelligence) is just about the first thing a worthy teacher will tell the student, and will usually have to keep on telling him for quite a while until the instinct habit is broken–which is not easy since instinct is closely related to intuition, which is something desirable.

Instinct is to intuition what infantile babble is to adult speech. The first must progress to the second. This is no small problem for the spiritual striver. "Feeling" can be either instinctive or intuitive, and he must learn to distinguish them. This is a major lesson in his development.

Few things are more destructive than constant dependence on some external authority for making our decisions in life. Unhappily, most religions and spiritual teachers foster this dependency and prevent real inner growth in their adherents. How will they survive without dependents? How will they be teachers without students? So, like a therapist who fears to lose his livelihood if his patients recover, they hold their members or students in thrall.

A truly aryan teacher or philosophy is like my father. He held on to my bicycle and walked beside me as I learned to ride. He kept me from falling, but he did something better: he gave me the confidence to ride on my own. How vivid is my memory of hearing him say: "You have been riding without me helping for the last three minutes. I was just barely touching the bike." I could do it! So I rode on alone, amazed and relieved. The great Master, Swami Sivananda of Rishikesh on occasion would tell a student after a two or three months: "Now I have told you everything you need to know. Go and gain experience on your own and make something of yourself." Another great yogi, Swami Rama of Hardwar (Ram Kunj) only met his teacher once, at the age of nine. He was playing in the village street when the yogi came walking through the village and said to him: "Come with me." He followed him a little distance beyond the village and there the sage gave him instructions in meditation, blessed him, and walked on. No more was needed. How rare are such great teachers. Most gurus are in the slave trade (emphasis on *trade*).

Awake

"Amongst the sleeping wide-awake"—such is the wise man. Before Buddha stated this, Krishna had told Arjuna: "The recollected mind is awake in the knowledge of the Atman, which is dark night to the ignorant. The ignorant are awake in their sense-life which they think is daylight. To the seer it is darkness" (Bhagavad Gita 2:69). There will always be this sharp division between human beings. Most sleep and dream they are awake, and some of them are halfway between sleep and waking, sleepwalkers. Though thinking they are living and acting, from a higher and more realistic perspective they are doing nothing. This is tragic.

Few are the wise, comparatively speaking. Yet this does not bother them, for though ignorance, like misery, loves company and the assurance of being part of a group or herd, wisdom is content with walking on alone if need be. Of course the wise are never alone, for they are walking in step with the awakened of all ages. In Mahayana Buddhism they say that the moment someone decides to seek higher awareness a multitude of Buddhas and Bodhisattwas become aware of him and begin blessing and helping him along the upward path. That is why Saint Paul said: "We are compassed about with a great cloud of witnesses" (Hebrews 12:1). In chapter six of *Autobiography of a Yogi*, the Tiger Swami tells that his guru finally said to him: "Enough of tiger taming. Come with me; I will teach you to subdue the beasts of ignorance roaming in jungles of the human mind. You are used to an audience: let it be a galaxy of angels, entertained by your thrilling mastery of yoga!"

Unfortunately for us, in the beginning our inner eyes are not fully opened so we do not realize what a great force is working on our behalf. Immersed in this world of darkness and ignorance we are only aware, often painfully, of the forces that try to prevent our striving upward and becoming aryas. We are like the servant of Elisha who, seeing the city surrounded by enemies, was terrified. Elijah assured him that they had more allies than there were enemies, but the servant thought he was speaking nonsense. Then "Elisha prayed, and said, Lord, I pray thee, open his eyes, that he may see. And the Lord opened the eyes of the young man; and he saw: and, behold, the mountain was full of horses and chariots of fire round about Elisha" (II Kings 6:17).

What is it to be awake? To be self-aware, centered in the consciousness that is our true nature. As Krishna indicated, the awareness of the Self is waking, in contrast to the fever-dream of absorption in sense-awareness. Of course, the sleepers will accuse *us* of being dreamers or unconscious, but that is to be expected. It is even a good sign.

It is said that Buddha was walking along the road when he met the first person he had seen after attaining enlightenment. Being sensitive to spiritual things, the man was astounded at the very appearance of Buddha. "Who or what are you?" he asked. "I am awake," replied Buddha. And walked on.

Leaving them behind

Transmigration of the soul is true. We move from the simplest of forms to the increasingly complex. Lower forms of life cannot exist outside a group, they are utterly interdependent. Higher life forms become increasingly independent, even solitary. But for some odd reason, perhaps because of their vulnerability, human beings revert to the herd instinct and live submerged in one or more groups, drawing their confidence and self-image from those around them. Look at the virtually absolute power of fashion and public opinion.

All types of claims and demands are made on us, but Buddha tells us that the wise person "leaves them all behind." *This is necessary.* We cannot sail in the sinking boat and expect not to drown. We cannot live amongst the diseased and suppose we shall remain healthy. We must separate ourselves and move beyond them. And that does not mean walking along parallel to them at a comfortably sociable distance. It means getting far away. To make sure we understand this, Buddha says "the intelligent man leaves them all behind, like a race-horse does a mere hack." Distance is the keyword here. The worthy steed does not mosey along with the bumbling and incompetent. He pulls out ahead and leaves them far behind. That is how he wins the race. It is drastic. And it is final. It is certainly unequivocal.

This separation and distancing need not be done externally, though in some cases it is absolutely necessary because of the negativity prevailing in the seeker's environment. But it must be done mentally and spiritually. This often results in the seeker being pushed away by the ignorant and finding himself separated involuntarily. Some of the less somnolent may sense the impending departure and try to stop it, even becoming accusatory and abusive. Regarding them Jesus said: "But whereunto shall I liken this generation? It is like unto children sitting in the markets, and calling unto their fellows, and saying, We have piped unto you, and ye have not danced; we have mourned unto you, and ye have not lamented" (Matthew 11:16, 17). This, too, is a good sign, though often a painful one. Such is the price that must be paid if we would be truly free, not just in abstraction and theory.

But here is the most important point in all this: There should be a vast, virtually infinite distance between us and the ignorant. How can this be accomplished and maintained? By moving forward, ever forward, never stopping until our last breath. That way we will continue on in higher worlds until we gain the Goal. Buddha was a perfect example of this. To the last day of his life he meditated for hours, even going into intense meditation retreats frequently. He begged his food like every other monk. He lived under a tree and followed the life he had taught to others. After his departure from the world many of his aspiring followers have gotten tangled up in trying to figure out exactly what level they have achieved (the technical terms are too tedious for us to bother with here). This signaled their loss of good sense, for Buddha's example was to keep on just like a beginner, the only difference between his life and others being the skill in which he conducted it. This is the truth: the way of life of a true Master and that of a fresh beginner is absolutely the same. Only the consciousness is different. The Master may give more time to the practices of spiritual life, but he does them all, omitting none and mitigating none. The difference is only in degree, not in the elements of daily life and practice. This is so important for us to understand, for keeping this in mind we will be able to discern what spiritual leaders are genuine and which are not. No enlightened person goes beyond even the most basic practices. "Baba doesn't need that anymore" means that Baba is deluded or an outright fake, and so are his followers. This applies to "Matajis" as well.

What the unenlightened do to attain,
The enlightened do to maintain.

Buddha demonstrated this by his perfect life.

Summing it up

In conclusion Buddha says the following that needs no comment:
**Careful amidst the careless, amongst the sleeping wide-awake,
the intelligent man leaves them all behind, like a race-horse does
a mere hack.**

**It was by attention that Indra attained the highest place
among the gods. People approve of attention, while carelessness
is always condemned.**

**A bhikkhu taking pleasure in being attentive, and recogniz-
ing the danger of carelessness, makes progress like a forest fire,
consuming all obstacles large or small in his way.**

**A bhikkhu taking pleasure in being attentive, and recogniz-
ing the danger of carelessness, is incapable of falling away. In
fact he is already close to Nirvana (Dhammapada 29-32).**

Chapter 3

THE MIND

Experience is surely the best teacher, but sometimes its lessons are discouraging. That is why Arjuna told Krishna: "Restless man's mind is, so strongly shaken in the grip of the senses: gross and grown hard with stubborn desire for what is worldly. How shall he tame it? Truly, I think the wind is no wilder" (Bhagavad Gita 6:34).

Buddha, who could not have been unaware of Arjuna's opinion, had this to say on the subject:

Elusive and unreliable as it is, the wise man straightens out his restless, agitated mind, like a fletcher crafting an arrow (Dhammapada 33).

Krishna replied to Arjuna: "Patiently, little by little, a man must free himself from all mental distractions, with the aid of the intelligent will. He must fix his mind upon the Atman, and never think of anything else. No matter where the restless and the unquiet mind wanders, it must be drawn back and made to submit to the Atman only" (Bhagavad Gita 6:25, 26).

The wayward mind

Buddha lists four characteristics of the mind that render it so difficult to deal with, much less master.

Elusive. How many people know their minds? Virtually no one. That is why self-analysis (swadhyaya) can be such a revelation. The mind, being a bundle of illusions, has progressed through many incarnations from being a lie to being a liar with an unsettling half-life of its own. I never thought my mind was worth much consideration, but when I began meditating, and it began to have an effect and thus endanger the mind and ego, I discovered that the mind was virtually a separate person inside me. (In reality, the mind *is* separate from the Self.) After meditating a while my mind would say: "I am bored. My legs hurt. Why not quit?" If I ignored or told it to shut up it would keep on fussing. One time I said: "That's right. I am bored. I am going to quit for now." And my mind became completely quiet. I meditated about twenty more minutes and again my mind announced that it was time to quit. Again I said that I was going to quit, and even said what I was going to do after quitting. Once more: silence of mind. And so it went. It might seem funny, but it is really frightening.

Within us is an entirely false self—completely false, not a distortion of our real self, though it can imitate it when it suits its purpose. We are all schizophrenic. Our ego/mind is the escaped lunatic that threatens us every moment. It is elusive because it is ever-changing. This is seen in the account found in the *Sri Devi Mahatmyam* (*Sri Durga Saptashati* or *Chandi*) of the manifestation of the Goddess Durga to vanquish the demon Mahishasura. No matter how much she struck at him with her weapons (and she needed a great many to deal with his many mutations), he kept changing and thereby eluding her. The mind's capacity to change shape and even become invisible and undetectable is genuinely miraculous. How do you deal with something that can differ from moment to moment and disappear at will? ("What problem?" "What illusion?" "*What mind?*") As we evolve, so does the mind. The bigger we get, the bigger grows the net.

Unreliable. It is astounding that people almost never face the fact of the mind's unreliability. (Actually, it never arises in their consciousness, so there is no question of facing it or not.) Again, the mind is a liar. It will tell us anything we want to hear or do not want to hear—whichever is the way to perpetuate its control over us. See how the likes and dislikes of the mind swing back and forth, ever changing. For many years people think they are so devoted to some spiritual ideal and in a moment they become either indifferent or inimical to it. It had always been no more than a puff of air. Buddha told his disciples that adherence to "views" was an obstacle. Why? Because they spring from the mind and are therefore nothing. Even an interest in Nirvana is meaningless when it comes from the mind rather than the deep intuition of the true Self. Most religion is nonsense because it is mind-based rather than spirit-based. We can count on nothing that the mind produces. "Well, I know one thing…," says the deluded individual as he teeters on the brink of completely changing his "knowing." The mind can never be trusted, the "spiritual" mind least of all.

Restless. Some translators prefer "difficult to guard." The mind is like a restless horse, a mad elephant, even. How can it be held in check or guarded when it is intent only on that which worsens its condition? The mind constantly demands diversion of all sorts, even delighting in pain and suffering if it can get nothing else as a distraction. As an addict requires larger and larger doses, so does the mind demand increasingly powerful objects and situations for its absorption.

Agitated. That is what the mind becomes when it does not get its addictions supplied *and* increased. The mind is desperate in its pursuit of…EVERYTHING. If it had some order to its goals then there might be a chance. But there is nothing it does not want at some time or other, and nothing that it does not equally despise or ignore at some time or other.

The wise man straightens out his mind

Who would not be overwhelmed at this panorama of determined chaos? Yet the wise man sets himself to the task of straightening out his mind just as a maker of arrows straightens the shaft so it can be sent unerringly to its target by the skilled archer. So after this awful picture we are given hope: the wise man can and does bring the mind under his mastery and renders it accessible, reliable, calm, and content. How? Krishna put it in the briefest possible way: "Become a yogi" (Bhagavad Gita 6:46). Meditation is the means by which we straighten and sharpen the arrow of the mind.

Comfort?

One of the goals of spiritual life is peace of mind, heart and life. But first there is often conflict, for spiritual life is a battle to the death with ignorance and ego. When we win that battle then there is peace, everlasting peace. But until then a lot of skirmishes and outright battles can occur. That is why Jesus declared so forthrightly: "Think not that I am come to send peace on earth: I came not to send peace, but a sword" (Matthew 10:34). And: "I am come to send fire on the earth;.... Suppose ye that I am come to give peace on earth? I tell you, Nay; but rather division" (Luke 12:49, 51) between truth and untruth, between wisdom and folly, between the ego and the true Self. "Therefore you must fight," Krishna told Arjuna. (Bhagavad Gita 2:18) "Fight, and have no fear. The foe is yours to conquer" (Bhagavad Gita 11:34). The outcome of the battle is assured, but until then:

Terrible struggle

Trying to break out of the Tempter's control, one's mind writhes to and fro, like a fish pulled from its watery home onto dry ground (Dhammapada 34).

This is a rather horrid picture. I am sure many of us remember the terrible distress we felt the first time we saw people we loved and trusted pull a helpless fish from the water and indifferently watch it suffocate as it desperately flopped about, trying to regain the water. How we wanted to let it live! But they looked on our compassion as childish, confident that in time we would grow up and become as callous as they. Is it any wonder that Jesus counseled his disciples to "become as little children" (Matthew 18:3)?

In time many of us came to lose compassion for the helpless innocent, at the same time developing compassion and indulgence for the guilty: our own false ego. As a consequence, when the ego-mind and emotions are pressured or pained we lapse into self-pity and begin looking for a way out as desperately as the poor fish struggles to get back into the water. We, however, are just opposite to the fish. Whereas its return to the water is necessary for its continued life, we have become so horribly addicted to the false realm of death, both psychically and physically, that we mistake death for life and life for death. Like an addict deprived of his addictive substance, we feel that we will die without it and are willing to do anything to avoid our cure and maintain the addiction. Free will complicates this a great deal, for as long as we will to remain distorted and ignorant, just so long shall we remain that way. We can understand why Krishna said: "How hard to break through is this, my Maya!" (Bhagavad Gita 7:14). *We* are our own Maya!

It can be done

"To achieve this certainty is to know the real meaning of the word yoga. It is the breaking of contact with pain. You must practice this yoga resolutely, without losing heart. Renounce all your desires, for ever. They spring from willfulness. Use your discrimination to restrain the whole pack of the scattering senses. Patiently, little by little, a man must free himself from all mental distractions, with the aid of the intelligent will. He must fix his mind upon the Atman, and never think of anything else. No matter where the restless and the unquiet mind wanders, it must be drawn back and made to submit to the Atman only" (Bhagavad Gita 6:23-26). How simple. But in the meantime, we must face it: the mind is going to writhe in agony. The crucial question is: will it strive to return to the sleep of death or will it awaken into real life? "Wherefore he saith, Awake thou that sleepest, and arise from the dead" (Ephesians 5:14). "The recollected mind is awake in the knowledge of the Atman which is dark night to the ignorant: the ignorant are awake in their sense-life which they think is daylight: to the seer it is darkness" (Bhagavad Gita 2:69),

The opponent

What are we struggling with? Richards employs the expression "the Tempter," but the Pali text says Mara. Mara is the force of cosmic evil, but let us consider a moment. Can we be tempted by any thing whatsoever unless we first have an inner affinity for it? If a person dislikes some kind of food or drink, can anyone tempt him to eat or drink it?

Not at all. Nor will it take any will power for him to refuse. If someone dislikes a certain activity, can he be tempted to engage in it? Never. In the same way the wise person who have seen through the tawdry and petty offerings of relative existence cannot be drawn toward them. He need not even resist, just ignore them as usual. Whether we call it Mara or Maya the truth is plain: if it cannot be found within us then it can move us not at all. This is why Jesus managed so easily when Mara-Satan tempted him. The secret? He was not tempted at all!

Could someone persuade us to once more do the things that so delighted us as infants or children? How interesting would our old toys seem if once more presented to us? Or the mindlessly repetitious games that we continually entreated our parents or other adults to play with us? Just look at children's Saturday morning television programs. We cannot stand them; there is no need for us to resist, they have no attraction at all.

Easy...

How easy it all sounds; but how tremendously difficult it is to pass from dream to awakening, from inner childhood to inner adulthood. It is a literal life-or-death struggle. And to succeed it must be constant. "You must know Him who is above the intelligent will. Get control of the mind through spiritual discrimination. Then destroy your elusive enemy" (Bhagavad Gita 3:43).

We are ourselves the answer, the secret of success in spiritual striving. "What is man's will and how shall he use it? Let him put forth its power to uncover the Atman, not hide the Atman: man's will is the only friend of the Atman: his will is also the Atman's enemy. For when a man is self-controlled, his will is the Atman's friend. But the will of an uncontrolled man is hostile to the Atman, like an enemy" (Bhagavad Gita 6:5, 6).

Self-freeing

We must free ourselves. None else can do it. Ascending the cross we must not come down until death has been transmuted into life.

"For this corruptible must put on incorruption, and this mortal must put on immortality. So when this corruptible shall have put on incorruption, and this mortal shall have put on immortality, then shall be brought to pass the saying that is written, Death is swallowed up in victory" (I Corinthians 15:53,54).

All the enemies that militate against us have been summoned by the One Enemy that flourishes within us. Once it is eliminated the enemies will not only be powerless against us, they will abandon the battlefield altogether. This is why more than once in the Bible we find the enemy vanquished without a single blow or stroke, fleeing and leaving behind everything. Also many aspects of our being that temporarily oppose us can be restored to us in peace as our own by right meditation. "Therefore you must first control your senses, then kill this evil thing which obstructs discriminative knowledge and realization of the Atman" (Bhagavad Gita 3:41).

How?

How do we do it? The simile of the fish tells us. The mind must be drawn out of the water of egoic life. That is, we must transfer our consciousness from the unreal to the Real, from darkness to the Light, from death to Immortality. We must transfer it from the kingdom of earth to the kingdom of heaven. And this is done in no haphazard manner but precisely and methodically through the sole transformer: meditation. "Yoga purifies the man of meditation, bringing him soon to Brahman" (Bhagavad Gita 5:6). "He should meditate on the Atman unceasingly" (Bhagavad Gita 6:10). "If he practices meditation in this manner, his heart will become pure" (Bhagavad Gita 6:12). "When, through the practice of yoga, the mind ceases its restless movements, and becomes still, he realizes the Atman. It satisfies him entirely....He stands firm in this realization. Because of it, he can never again wander from the inmost truth of his being" (Bhagavad Gita 6:20 21). "Make a habit of practicing meditation, and do not let your mind be distracted. In this way you will come finally to the Lord, who is the light-giver, the highest of the high" (Bhagavad Gita 8:8).

When we do this, we ensure that the fish of the mind will not be able to twist and flop its way back into the waters of samsara. "On earth there is no purifier as great as this knowledge. When a man is made perfect in yoga, he knows its truth within his heart. The man of faith, whose heart is devoted, whose senses are mastered: he finds Brahman. Enlightened, he passes at once to the highest, the peace beyond passion" (Bhagavad Gita 4:38, 39).

"If a yogi has perfect control over his mind, and struggles continually in this way to unite himself with Brahman, he will come at last to the crowning peace of Nirvana, the peace that is in me" (Bhagavad Gita 6:15).

The real "pursuit of happiness"

Through the ages people have been chasing after the silliest of things and situations in the belief that they will bring them happiness. But Buddha cuts through the nonsense and shows the only way, saying:

It is good to restrain one's mind, uncontrollable, fast moving, and following its own desires as it is. A disciplined mind leads to happiness (Dhammapada 35).

Both the Bhagavad Gita and the upanishads are echoed in this passage listing the problems of the mind: uncontrollable, fast moving, and following its own desires. Buddha adds to the list, continuing:

A wise man should guard his mind for it is very hard to keep track of, extremely subtle, and follows its own desires. A guarded mind brings happiness (Dhammapada 36).

In his translation Harischandra Kaviratna lists the mind as "incomprehensible," and Max Muller employs the expression: "very artful." How true that is. The mind is a mystery beyond mystery—actually more of a mystification. And in its tricky ways it truly is extremely artful. Yet we must outsmart it. The next verse tells how.

The mind goes wandering off far and wide alone. Incorporeal, it dwells in the cavern of the heart. Those who keep it under control escape from Mara's bonds (Dhammapada 37).

The "cave of the heart" is the lair of the mind. So those who track it down to the core of their being will be able to tame it. There is no drawing near to the cave of the heart except through meditation. As T. Byrom renders this verse: "With single-mindedness the master quells his thoughts. He ends their wandering. Seated in the cave of the heart, he finds freedom." Through meditation all this is accomplished, and the pursuit of happiness ends in the eluding of delusion and death.

Wasted wisdom

If he is unsettled in mind, does not know the true Teaching, and has lost his peace of mind, a man's wisdom does not come to fulfillment (Dhammapada 38).

Getting wisdom is hard enough, but that is not the ending of the matter. Those who have no real focus or knowledge of The Way—without which peace of mind is impossible—cannot bring their wisdom to fruition. A tool is valueless if there is no knowledge of its purpose or how to use it.

Fearlessness

There can be no happiness where there is fear. So Buddha tells us:

With his mind free from the inflow of thoughts and from restlessness, by abandoning both good and evil, an alert man knows no fear (Dhammapada 39).

When we are no longer assaulted by thoughts and agitated by them, and when we feel no compulsion to do either good or evil but in perfect freedom of will do that which is RIGHT—that which is accordance with our true nature. Then, being awake even in the dark night of material existence, we shall have no fear. For that which makes fear possible shall have melted away in the flame of spiritual reality.

This is a beautiful thought, but Buddha did not come into the world to give pretty ideas, he came to show The Way. So he continues.

Understand the body

Seeing your body as no better than an earthen pot, make war on Mara with the sword of wisdom, and setting up your mind

as a fortress, defend what you have won, remaining free from attachment (Dhammapada 40).

Foolishly we identify with the body and therefore order our lives according to its whims, demands, and even its addictions. What a preposterous basis for the conduct of our life. But Buddha exhorts us to see that the body is no more than an earthen pot, ready at any moment to break and to be as nothing.

Far greater than the body is the indwelling consciousness, indeed it is for the sake of the consciousness that the body has been assumed. Therefore we should seize the sword of wisdom which cuts through the veils of ignorance, and make war on illusion and delusion (Mara), an enemy that dwells within, not without. This is why the only remedy is an internal process. Certainly, because the body so affects the mind, we need to provide external measures to make the internal process easier and more effective. This includes right conduct in all its aspects, which is the way to fortify the mind. Rousing up and honing the sword of wisdom in the mind, we shall conquer Mara; there is no doubt, for Mara itself is an illusion.

Defend yourself

One of the saddest experiences in human life is to see someone who has attained some measure of spiritual development slip back and lose the gained ground. Why does it happen? Simply because he did not defend what he had won, mostly because he had no idea of his danger. Having lived so long in the swirling waters of spiritual heedlessness, he felt secure as would a child.

One of the most important elements of spiritual awakening is awakening to the real dangers inherent in the world and in ourselves, since we are conditioned by the world. Once we begin walking the path to liberation in this world whose very nature is bondage, we are moving against an inexorable current of downward-moving force with which there can be no compromise or accommodation if we are not to fall back and be once more carried along in the descending stream. As Krishna urged Arjuna: "Stand up and fight!" (Bhagavad Gita 2:37).

Buddha does not outline for us an easy or lackadaisical path any more than did Krishna or Jesus.

Free from attachment

But there is more. Buddha tells us to be free from attachment. This has two aspects. One is the common failing in which a person becomes satisfied with what has been gained, however small, and clings to that in self-congratulation with no intent of pressing onward to wider horizons of consciousness. The wise are never satisfied with their gains, but keep on seeking more. The other problem is becoming attached to our self-image as a seeker after enlightenment, and cultivating all that gives us the appearance of being so—with no interest as to whether we really are seeking, and even less interest in really attaining. One of the worst illusions of human beings is the belief that they are what others—and they themselves—think they are. They consider that if they look or act the part, then they are that which they look and act like. And being caught up in this costume drama, they can be distracted from reality for all of their life.

No more than wood!

Before long this body will be lying on the ground, discarded and unconscious, like a useless bit of wood (Dhammapada 41).

Buddha knows that body identification is at the root of so much of our suffering. He has already pointed out its fragility, but knows that many can shrug that off, feeling that they will be healthy forever. So he makes us face our mortality, for although we may ignore our mortality, we cannot deny it.

Yet he points beyond the body when he speaks of it as "discarded." Surely he has in mind the words of Krishna in the Bhagavad Gita: "Even as a man casts off his worn-out clothes and then clothes himself in others which are new, so the embodied casts off worn-out bodies and then enters into others which are new" (Bhagavad Gita 2:22).

It is true. In time our body will be discarded, bereft of life and consciousness (which are really the same), as useless to ourself and others as scrap wood. Yet we shall be alive and conscious, immortal beings. And that is the most important reason to heed the Buddha's teachings. For he shows us the way to unveil our immortality—our eternity.

Mind: enemy/friend

"He should lift himself by the Self; he should never degrade himself; the Self is indeed the self's friend, and the self's only enemy. For him who has conquered himself by the Self, the Self is a friend; but for him who has not conquered himself, the Self remains a foe" (Bhagavad Gita 6:5, 6). So said Krishna. Some centuries later, Buddha told his hearers:

One's own misdirected thought can do one more harm than an enemy or an ill-wisher (Dhammapada 42).

Harischandra Kaviratna renders it: "An ill-directed mind does greater harm to the self than a hater does to another hater or an enemy to another enemy."

Sri Ramakrishna frequently said: "The mind is all." Of course by "mind" he is including both the basic consciousness and its instruments, which would include the senses, at least on a subtle level. The body certainly dominates our awareness, but it is continually seen that the mind dominates the body as well. In crisis situations, for example, people can do things that are supposedly beyond the capacity of the body. The mind is the ruler in the plane of relative existence.

The history of mankind in general and the personal history of just about every human on the earth demonstrates the destructive capabilities of a misdirected or uncontrolled mind. Why expound it? Anyone who is not aware of the facts is either subhuman or superhuman.

There are some points in which the fact of duality becomes advantageous, and this is one. For the same mind which harms can also do good. So Buddha continues:

Even your mother, father or any other relative cannot do you as much good as your own properly directed thought (Dhammapada 43).

"Not a mother, not a father will do so much, nor any other relative; a well-directed mind will do us greater service" is the Max Muller translation. The reason should not be hard to figure out. Mother, father, or any other human being is outside us, whereas the mind is within us.

So in these few verses Buddha has shown the way to the fulfillment of our pursuit of true happiness, of that true bliss (ananda) that is our Self.

Chapter 4

FLOWERS

Fear of death is the most widespread and deep-seated fear within the hearts of the human race. All religions pay a great deal of attention to the subjects of death and immortality, and they all claim to have the way to avoid death and enter into immortality. These ways consist of avoiding wrong action and cultivating good action, faith in and worship of their gods, and material contribution.

Buddha stands in contrast to all this. As any responsible spiritual teacher would do, he places the matter solely upon the individual. First he sets forth the relevant question:

Who shall gain victory over this earth together with the domain of Yama [ruler of the underworld] with its gods? Who shall find the well-proclaimed Dhammapada [Path of Truth], even as the expert gardener selects the choicest flower? (Dhammapada 44).

This world and the next

To begin with Buddha lets us know that there is no mastery of a future world until we attain mastery in this world. It is the failing of every major religion on the earth to despise this earth in some degree, whether spoken or not. Everyone is so intent on getting beyond this world that they ignore its absolute necessity, and this includes popular Hinduism, which is a major offender in this matter. The result is a guaranteed return here. "This old world of sin and sorrow" happens to be as much the kingdom of God as the highest spiritual world. It is our ignorance that produces the sin and sorrow, not the world. That is like calling the weapon of a murderer "a vicious killer." But we are just that crazy. Buddha points the way to sanity.

Wisdom

The conqueror of both life and death is he who will seek and find the path of dharma, using his intelligent discrimination to distinguish true dharma from the false, "even as the expert gardener selects the choicest flower." The Venerable Thanissaro Bhikkhu translates this verse in the following manner: "Who will penetrate this earth and this realm of death with all its gods? Who will ferret out the well-taught Dhamma-saying, as the skillful flower-arranger the flower?"

To "penetrate" something means to know it thoroughly, and by that wisdom to master it. Here, too, we see that to minimally live in this world and minimally deal with it—an ideal also set forth by nearly all religions—is to miss the mark completely. We must *comprehend* this world. And to do that we must diligently seek—literally ferret out—the way of dharma. Then we must put ourself in control and order things accordingly, "as the skillful flower-arranger the flower." This is not the picture of some pious nitwit proudly proclaiming his ignorance and declaring his total dependence on God or gods. In the Bhagavad Gita Krishna tells Arjuna to take refuge in God, but also he tells him to stand up and fight. The two go together. One without the other is nonsense, producing chaos.

And the winner is…

Who, then, will conquer?

The disciple will gain victory over the earth and the realm of Yama together with its gods. The true disciple will indeed find the well-proclaimed Dhammapada, even as the expert gardener selects the choicest flower (Dhammapada 45).

"Disciple" has a lot of connotations, most of them negative and erroneous as applied in the religions that seek to dominate their adherents. The Venerable Thanissaro Bhikkhu translates it "learner-on-the-path" which gives a much better idea than mere "disciple." For it is the path itself that teaches the worthy disciple as he applies what he has learned from a worthy teacher.

Seeing true

Recognizing this corporeal body to be evanescent as foam, comprehending this worldly nature as a mirage, and having broken the flower-arrows of Mara, the true aspirant will go beyond the realm of the Evil One (Dhammapada 46).

What characterizes a learner-on-the-path? Three major traits.

Recognizing this corporeal body to be evanescent as foam. Older people who have not seen through the world envy the young. Naturally, the state of health and the prospect of years ahead in which to attain goals is desirable, but the terrible delusions and illusions of youth far outweigh that. One of the worst blindnesses of youth is the heedlessness of death, the baseless feeling of assured life and well-being in the future. Long ago the sages of India stated that one of the most amazing things about human beings is their inability to grasp their own mortality although they see others dying around them. This of course comes from an intuitional grasp of our innate immortality, but the placement is mistaken. Only the Self is immortal. The incredible fragility of life must be grasped by those who would learn on the path, not in a pessimistic manner but in a realism that cannot be clouded by false confidence. Think of all we accomplish when we realize we have little time in which to do it. Awareness of the brevity and fragility of life can be positive if it spurs us on to wisely-directed action.

Comprehending this worldly nature as a mirage. Life is not only fragile, it is insubstantial, even illusory. The right attitude toward the world and its nature, as well as the earthly aspects of our own being, is absolutely necessary for us, and a simplistic view will not suffice–it will get us into major difficulties.

In India we find two conflicting statements: 1) the world is real; 2) the world is unreal. And so the wrangle goes on, and we are supposed to choose which we think is right. I can help you on this. *They are both wrong and they are both right.*

In our modern times we have many advantages over the ancient philosophers because a great deal of our modern science and technology actually makes easy the knots they found so hard to loosen and eliminate. One of our most inspired examples is the motion picture. It is real and it is not real. The filmmakers and film students and film historians take motion pictures quite seriously. Yet what is a motion picture but a series of images that do not move but appear to move and speak?

It was motion pictures that revealed the unreal nature of "reality" to me when I was just a child of seven or eight. First I noticed that at the start of the movie I would hear the sound coming from speakers on the walls at either side, but in just a few minutes I would hear the sound coming from the screen, and not just from the screen but from the projected images of the characters that were speaking. This was obviously an illusion created by my mind, and it disturbed me somewhat. Next I saw that when spoked wheels (as on a stagecoach) turned rapidly they appeared to stand still and then begin to move backwards. Again, an obvious illusion showing that the senses were not reliable in perceiving reality. The most amazing thing was my discovery that the perception of passing time was completely subjective. One evening I liked a motion picture so much I decided to stay on and watch it a second time. To my bewilderment the picture seemed to take only half the time it had the first time through. Again, it was all in my head—an idea I did not like very much, because everything was then seen as unstable and, as I say, mostly subjective.

By studying our experience of motion pictures (and now television) we can get some idea of the unreality of "reality," understanding that even an illusion is real. Reality is unreal and unreality is real! No ancient sage of India ever demonstrated this as clearly as Edison's Wonder.

Our cooperation with and creation of illusion is also shown by motion pictures. We know it is all illusion, yet we react as though we were witnessing something real. We respond with a range of emotions, liking and disliking characters and situations that are nothing but light patterns on a screen. (And how profound is the insight that the relationship between picture and screen perfectly mirrors Purusha and Prakriti, samsara and the atman, matter and consciousness.) Even stranger, no matter how many times we see a movie, we still react to it. Although we know exactly what the outcome will be, we find ourselves involuntarily feeling tense, even anxious, about what may happen. We laugh as much at a comic situation as we did the first time—maybe even more—and even jump at a no-longer-unexpected development. Why? Because it is the nature of the mind to fool and be fooled. We truly are Dwellers In The Mirage, and voluntarily so. So we not only come to realize that the world is ultimately a mirage, so is the mind that perceives it. The capacity of the mind to create a world in dream drives the point even deeper home. A dream is totally unreal and yet is real at the same time.

Having broken the flower-arrows of Mara. Cosmic Delusion hooks us like the gullible fish takes the tasty bait unaware of the horrible steel beneath. If you have ever seen a fish that has not just been hooked in the mouth but has completely swallowed the hook then you have some idea of the consequences of being struck by the flower-arrows of Mara. How we like being hit! Poor fools. As the Gita points out, we live "desiring desires" (Bhagavad Gita 18:24), or as Swami Prabhavananda put it: "under the whip of lust and the will of the ego." "The man who stirs up his own lusts can never know peace" (Bhagavad Gita 2:70), yet we keep right on. In India they cite the example of camels that keep chewing on thorns however much their mouths are pierced and bleeding. But "He knows peace who has forgotten desire. He lives without craving: free from ego, free from pride" (Bhagavad Gita 2:71).

Buddha does not speak of someone who has learned to evade the flower-arrows or who has become impervious to them. Rather he speaks of those who have *broken* the arrows. That is, they have rendered them ineffectual and, practically speaking, non-existent. He has destroyed them. For "when a man enters Reality, he leaves his desires behind him" (Bhagavad Gita 2:59). Thus—and only thus—he has gone beyond the realm of death. He has gone "where the King of Death [Yama] cannot see," as Thanissaro Bhikkhu translates it.

"Cravings torment the heart: he renounces cravings....Free from the things of desire,...the bonds of his flesh are broken" (Bhagavad Gita 2:55-57). "When he has no lust, no hatred, a man walks safely among the things of lust and hatred....Sorrow melts into that clear peace: his quiet mind is soon established in peace" (Bhagavad Gita 2:64, 65).

Seeking death

This is a happy picture, but truth is both happy and sad. So Buddha shows us another view in conclusion, perhaps because it is the situation of the majority of human beings—and of us if we are not vigilant. Worthy teachers do not hesitate to tell us or show us what we may not like, but which must be changed if we would pass from death unto life. Here are his words:

The hedonist who seeks only the blossoms of sensual delights, who indulges only in such pleasures, him the Evil One carries off, as a flood carries off the inhabitants of a sleeping village (Dhammapada 47).

What a horrible truth! We can be carried off by Death while sleeping and dreaming just the opposite. "It shall even be as when an hungry man dreameth, and, behold, he eateth; but he awaketh, and his soul is empty: or as when a thirsty man dreameth, and, behold, he drinketh; but he awaketh, and, behold, he is faint, and his soul hath appetite" (Isaiah 29:8). It is worldly life and not religion that is the opium of the people, though of course worldly religion is part of the poppy field. There is more:

The hedonist who seeks only the blossoms of sensual delights, whose mind is agitated, him the Evil One (Mara) brings under his sway even before his carnal desires are satiated (Dhammapada 48).

Now this is the truth. Delusion never really comes through or pays off. Oh, yes, just like crooked gamblers, for the first few times the forces of Mara let us "win." Then, when we are addicted, the sorrow sets in. All we really end up with is addiction and the inevitable frustration of that addiction. What an awful trap, and what an awful willingness to be trapped. Nevertheless, if we hearken to Buddha's wisdom and follow it we shall transcend delusion and death.

The holy "bee"

A holy man [muni] should behave in the village like a bee which takes its food from a flower without hurting its appearance or its scent (Dhammapada 49).

It is generally assumed that this is an instruction for the wandering monk that begs for his food, telling him that he should not take advantage of those who provide his food by putting an undue burden on them, that he should take a little from many places rather than expect one or two people to provide him with all his food, unless some specifically ask him to take their whole meal from them.

But considering that the four hundred and twenty-two other verses are philosophical in nature and applicable to all types of aspirants, I think it is safe to interpret this verse differently. It seems to me that this verse is telling us how to pass through the world, benefiting from it in many ways—especially in the fulfilling of karma and dharma—and burdening it in no way. The great Mughal emperor, Akhbar, in 1601 A.D. built a gate at Fatehpur Sikri on which he had written in Persian: "Jesus, son of Mary, said: The world is a Bridge, pass over it, but build no houses upon it." The Bhagavad Gita puts it this way: "He by whom the world is not agitated and who cannot be agitated by the world, and who is freed from joy, envy, fear and anxiety—he is dear to Me" (Bhagavad Gita 12:15). And Saint Paul: "The world is crucified unto me, and I unto the world" (Galatians 6:14). These fully support the picture given in the translation of the Venerable Thanissaro Bhikkhu: "As a bee—without harming the blossom, its color, its fragrance—takes its nectar and flies away: so should the sage go through a village." We should pass through this world without injuring or exploiting it in any way. And especially we should keep moving on, not trying to settle down at any point or trying to carry any of it along with us.

The right focus

It is not the shortcomings of others, nor what others have done or not done that one should think about, but what one has done or not done oneself (Dhammapada 50).

The meaning is obvious, so I need only point out that Buddha is telling us that we *ought* to think about our actions—not to egotistically brood, but to examine and learn how better to act or abstain from action. We are not to shrug off our past actions without a thought and move on heedlessly. This also means that we must ponder our shortcomings so they will not be repeated.

Actions alone matter

Like a fine flower, beautiful to look at but without scent, fine words are fruitless in a man who does not act in accordance with them.

Like a fine flower, beautiful to look at and scented too, fine words bear fruit in a man who acts well in accordance with them (Dhammapada 51, 52).

High ideals are nothing if they are not lived out by those who speak or advocate them. There is simply no value in theory that is not carried out successfully in practice. What a pity that Buddha needs to point this out, but he certainly does. Look at politics, for proof.

Creating destiny

Just as one can make a lot of garlands from a heap of flowers, so man, subject to birth and death as he is, should make himself a lot of good karma (Dhammapada 53).

Human beings can turn any wisdom into foolishness, and karma no doubt tops the list. Karma is proof that we have the power to completely create our life situations, but nearly everybody acts like it is some kind of imposed fate. We easily say "my karma" while ignoring the implication: it is *ours*, not an external factor, and it is totally under our control. It exists only because we make it exist. It is always right in our hands, and nowhere else.

"Just as from a heap of flowers many garland strands can be made, even so one born and mortal should do—with what's born and is mortal—many a skillful thing" (Thanissaro Bhikkhu).

"As many a garland can be strung from a mass of flowers, so should mortal man born in this world perform many wholesome deeds" (Harischandra Kaviratna).

The power of goodness

The scent of flowers cannot travel against the wind, and nor can that of sandalwood or jasmine, but the fragrance of the good does travel against the wind, and a good man perfumes the four quarters of the earth (Dhammapada 54).

World history bears this out. Nero, Hitler, Stalin, and suchlike are ugly memories, but Krishna, Buddha, and Jesus are living presences, changing and preserving lives. How many times do the corrupt and degraded exhort the good and true to "wake up and see how things are" and "go with the flow." But Buddha assures us that the good absolutely are able to move against the flow and exert great influence around them. History also shows how much a single person can change the world, altering the course of culture and history.

Sandalwood, tagara, lotus, jasmine—the fragrance of virtue is unrivalled by such kinds of perfume.

The perfume of tagara and sandalwood is of little enough power, while the supreme fragrance, that of the virtuous, reaches even up to the devas (Dhammapada 55, 56).

There is no ceiling to the power and glory of virtue.

No fear

Fear has no place in spiritual life, although caution and wariness often do. Yet most religion thrives on fear, especially in relation to evil. The three Western religions, Judaism, Christianity, and Islam keep their adherents in line by threatening them with the power of Satan or the wrath of God if they do not follow along. But Buddha has no need for such manipulative mythology. Instead he assures us that:

Perfect of virtue, always acting with recollection, and liberated by final realization—Mara does not know the path such people travel (Dhammapada 57).

In other words, evil cannot even figure out what the virtuous are doing. Only those whose minds and hearts live in the realm of metaphysical evil will be bothered by it. What if it is their karma from the past? Virtue will dissolve it. This is another major liberating truth of Buddha's teaching as contrasted with the modern idea that karma is some inexorable entity that must be worked out or fulfilled. Buddha assures us we can dispel karma along with the ignorance and defilement that produced it. Again: we can undo what we have done.

The contrast

Saint Paul told his disciples: "In the midst of a crooked and perverse nation [generation] ye shine as lights in the world" (Philippians 2:15). But Buddha gives a much more colorful picture, saying:

Like a beautiful, fragrant lotus, springing up on a pile of rubbish thrown out on the highway, so a disciple of the Enlightened One stands out among rubbish-like and blinded ordinary people by virtue of his wisdom (Dhammapada 58, 59).

Oh, oh! Can we believe that "the Compassionate Buddha" said such harsh words? Yes, indeed. He had compassion for human suffering, but not for human stupidity. He says flat out that those who follow the Buddha Way, whatever their religious label or lack thereof, are exquisite blossoms of enlightenment in contrast to the "rubbish-like and blinded ordinary people." It is a simple matter of wisdom, of those who have it and those who do not. May the wisdom of Buddha be made ours so we, too, can bloom.

Chapter 5

THE FOOL

In the drug-soaked 'sixties of the last century, one interesting phenomenon was that of "underground comics." Usually incoherent or obscene, on occasion they were discomfitingly insightful. One such was a brief comic strip called "Shuman the Human." It began: "Shuman the Human went searching for God. And believe me, he packed a lunch," the idea being that Shuman was not that interested in finding God, just in passing time; but if he should find God, he hoped it would not be right away.

In the same way, when Buddha decided to expound the nature of a spiritual fool in the Dhammapada, he took sixteen verses, a number that in India signifies completeness. So he will be describing a Complete Fool to us. It should not be missed that he will next take fourteen verses to describe a wise man, and only ten to describe an enlightened one. There has to be a meaning here.

Why do we need to know the traits of a fool? For two very crucial purposes: 1) so we can find out if we ourselves are fools and amend–not just our ways, but our minds; and 2) so we can tell when others are fools, and avoid and ignore them. This latter is very hard, since there so many of them, and they run all aspects of public life and set the tone for the pathetic mess *they* call culture.

Now Buddha speaks:

Blind to wisdom

Long is the night for the sleepless. Long is the road for the weary. Long is samsara [the cycle of continued rebirth] for the foolish, who have not recognized the true teaching (Dhammapada 60).

The word translated "true teaching" is *saddhammam*, true dharma. There are many definitions of dharma, but fundamentally dharma is that which unfolds or evolves relative nature and reveals transcendent Reality. It may take the form of many do's and don'ts, but essentially it is that which reveals the inmost reality, which is why we have the Sanskrit term *swadharma*: "the dharma of the Self."

No thing, no matter how desirable it may seem, is dharma (or dharmic) if it does not reveal the Self or further the possibility of that revelation. What may accomplish that in one person may have the opposite effect in another. For example, a great deal of social interaction may be just what one person needs for his development, but it may be detrimental to another person, whose swadharma would be solitude. This is extremely valuable to keep in mind, lest we try to coerce others into doing what may only be beneficial for us. It is a trait of childish individuals to consider that anything good, bad, or indifferent for them is good, bad, or indifferent for everyone.

True dharma, then, is that which reveals the truth of our own being to us. Without the knowledge and the practice of this dharma, life itself is nothing but weariness, like waking for the sleepy and walking for the weary. Human beings engage in all types of frantic activity to cover up this weariness and invent so many things to hide the truth of their own inner misery from themselves and others. If they cannot find an adequate mask, they merely engage in stubborn denial of the truth. And the weariness increases apace with their distraction and denial.

Life is death for such people. Some close friends of mine trained for a long time to be telephone counselors for suicidal people, wanting to be of help to suffering souls. But within two weeks of counseling they resigned because they could think of no reason why most people should continue their lives if they were not going to change. Why prolong the agony? "The only way their lives could be worth living would be for them to wake up spiritually and change their whole way of thinking and acting," one of them told me, "but according to the 'rules' we were not allowed to speak about spiritual or even philosophical things with them. How could we help them? So we quit. It was all a sham." Human beings frantically run from the only solution there is: spiritual consciousness. So their lives drag on horribly. They live and die in hopelessness, for only dharma can give them life and hope.

Worthless association

Human beings are sometimes described as "social animals," and they do not change when they take up spiritual life. Recognizing this, Buddha then says:

If on one's way one does not come across one's better or an equal, then one should press on resolutely alone. There is no companionship with a fool (Dhammapada 61).

This echoes the Gita: "Adore me only with heart undistracted; turn all your thought toward solitude, spurning the noise of the crowd, its fruitless commotion" (Bhagavad Gita 13:10).

There is no place in the psychology of Buddha for the "I'm as good as anyone else" fantasy. There are a lot of people is this world much better than us in a myriad of ways, and only the inveterate fool refuses to recognize this and give them their due. We should certainly seek for those who have progressed further along the path than ourselves and learn from them. If we cannot find such people, then let us find those that at least have the same degree of resolve and understanding as ourselves. If we cannot find either kind, then let us go on alone with strong intention. We are never alone on the path, for as mentioned before whenever someone decides to follow the Buddha Way, a multitude of Buddhas and Bodhisattvas become aware of the fact and begin helping him.

Buddha is warning us against association with the foolish, telling us that there is no real companionship with them. This is a bitter dose to swallow and digest, but we must if we would not relapse into foolishness ourselves. Company is greater than will power. In an unsuitable or hostile environment no seed can grow or plant continue to live. So following Buddha's counsel is a matter of survival. I know myself that this is true. At the beginning of my yoga practice I was literally over a hundred miles from the nearest yogis, and did not know about them at that time. So I nobly but stupidly decided that I should at least seek out people locally who were sincere and trying for higher life. That was a mistake, and one that nearly cost me my spiritual life. The story is too long to recount here, but I assure you my danger was very real. It is the same with any aspirant. Sri Ramakrishna used the simile of the brick enclosure put around a sapling to keep goats and cows from eating it. We must protect ourselves from our vulnerability to the influence of others. If need be, we must walk on alone. That is a much better choice than it may seem in the beginning.

And remember: the spiritually unconscious and indifferent can be much more harmful than the overtly wicked, for their negative influence is not readily perceived. They can infect us with their inertia, even if not with outright evil. As Jesus said: "He that is not with me is against me; and he that gathereth not with me scattereth abroad" (Matthew 12:30).

"Mine!"

"I've got children," "I've got wealth." This is the way a fool brings suffering on himself. He does not even own himself, so how can he have children or wealth? (Dhammapada 62).

Another good translation is that of Harischandra Kaviratna: "'I have children, I have wealth,' thinking thus, the fool torments himself. But, when he is not the possessor of his own self, how then of children? How then of wealth?"

The belief that any *thing*, internal or external, is ours is the terrible snare of samsara. But we are not helpless victims; rather, we are willing enslavers of our own selves. There is an internal aspect to Jesus' statement that "a man's foes shall be they of his own household" (Matthew 10:36).

We often, and glibly, speak of someone as his own worst enemy, but fail to realize that this is the truth about all of us. Consequently Krishna says: "Man's will is the only friend of the Atman: his will is also the Atman's enemy. For when a man is self-controlled, his will is the Atman's friend. But the will of an uncontrolled man is hostile to the Atman, like an enemy. That serene one absorbed in the Atman masters his will" (Bhagavad Gita 6:5-7).

But we willfully torment ourselves with the "mine" whip, driving ourselves from absurdity to absurdity. "I must fulfill my...;" "I must satisfy my ...;" "I must protect my...;" "I must look after my...;" "I must pay attention to my...;" "But I have my...;" "I must increase my...;" "It is my duty to love and care for my...." There are thousands of "my's" that demand our attention, none of them real and therefore none of them legitimate. Who will heed the insistence of Jesus that only "one thing is needful" (Luke 10:42)? And who will adopt as his own the wise words of David: "One thing have I desired of the Lord, that will I seek after; that I may dwell in the house of the Lord all the days of my life, to behold the beauty of the Lord, and to enquire in his temple" (Psalms 27:4). We are ourselves the temple of God, "the house of the Lord" (I Corinthians 3:16). Those who cultivate interior consciousness through meditation and purification will find this to be so. This is the only way to freedom from fear and sorrow.

Yet the fool stumbles on, increasing his fears and sorrows, truly "dreaming the impossible dream," for Buddha asks: "But, when he is not the possessor of his own self, how then of children? How then of wealth?"

No thing is ours, because the "me" who cries out "Mine!" is the ego, itself a mirage. How can a dream possess a dream? Awakening is the only course for us. All shall come to it in time, but until then fools pursue folly with the avidity of madness.

A "tough truth"

In the annals of all authentic religions the rosters of saints are filled with the names of monastics, with very few non-monastics named. Why so? Monastic life is no guarantee of enlightenment; millions (or even billions) of ignorant monks and nuns are proof of that. Nevertheless history shows that monastics have a better chance, a better percentage, at winning the race and gaining the prize. In this verse Buddha has shown us why. Monastics are free from the delusions: "I've got children," "I've got wealth." And these are the strongest delusions a human being can indulge. It is not external monasticism that is the key, but rather freedom from the psychology that is inherent in secular life. It is not family and money that does the harm, but their effects on the mind and heart of those who mistakenly think they possess them. Few are those who can resist and rise above that error. This sad fact is seen every day. Materiality is the School of Fools.

A real fool

A fool who recognizes his own ignorance is thereby in fact a wise man, but a fool who considers himself wise–that is what one really calls a fool (Dhammapada 63).

Is there really a need to comment on this? The problem is that we are in the grip of utter inconsistency. We may have the most sophisticated philosophy while living the most primitive or degraded lifestyle. "As a man thinketh, so he is," is outright bunkum. We should not disregard or deny our wisdom, but we must also recognize the presence of ignorance in our minds as well. Otherwise we will be unable to cultivate the one and eliminate the other. Constant vigilance is needed; we must be always sensitive to the arising of foolishness, for a great deal is hidden in our heart. The Kena Upanishad gives a fine exposition of the problem of "knowing." I will relay it here and nothing more will be needed on the subject.

"If you think that you know well the truth of Brahman, know that you know little. What you think to be Brahman in your self, or what you think to be Brahman in the gods—that is not Brahman. What is indeed the truth of Brahman you must therefore learn.

"I cannot say that I know Brahman fully. Nor can I say that I know him not. He among us knows him best who understands the spirit of the words: 'Nor do I know that I know him not.'

"He truly knows Brahman who knows him as beyond knowledge; he who thinks that he knows, knows not. The ignorant think that Brahman is known, but the wise know him to be beyond knowledge.

"He who realizes the existence of Brahman behind every activity of his being whether sensing, perceiving, or thinking—he alone gains immortality. Through knowledge of Brahman comes power. Through knowledge of Brahman comes victory over death" (Kena Upanishad 2:1-4).

The company of the wise

Sri Ramakrishna often spoke of the legend that when the Malaya breeze blew all trees turned into sandalwood trees except the ironwood trees. Some people, he commented, were ironwood trees. No matter how beneficial the company or environment, they would not learn or progress an inch. We see this in the lives of great master teachers like Krishna, Buddha, and Jesus. Comparatively few struck fire from their company, sometimes the most incorrigible seeming to be close disciples.

Buddha was speaking from experience when he said:

Even if a fool lived with a wise man all his life, he would still not recognize the truth, like a wooden spoon cannot recognize the flavor of the soup (Dhammapada 64).

All the "wisdom" and the "wise" in the world mean nothing as long as they remain external to us. There must be an inner awakening for us to even recognize either wisdom or the wise. It truly does take one to know one. That is why Buddha continues:

Even if a man of intelligence lives with a wise man only for a moment, he will immediately recognize the truth, like one's tongue recognizes the flavor of the soup (Dhammapada 65).

The question is: Are we tongues or spoons?

The old adage is true: "A fool and his money are soon parted." But the fool clings to his folly with great tenacity. So Buddha is now going to expound the deeds of a fool.

Their own enemy

Stupid fools go through life as their own enemies, doing evil deeds which have bitter consequences (Dhammapada 66).

Human beings are astonishing, including in their foolishness. One of the most astonishing follies is their insistence on doing things which bring them nothing but bitterness inwardly and outwardly. "Aren't we having a good time?" they ask their fellow-fools, shuffling through their little dreary lives that are crammed with activity that is really doing nothing in the end result.

A friend of mine challenged her father as to what his way of life—which he cordially hated, but which made him a lot of money—had ever done for him. Indignantly he took a deep draw on his cigarette (as he habitually did) as his hands shook (as they habitually did), and stammered out: "Why...it has made me very happy!" She was speechless at this response. Truly, he was the most miserable person I have ever seen. He was not an evil man, but had foolishly chosen a way of life completely galling to him just so he could make money and be respected by people he despised. As a result he was friendless and respected by no one, including his wife and children. But he did have money—which he used to endow scholarships so others could take up the career he wished he had adopted.

I have already referred to the camel that chews on thorns that pierce its mouth and make it bleed, but keeps on chewing. People are the same. Over and over they do what makes them suffer, often resolving to never do it again, but just as often repeating their folly. Many more people are destroying themselves without any idea they are doing so. They are bewildered as to what the problem is, and keep on piling up the pain. Others have somehow anesthetized themselves so they do not even know they are suffering. That is why Buddha said the first step we must take is the acknowledgment of the fact of our suffering.

The self-revealing nature of action

In Hinduism and Buddhism acts are not classed as right or wrong because some divine revelation has said so, as is the case in Western religion. In the East the character of an action is determined solely by its effect on the actor, not on the whim of a deity or prophet. So Buddha further says:

A deed is not well done if one suffers after doing it, if one bears the consequences sobbing and with tears streaming down one's face.

But a deed is well done if one does not suffer after doing it, if one experiences the consequences smiling and contented (Dhammapada 67, 68).

Of course Buddha is speaking of the long-term or ultimate consequences of a deed. Many people rejoice at the successful accomplishment of an evil deed, but in time—even in another incarnation—the suffering will result. On the other hand, some people are unhappy at doing good because they do not understand the principle of karma. But in time they rejoice at the good they did. The important principle is the fact that all actions in time reveal their true nature. But until then:

A fool and his karma...

A fool thinks it like honey so long as the bad deed does not bear fruit, but when it does bear fruit he experiences suffering (Dhammapada 69).

"I got away with it!" so thinks the fool. Consequently, when the suffering starts he wails: "What did I do to deserve this?" Never learning, he keeps on perpetuating his misery. When will it end? That is all up to him.

Ascetic fools

There are not only self-indulgent fools, there are self-denying fools who think that by coercing and tormenting the body they will somehow become spiritual. Engaging in physical discipline enables them to stay intent on their favorite subjects: their bodies and their egos. The ascetic struggle takes up all their attention so they can utterly forget their true selves, their spirits. Of such persons Buddha remarks:

Even if a fool were to take his food month after month off the tip of a blade of grass, he would still not be worth a fraction of those who have understood the truth (Dhammapada 70).

Narada Thera translates this verse: "Month after month a fool may eat only as much food as can be picked up on the tip of a kusha grass blade; but he is not worth a sixteenth part of them who have comprehended the Truth [Dharma]."

If we saw someone who would eat each day only as much food as could be contained on the tip of a blade of grass, we would consider that he was living on–and in–spirit. But we would be wrong. He would only be an amazing fool. His incredible discipline and dedication would be only so much stupidity, but other fools would admire it greatly. (If you do not believe me, just go to India for a while.)

The expression "sixteenth part" is significant. In Indian thought, sentient beings upon the earth are classified in sixteen categories, from the most elementary to the most developed. To only be worth a sixteenth of a fully perfected human being is to be rated with the most elementary plant life such as moss or mold. And to not be even worth that would be as of no more worth than a pebble–not even alive. In the spiritual sense, those without awakened consciousness are not alive. They are insentient, though technically sentient.

It is easy to look at this negatively, as though Buddha is saying what worthless people such ascetics would be. But actually he is saying how great is the awakened person. It is a matter of praise, not blame. We should admire the wise, not despise the foolish.

Inevitable karma

Like fresh milk a bad deed does not turn at once. It follows a fool scorching him like a smoldering fire (Dhammapada 71).

Narada Thera renders it: "Verily, an evil deed committed does not immediately bear fruit, just as milk curdles not at once; smoldering, it follows the fool like fire covered with ashes."

As already mentioned, the unwise think that they have gotten away with wrong action if it does not immediately rebound on them. Although there is such a thing as rapid karmic reaction, karma usually ripens like fruit before it falls off the universe-tree and hits us. It also takes a well-ripened mind to intuit this and know that "whatsoever a man soweth, that shall he also reap" (Galatians 6:7). Believing in one's own immortality—actually eternity—carries a lot of connotations.

Beneath the ashes of our forgetfulness, especially forgetfulness of past lives, the karmas lie smoldering. We may feel their heat in a vague way and feel unease, but in time, as Harischandra Kaviratna translates it, the karma "suddenly blazes up" and burns us, much to our bewilderment, for we have long ago forgotten what we did to produce this result. No wonder human life is utter confusion most of the time.

A knowledge worse than ignorance

A fool acquires knowledge only to his own disadvantage. It destroys what good he has, and turns his brains (Dhammapada 72).

Narada Thera: "To his ruin, indeed, the fool gains knowledge and fame; they destroy his bright lot and cleave his head."

All around us we see fools whose knowledge, little or great, is completely destructive. Consider how many scientific discoveries have rebounded to our detriment. Nothing good whatsoever has come from nuclear energy. There is hardly a greater or more harmful fraud than nuclear power plants. Like demons from a hideous fantasy they brood over the landscape, subtly poisoning everything in sight. Every single one is built at a cost ruinous to the economy and we have yet to see the "cheap" and "clean" power promised to us. Yet, addicted to death, governments will not learn and give them up. The very fact of nuclear waste should terrify them into abandoning such folly, but it never happens. And now we face the holocaust of genetic engineering.

In religion we find the most obvious evidence of Buddha's assertion. The New Age is a carnival of foolishness, of idiocy based on fragmentary knowledge. Rare is the oyster who produces a round pearl; most oysters make misshapen globs. It is the same with fools; in them the seed of knowledge mutates into distorted ideas and actions. Tell a fool that Krishna says it is a delusion to think we have the power to kill or the capacity to be killed, and he will instantly state that murder is not so bad, then, especially murder of the unborn. "It's all one" and "We are all God" are the slogans of spiritual and moral stupidity, even though they are statements of truth when in the mouth of the wise.

As a yogi once told me: "Never teach either meditation or philosophy to crazy people. It will just compound their craziness, and add another tool for them to express their insanity. And it will give a bad reputation to what should be respected." As Buddha says, it will crack their heads open. As an Eastern Christian priest once said to me about some mentally and morally degenerate people: "Those animals need a religion. But not *my* religion!" Just see what fools in the West are doing daily to utterly muddle and even destroy the great values of Hinduism and Buddhism.

Look at me, everybody!
One may desire a spurious respect ["undue reputation"– Narada Thera] and precedence among one's fellow monks, and the veneration of outsiders. "Both monks and laity should think it was my doing. They should accept my authority in all matters great or small." This is a fool's way of thinking. His self-seeking and conceit just increase (Dhammapada 73, 74).

Success also ruins a fool. One achievement and he swaggers and boasts for life. These are the last people in the world that should have self-esteem or high self-image, but many are eager to bestow such nonsense on them. As the upanishad says: "Living in the abyss of ignorance yet wise in their own conceit, deluded fools go round and round, the blind led by the blind" (Katha Upanishad 1:2:5; Mundaka Upanishad 1.2.8).

Aryas have a healthy and reasonable desire to improve themselves and to succeed in worthwhile endeavors, but fools only want to glorify themselves and justify their egotism and arrogance. Here, too, a multitude of fools await to boost their morale and give them self-confidence and make things even worse for them and those unfortunate enough to come into contact with them. Only take a good look at politics throughout the world to see a riot of such fools.

The two ways

Buddha is not taking pleasure in delineating the ways of fools. He has a very positive and constructive purpose: finally pointing us to the way of wisdom. So he concludes by saying:

One way leads to acquisition, the other leads to Nirvana. Realizing this a monk, as a disciple of the Buddha, should take no pleasure in the respect of others, but should devote himself to solitude (Dhammapada 75).

Narada Thera gives a more accurate rendering: "Surely, the path that leads to worldly gain is one, and the path that leads to Nirvana is another; understanding this, the bhikkhu, the disciple of the Buddha, should not rejoice in worldly favors, but cultivate detachment [viveka]."

A disciple of the Buddha is one who is intent on the revelation of his own Buddhahood, his Buddha Nature. Seeing that the accolades of others lead only to addiction and hunger for more, he disregards all such and practices discrimination (viveka), seeing truly that the ways of the world are hollow, but filled with poison, in contrast to the Buddha Way which concentrates on real spiritual attainment rather than mere spiritual reputation. He finds his fulfillment in nothing less than the perfection of Nirvana.

"Only that yogi whose joy is inward, inward his peace, and his vision inward shall come to Brahman and know Nirvana. All consumed are their imperfections, doubts are dispelled, their senses mastered, their every action is wed to the welfare of fellow-creatures: such are the seers who enter Brahman and know Nirvana. Self-controlled, cut free from desire, curbing the heart and knowing the Atman, man finds Nirvana that is in Brahman, here and hereafter" (Bhagavad Gita 5:24-26).

Chapter 6

THE WISE MAN

Buddha has given us a portrait of the foolish man, and now he begins to speak of the wise man.

We all begin foolish, but after a while we aspire to become wise. If we are fortunate, the first step in this process will be to meet with someone wise who will point out to us the way to wisdom. If we cannot meet such a person—and they are rare, especially in the West—then we should search for the written wisdom of a wise teacher (or even more than one). It is glibly said that spirituality cannot be gotten from books, but the truth is, spiritual awakening or spiritual recognition has resulted from books far more than from meetings with a living teacher. That is because over the centuries the teachings of many wise men have been preserved, whereas the living teachers are always few in comparison. As the Venerable Master Chin Kung, a contemporary Chinese Buddhist teacher, has said, by studying and applying the teachings of any great teacher, no matter how long ago he lived, you can become his student. So now let us look at Buddha's teaching on the matter of a teacher, keeping in mind that his words apply equally to living teachers and books of teachings.

Like one pointing out hidden treasure
Like one pointing out hidden treasure, if one finds a man of intelligence who can recognize one's faults and take one to task for them, one should cultivate the company of such a wise man.

He who cultivates a man like that is the better for it, not worse (Dhammapada 76).

Obviously Buddha's idea of a worthy teacher is not the one popularly held today. Buddha is not at all interested in a teacher who is totally accepting—just the opposite. He extols a teacher who is not at all tolerant of our faults or our sore-ego sensitivity to having them revealed or prodded at. In the twelfth chapter of *Autobiography of a Yogi*, Paramhansa Yogananda tells of his experience as a disciple of Swami Sriyukteswar Giri. Here are some bits that give a general idea. We will begin with the sweet, and go directly to the bitter.

"Lifelong shadow lifted from my heart; the vague search, hither and yon, was over. I had found eternal shelter in a true guru....Discipline had not been unknown to me: at home Father was strict, Ananta [Yogananda's elder brother] often severe. But Sri Yukteswar's training cannot be described as other than drastic. A perfectionist, my guru was hypercritical of his disciples, whether in matters of moment or in the subtle nuances of behavior. ...my ears were no strangers to reproof. My chief offenses were absentmindedness, intermittent indulgence in sad moods, non-observance of certain rules of etiquette, and occasional unmethodical ways....Under Master's unsparing rod, however, I soon recovered from the agreeable delusions of irresponsibility.

"My guru could never be bribed, even by love. He showed no leniency to anyone who, like myself, willingly offered to be his disciple. Whether Master and I were surrounded by his students or by strangers, or were alone together, he always spoke plainly and upbraided sharply. No trifling lapse into shallowness or inconsistency escaped his rebuke. This flattening treatment was hard to endure, but my resolve was to allow Sri Yukteswar to iron out each of my psychological kinks. As he labored at this titanic transformation, I shook many times under the weight of his disciplinary hammer.

"'If you don't like my words, you are at liberty to leave at any time,' Master assured me. 'I want nothing from you but your own improvement. Stay only if you feel benefited.'"

Please read the entire chapter to see the characteristics of a worthy teacher. It is so perfect, that I will say no more except to point out that Buddha evidently thinks that having our faults exposed to us and undergoing reprimand for them is the finding of treasure. Yogananda agrees, for he further says: "For every humbling blow he dealt my vanity, for every tooth in my metaphorical jaw he knocked loose with stunning aim, I am grateful beyond any facility of expression. The hard core of human egotism is hardly to be dislodged except rudely. With its departure, the Divine finds at last an unobstructed channel." What a treasure indeed!

There are many kinds of intelligence, but spiritual intelligence is the highest, for it alone frees us from our age-long bondages. A teacher possessing such intelligence has only their freedom in mind when dealing with students. "He who cultivates a man like that is the better for it, not worse."

Two reactions

In our egotism we think that our opinions are discernments of truth regarding things. But usually they are only revelations of our own worth or lack of it. I read of a woman who remarked aloud that a painting in an art museum was worthless. A guard standing by said, "Madam, the merit of this painting was established long ago. What is on trial here is the worth of your perceptions." Krishna, too, indicates in the Gita that our reactions are according to the quality of our inner makeup. "Even a wise man acts according to the tendencies of his own nature. All living creatures follow their tendencies. What use is any external restraint?" (Bhagavad Gita 3:33). So by analyzing our opinions we can discern the true quality of our intellect.

Much less philosophical was part of the theme music for a favorite television program of my (much) younger years. Every week before Richard Greene swung across the screen as Robin Hood, the words boomed out: "Feared by the bad; loved by the good...." Buddha had the same conviction, for he further said:

If a man disciplines, instructs and restrains them from what is not right, he will be dear to the good, and disliked by the bad (Dhammapada 77).

The students' declarations that the worthy teacher is good or bad is a revelation of their own inner condition. Here, too, Yogananda helps us to understand.

"But divine insight is painful to worldly ears; Master was not popular with superficial students. The wise, always few in number, deeply revered him. I daresay Sri Yukteswar would have been the most sought-after guru in India had his words not been so candid and so censorious.

"'I am hard on those who come for my training,' he admitted to me. 'That is my way; take it or leave it. I will never compromise.... Tender inner weaknesses, revolting at mild touches of censure, are like diseased parts of the body, recoiling before even delicate handling.' This was Sri Yukteswar's amused comment on the flighty ones. There are disciples who seek a guru made in their own image....

"Students came, and generally went. Those who craved a path of oily sympathy and comfortable recognitions did not find it at the hermitage. Master offered shelter and shepherding for the aeons, but many disciples miserly demanded ego-balm as well. They departed, preferring life's countless humiliations before any humility. Master's blazing rays, the open penetrating sunshine of his wisdom, were too powerful for their spiritual sickness. They sought some lesser teacher who, shading them with flattery, permitted the fitful sleep of ignorance.

"...But toward students who sought his counsel, Sri Yukteswar felt a serious responsibility. Brave indeed is the guru who undertakes to transform the crude ore of ego-permeated humanity! A saint's courage roots in his compassion for the stumbling eyeless of this world.

"When I had abandoned underlying resentment, I found a marked decrease in my chastisement. In a very subtle way, Master melted into comparative clemency. In time I demolished every wall of rationalization and subconscious reservation behind which the human personality generally shields itself. The reward was an effortless harmony with my guru. I discovered him then to be trusting, considerate, and silently loving."

The love of such a one is the only love worth seeking and finding. Actually, it is the only love there is. Unconditional love is only given by those who have themselves transcended all conditions and conditionings.

Determining association

Over and over in the teachings of Buddha we find that he is giving us only that which can be applied in our daily lives in order to fit ourselves for freedom from all that bind us. Never does he waste a single moment of our time with metaphysics that, by their abstract nature, have no practical use. Again and again we see from his words that dharma is a matter of here and now. Anything outside the here and now is meaningless.

Paramhansa Nityananda said: "When a man takes birth, he is not born with a book in his hand but he is born with a brain" (Chidakasha Gita 41). In modern India it certainly seems like the popular teachers were born with a book instead of a brain–a book of platitudes and truisms that someone once rightly labeled "fortune cookie omniscience." In the West we are raised in such abysmal ignorance that when we first hear the fortune cookie platitudes we are overwhelmed with their wisdom. We are like a starving person to whom junk food tastes heavenly. The sad thing about many Western seekers is that they never come to see the flimsy character of the platitudes but stick with them and their robotic dispensers for all their life.

Fortunately for me, my initial contact with Sanatana Dharma was the unparalleled translation of the Bhagavad Gita by Swami Prabhavananda. There is not a single syllable in the spiritual teaching of the Gita that is not essential; for me the Gita was a door into a whole new world. My next contact moved me forward into that new world and told me what I needed to acclimatize and expand into it. That contact was Yogananda's *Autobiography of a Yogi* and his other writings that are worthy of a lifetime of study and analysis. His commentary on the

Bhagavad Gita presents the Sankhya philosophy in an unequaled manner, and his commentary on the Christian Gospels is the prime source for the real teachings of Jesus. No matter how many excellent books I have read over the intervening years, I always find myself going back to Yogananda to find the first, middle, and last words on spiritual life. Over and over he illuminates practical aspects of both inner and outer life that other teachers never even mention. One of the first aphorisms of Yogananda that I learned deeply affected me. It was: "Company is greater than will power." I took it seriously and applied it seriously in my life. It still comes to mind in many instances. So it naturally came to mind when I read the seventy-eighth verse of the Dhammapada:

Companions good and bad
Don't cultivate the company of bad companions. Don't cultivate depraved men. Cultivate companions of good character. Cultivate superior men (Dhammapada 78).

Here are three other translations that bring out the shades of meaning:

"Do not keep company with evildoing friends nor with people who are base; associate with the good, associate with the best of men" (Harischandra Kaviratna).

"Do not have evil-doers for friends, do not have low people for friends: have virtuous people for friends, have for friends the best of men" (Max Muller).

"Don't associate with bad friends. Don't associate with the low. Associate with admirable friends. Associate with the best" (Thanissaro Bhikkhu).

Buddha, as we would expect, is not in the least afraid of being thought a snob or a self-righteous prig. The only people who would accuse him of that on the basis of this words are the very people he tells us to avoid.

Bad companions
What makes someone a bad companion? Obviously evil-doers are bad companions, but we have to define evil. There are a lot of things

that never come to mind as outright evils, but for the sadhaka they can be deadly. Laziness, ignorance, lack of interest in higher life, material-mindedness, trivial-mindedness, mundane-mindedness, arrogance, selfishness, egotism, lack of spiritual motivation–all these are evils for the seeker of enlightenment, especially since we rarely consider them as such. People who have these traits are bad companions, since these things are contagious. Company *is* greater than will power.

Wagner wrote the symbolic music-drama called *Parsifal*. One of the major characters is a woman named Kundry. She divides her time between association with the holy knights of the Grail and the vile Klingsor, a renegade Grail knight that has become a sorcerer. When she is with the Grail knights, Kundry behaves in a positive manner, but when she is with Klingsor she behaves in a negative, destructive manner. Many people are like Kundry, being influenced profoundly by the psychic character of whomever they are with. "Evil company corrupts good manners" is true, but the worst of it is the condition of being so susceptible.

None of us should feel beyond the influence of others. Some people do not succumb immediately, but in time the citadel of their good state falls, often to never rise again in this lifetime. So this is a matter of life and death.

The depraved

The fact that Buddha distinguishes between the bad and the depraved bears out my contention that the bad are those we never think of as bad, only spiritually out of the picture. The depraved are those who do evil by choice–choice which rapidly escalates into addiction and eventual enslavement. These people can usually be identified by anyone with good moral sense, but many of them operate under a veneer of benevolence and even goodness. This is why so many morally corrupt people at the present time are avidly engaging in social action and are exaggeratedly concerned about ecology and the pollution of the atmosphere. These are fake, "noble" moralities, requiring no moral strength whatsoever, that are only a cover for their depravity.

These, too, must be avoided assiduously. (Good and worthy people are also sincerely involved in these concerns, but that is a different matter altogether.)

How to define a depraved person? First, anyone who is addicted to anything. Second, anyone who encourages addiction in others. It is incumbent on aspirants to higher awareness to develop the intuition to detect hidden depravity.

Those of good character

What makes a person one of good character? Absence of the negative qualities we have discussed is necessary, but not enough. There must be the presence of active, positive elements. We can take our former list and reverse it. Good people are diligent, disciplined, wise, oriented toward higher consciousness, spiritual-minded, substantial of character, possessing intelligent values, generous, unselfish, and valuing things of the spirit above all else.

Someone once asked Anandamayi Ma how to define "good" and "friend." She replied that good was anything that enables someone to remember God and that a friend was someone who inspired you to remember God. Anything or anyone else was bad and an enemy. To grasp this truth and act upon it, bringing into our life the good and ruthlessly eliminating the bad—and doing it right now, not gradually easing into it or putting it off to some vague or convenient future—is not just the beginning of wisdom, it is the guarantee of wisdom.

The superior

Superior people are those of conscious spiritual evolution who are constantly moving forward to higher and deeper realms of personal consciousness. They are dedicated wholeheartedly to the path of progress. Obviously they are yogis in the truest sense. A superior person not only elevates himself, but elevates those who come in contact with him. Vibrating to truth, he awakens others to truth by his mere presence. Those who cannot be so uplifted are indifferent to him and he is indifferent to them. "He by whom the world is not agitated and who cannot be agitated by the world—he is dear to Me" (Bhagavad Gita 12:15). "I pray not for the world, but for them which thou hast given me" (John 17:9).

Great saints and masters can produce spiritual consciousness in others simply by entering the room. I have known such myself, and have lived with some. However, only those who get busy and cultivate their own spiritual consciousness will benefit from them in a lasting manner. It always comes back to us.

Take it within
He who drinks in the Dharma will live happily with a peaceful mind. A wise man always delights in the Dharma taught by the Aryas (Dhammapada 79).

Water is essential to life, possessing many aspects necessary to the maintenance of form and function. We can live a long time without food, but not without water. Dharma is equally necessary for the true life of the inmost consciousness. But both water and dharma are valueless if they are not internalized–and not drop by drop, but by continual, deep drinking. Buddha is explaining to us that we must drink up dharma as the thirsting man seizes water and drinks it with urgency and delight. Just as the most virulent poison will not harm us or the best medicine will not cure us if we do not swallow it, in the same way dharma will have no effect unless we make it part of our very being by taking it into our consciousness.

Looking at, touching, applying, or even immersing ourselves in water is useless if we do not drink it. And just talking about it is the most useless of all. It is the same with dharma. That is why Saint Paul spoke of "Christ *in* you, the hope of glory" (Colossians 1:27). An external Christ is of no value whatsoever. That is why Jesus spoke of eating and drinking the flesh and blood of Christ–in other words, internalizing and absorbing Christ. It is the same with dharma.

Work on yourself; change yourself
Irrigators channel water, fletchers shape arrows, and carpenters bend wood, but the wise discipline themselves (Dhammapada 80).

This verse conveys a tremendous amount of information in a very concise manner. It is a marvel. And if we follow it, we will ourselves become marvels.

Irrigators channel water. First, they find a source of water. Then they dig a channel to the place where water is needed. Finally, they remove the barrier between the water and the channel, and the water flows in and their work is done. It is hard work that demands perseverance and good engineering. Sri Ramakrishna speaks about it this way:

"There happened to be drought in the country. All the peasants began digging channels to bring water. One of them was stubbornly determined. One day he vowed that he would go on digging a channel until it became connected with the river and water began to flow into it. He proceeded digging. The time came for his bath. The wife sent the daughter to him with oil. The daughter said, 'Father, it is late already. Finish bathing quickly after rubbing the body with oil.' He told her to go away for he still had work to do. It was past midday and the farmer still kept working. No thought at all of taking a bath. Then his wife came to the field and said, 'Why haven't you bathed as yet? The food is getting cold. You carry things too far. You may finish it tomorrow or even after taking your meal.' Scolding, the farmer ran after her with spade in hand and said, 'Have you no sense? There has not been any rain. There has been no farming at all. What will the children eat? You will all die of starvation. I have taken the vow that I will bring water to the field today and then worry about bath and food.' Observing his mood the wife fled running. After a whole day's bone-breaking labor the farmer connected the channel with the river. Then he sat down for a while and watched the water from the river flowing into the field with a pleasant gurgle. His mind was at peace and filled with joy.

"Now there was another farmer who was also trying to bring water to his field. His wife went to him and said, 'It is very late. Come now, there is no need for overdoing things so much.' He dropped the spade without much protest and told his wife, 'Let's go, since you say so.' That farmer did not ever succeed in bringing water to his field."

So we have to know where the water of life is to be found, how to remove the barriers between it and us, and how to channel it into ourselves. This is what dharma really is, and its most important component is meditation.

Fletchers shape arrows. It is no easy thing to make an arrow. The wood must be strong, free from defect, and of the right density or weight. It must be shaped in such a way that it will move through the air at maximum speed. More important, it must be absolutely straight so it will fly unerringly to its target. Obviously this is a symbol of the mind itself.

The mind is a field of energy, and the quality of that energy is crucial for the sadhaka. Just as a machine can have gears of tempered steel or cheap shoddy plastic, in the same way, although everyone has a mind, the character of the mind substance, the manasic energy, varies greatly. Even intelligence counts for little if the mind itself is of inferior energy. As Yogananda pointed out, Handel took a sequence of notes and got the opening of the Hallelujah Chorus, while an American composer took the same notes and got "Yes, We Have No Bananas."

The Chandogya Upanishad explains: "Mind consists of food. That which is the subtle part of milk moves upward when the milk is churned and becomes butter. In the same manner, the subtle part of the food that is eaten moves upward and becomes mind. Thus, mind consists of food" (Chandogya Upanishad 6.5.4; 6.6.1, 2, 5).

The type of thoughts habitual to a person also determines the rate of vibration of his mind. The mind must be strong and steady, yet at the same time it must be fluidic, responsive, and capable of mirroring correctly that which is presented to it. Without yoga this is simply impossible.

Carpenters bend wood. It is interesting that Buddha refers to the bending of wood. We usually think of carpenters cutting or planing wood, but wood is bent in the making of furniture, and even in the making of yokes for oxen and other animals that pull carts. (It is said that Saint Thomas the Apostle was especially skilled in this.) To bend wood it is necessary to soak it and soften the fibers to the right degree and then to ever so slowly bend it to the desired shape, affix it in that shape, and then let it dry. If everything was done right, it will permanently hold that configuration. It is the same with us. Great care and skill are needed for us to rework and reshape ourselves, particularly our minds, so there will be a permanent change for the better. As Buddha concludes: "The wise discipline themselves."

Irrigators, fletchers and carpenters all work with external things, but the wise work with themselves, shaping and changing themselves. At the end of life they take the results along with them, having produced lasting change in their consciousness, and will build on that in future lives until Nirvana is reached.

Wise indifference

As a solid rock is not shaken by the wind, so the wise are not moved by praise or blame (Dhammapada 81).

A rock is not shaken by wind because it is so substantial and firmly settled on the earth. In the same way, a person who possesses self-knowledge as well as knowledge as to what is *not* himself is not moved by praise or blame, since neither mean anything, for the true Self is beyond anything that can be said about it. Also, knowing that whatever occurs in the outer world is only a passing show, the wise take nothing seriously that is said or done in relation to them. A perfect example of this was the holy Metropolitan Philaret of New York, head of the Russian Orthodox Church Outside Russia. I had the great blessing of meeting him a few times and will never forget the experience. An acquaintance of mine told me that when he was first made the chief hierarch of the Russian Church Abroad, he visited all the churches in America and Canada. When he came to Boston he was accompanied by Archbishop Nikon, himself a spiritually remarkable person. At the Divine Liturgy, Archbishop Nikon introduced the Metropolitan, praising him fulsomely and eloquently, virtually proclaiming him a saint (which he was). Any other person would have made some protest of modesty, but he just stood there, looking downward and indrawn in prayer, completely indifferent to the praise. As another friend of mine said regarding him: "He was alone with God and absorbed in God."

The way to peace

The wise find peace on hearing the truth, like a deep, clear, undisturbed lake (Dhammapada 82).

Already wise in their inmost consciousness, the wise need only hear the truth of dharma to instantly recognize it and to come to the end of their search for realities of life–and beyond. The mind of a truly dharmic person is deep, clear, and undisturbed by any phenomena arising either from within or without. We usually think about peace of mind, but there is also peace of will. That is, once a person has fixed his intention on the attainment of higher consciousness, and resolved to do all that is necessary to attain that precious thing, then nothing can shake him from that steadiness of will (sankalpa). Inwardly he will have peace, even if he is somewhat affected by fluctuations in his emotional or intellectual levels. Those who keep their mind's eye steadfastly on the goal, like an archer aiming at the target, will know peace that is unshakable.

The Wisdom of Renunciation

The good renounce everything. The pure don't babble about sensual desires. Whether touched by pleasure or pain, the wise show no change of temper (Dhammapada 83).

This eighty-third verse is not a simple one, and the translations of even very qualified scholars can vary. Rather than pick what seems to me to be the best, I am going to give the differing translations so you can see what I mean.

The good

Jesus said: "There is none good but one, that is, God" (Matthew 19:17). At that time in parts of the Mediterranean world the word "good" was never applied to anything or anyone but God. That is why the Eastern Orthodox compendium on mystical life is called *Philokalia*, "Love of the Good"–that is, Love of God. So the good are the godly. Buddha has something to say about them: "They renounce everything." So translates John Richardson. Narada Thera has: "The good give up everything." Harischandra Kaviratna: "Good men abandon lusting after things."

There is no use ignoring the fact that we live in a thing-obsessed society. And it is risky indeed to assume that we have not been influenced by its material philosophy, both consciously and subliminally. So when people hear about giving up or renouncing they become unsettled, unless at the moment they are unhappy through being let down by something or someone. Then they agree and make noise about "chucking it all away" and suchlike. It will not be long, though, before they are pursuing another form of what made them miserable.

The plain truth is, we cannot live without material things. Even if we could remain forever in samadhi without breathing or eating, we would still be in the body and would have to sit or lie upon the earth. So good sense tells us that whether we externally rid ourselves of many things or whether we retain them, Buddha is definitely speaking of our attitude toward them. Perhaps the best explanation of this is to be found in the words of Sri Ramarkrishna:

"If one is sincere one can realize God even in the world. 'Me and mine' make ignorance. 'O God! You and yours.' This is knowledge! Live in the world like the maid servant of a wealthy man. The maid servant does all household work, brings up children and calls the master's son, 'My Hari,' but she knows very well at heart that neither the house nor the boy belongs to her. She does all the chores but her heart is always in her country home. Likewise do all the work of the household but keep your mind on God. And know that the house, the family, the son and all the rest are not yours but God's. And that you are only God's servant.

"I ask people to renounce mentally. I do not ask them to renounce the world. If one lives in the world with detachment and longs for God from the heart one can realize him" (*The Gospel of Sri Ramakrishna*, Volume 2, Part 15, Chapter 2).

"The tortoise moves about in water but do you know where its mind is? It is on the land where its eggs are. Do all the duties of the world but keep your mind on God" (*The Gospel of Sri Ramakrishna*, Volume 1, Part 1, Chapter 5).

"I say to those who come to me, 'Live in the world; there is no harm in that. But keep your mind on God while living in the world. Know that house, home, family are not yours. All these belong to God. Your home is near God.'" (*The Gospel of Sri Ramakrishna*, Volume 1, Part 10, Chapter 8)

This is possible only to the yogi. For all others this is mere juggling with the mind.

The Venerable Thanisarro Bhikkhu's translation sums it up very well: "Everywhere, truly, those of integrity stand apart." Integrity means self-containment, self-sufficiency. This the wise always strive for: not to be scattered or diluted or weak and dependent. The worthy find all they need within. By their very nature they stand apart. The Gita gives a perfect picture of them: "Master of ego, standing apart from the things of the senses, free from self; aware of the weakness in mortal nature, its bondage to birth, age, suffering, dying; to nothing be slave, nor desire possession of man-child or wife, of home or of household; calmly encounter the painful, the pleasant; adore me only with heart undistracted; turn all your thought toward solitude, spurning the noise of the crowd, its fruitless commotion; strive without ceasing to know the Atman, seek this knowledge and comprehend clearly why you should seek it: such, it is said, are the roots of true wisdom: ignorance, merely, is all that denies them" (Bhagavad Gita 13:8-11).

The pure

"The pure don't babble about sensual desires." Narada Thera: "The saintly prattle not with sensual craving." Harischandra Kaviratna: "They take no pleasure in sensual speech." This is really quite clear. The truly pure do not talk about sensual things because they do not think about them. Speech can deceive but it can also greatly reveal the hidden contents of the mind. For example, it is amazing how many yoga gurus use sex or sexually related examples when wanting to make a point. Obviously that is what habitually springs to their minds. Our monastic group used to visit the monastery of another tradition. The head of the ashram was highly intelligent and the author of many books. We profited greatly from conversation with him about the meditational and philosophical aspects of his tradition. But every single time we visited he would bring up some aspect of sex, and always made reference to male sexual organs. He was amazingly creative in coming up with ways to do this. So you can imagine that we had little interest in anything more than intellectual contact with those people. And eventually we just faded away from their orbit.

"Where your treasure is, there will your heart be also," said Jesus (Matthew 6:21). And, as he also said: "Out of the abundance of the heart the mouth speaketh" (Matthew 12:34). This applies to teachers who under the guise of teaching morality really only expound immorality, just as others who under the guise of teaching truth only go on and on disproving and denouncing heresy. Even worse are those that instead of speaking of God and angels talk only about the Devil and demons. What we love, that we think and speak about.

Even-mindedness

"Whether touched by pleasure or pain, the wise show no change of temper." Narada Thera: "Whether affected by happiness or by pain, the wise show neither elation nor depression." Harischandra Kaviratna: "When touched by happiness or sorrow, the wise show no elation or dejection."

This has a great lesson for us. The idea is current among many yogis that the wise are simply numb to pleasure or pain, that they never experience such things. But Buddha indicates otherwise. He says that they are touched by these things, but they do not respond to them with elation or depression. Krishna said: "Water flows continually into the ocean but the ocean is never disturbed: desire flows into the mind of the seer but he is never disturbed" (Bhagavad Gita 2:70). This is the state we should seek.

Hard sayings

Great Masters are fearless, and so must those be who would benefit from their teachings. For Masters and (true) disciples see things exactly opposite to the world and the worldlings. Certainly greed and desire for control over others bring about the inner destruction of religion, but an equally pernicious factor is the insistence that the principles of religion be made to accommodate, please and motive the common crowd rather than the worthy few–the only ones to whom the Masters really speak. That is why Jesus prayed, saying: "I pray for them: I pray not for the world, but for them which thou hast given me; for they are thine.…I have given them thy word; and the world hath hated them, because they are not of the world, even as I am not of the world" (John 17:9, 14). On one occasion when Jesus had given a particularly thorny discourse: "Many therefore of his disciples, when they had heard this, said, This is an hard saying; who can hear it?…From that time many of his disciples went back, and walked no more with him" (John 6:60, 66). Now we are ready to look at one of Buddha's hard sayings.

If a man does not seek children, wealth or power either for himself or for someone else, if he does not seek his own advantage by unprincipled means, he is a virtuous man, a wise man and a righteous man (Dhammapada 84).

Narada Thera: "Neither for the sake of oneself nor for the sake of another: he should not desire son, wealth, or kingdom. By unjust means he should not seek his own success. Then such a one is indeed virtuous, wise and righteous." The translation of the Venerable Thanissaro Bhikkhu says that such a one "is righteous, rich in virtue, [and] discernment."

Applied to everyone

Although it is so common to hear someone say regarding an unpalatable discipline: "Oh, that is just for you monks," in this case it has to be pointed out that Buddha's teaching is not just for non-monastics. For sad to say a lot of monastics are greedy and scheming, though supposedly for the sake of others: family, friends, church, monastic order, etc. Under the guise of personal poverty, Christian monks for centuries have amassed fantastic amounts of money and land holdings, often owning slaves and bond servants including peasants in imperial Russia. One famous monk in Thailand actually raised enough money to pay off the national debt, then realized that everyone in the government were such crooks that they would grab it and not pay off the debt. So the money sits idle to no purpose. Monks are often matchmakers. I knew a Greek Orthodox nun that travelled around raising thousands of dollars for her nieces' dowries.

Even more absurd, consider the number of monks (especially in India) who are credited with the miraculous power to ensure pregnancy, gain wealth for devotees, and get employment and university degrees for others. Some activity for world-renouncing teachers of dispassion and non-materialism! Buddha never did such things. He is a perfect example for all humanity. In the case of this eighty-fourth verse, one size truly does fit all.

Children, wealth, and power

Children, wealth, and power; in themselves these three items have no defect. After all, if we had not been children we would not be here at all. And if we had no money, what kind of existence would we have? It is the same with some power or influence; it would be impossible to live a worthwhile human life without it. What, then, is the problem? As always: the ego. The trouble is with the rascal that says: My children, My money, My influence. Or an ego so twisted that it thinks getting those things for others–which will all be labeled Mine in some way–is acceptable. Ego is at the bottom, the middle, and the top.

Buddha is warning us away from actively seeking those things in an ego-involved way. Actually, he is warning us about seeking anything in a self-centered manner rather than to approach life as a worthy karma yogi: do our best and leave the rest to the cosmic laws. It is true, as the Gita points out to us, that there is a positive form of indifference to these things that renders them safe for us. Buddha does not want us to hate or despise them, for then we would be thinking and obsessing about them. The idea is that we should live life with the central purpose of spiritual evolution and let these other factors be, or not be, as they are. We are to seek the Paramartha, the Supreme Attainment, of enlightenment.

Let us not forget that Buddha gave up all these three. And because of his renunciation billions have understood the truth about this life and have attained higher consciousness. Just think: one man has done all this through his renunciation!

Unprincipled means

The end does not justify the means. Rather, the end can invalidate or corrupt the means. Buddha is aware of the slippery nature of the ego. It may seem to agree to not seek for vain things, but it will certainly consider that it can adopt any strategy it wants for the accomplishment or gain of something that is seen as necessary or beneficial. The ego loves to Do Good in a Not Good manner, thinking it is justified to do so. This type of hypocrisy is common on all levels of life. Sometimes the religious people are the worst. In the 1960's an acquaintance of mine discovered that officials of the Russian Orthodox Church in New York City were paying someone who lived right there in New York City to write accounts of fictitious "new martyrs" in Russia–as if the Communists were not continually making enough real ones! These fabrications were then presented as "accounts recently smuggled out of the Soviet Union." When the priest (later a bishop) in charge of the fraud was challenged by her regarding this, he responded with polished cynicism: "It accomplishes what we want." And the conversation was at an end.

But the good and true person will never cut corners or compromise integrity or moral principles to gain something that of itself may seem desirable. As an Eastern Christian writer has said: "If you have to employ an unjust means, then the end is unjust, as well."

Virtuous, wise, and righteous

Diogenes may have searched for a good and wise man with a lantern, but only two things will enable us to find such a one: a) by that person really being good and wise; and b) by ourselves being good and wise so we can recognize them. It is true: it takes one to know one.

Those who live according to the principles so clearly presented by Buddha will be all those things: virtuous, wise, and righteous. It is easy for the real person, but impossible for the ego.

Running along the bank

Few are those among men who have crossed over to the other shore, while the rest of mankind runs along the bank (Dhammapada 85).

Narada Thera: "Few are there among men who go Beyond; the rest of mankind only run about on the bank." It is a fact: people live their lives like ants whose hill has been disturbed; rushing about aimlessly and uselessly.

"Then said one unto him, Lord, are there few that be saved? And he said unto them, Strive to enter in at the strait gate: for many, I say unto you, will seek to enter in, and shall not be able" (Luke 13:23,24). Jesus was surely familiar with the Dhammapada, considering the amount of time he spent in Buddhist monasteries and centers in India, and no doubt had these very verses in mind when he gave his answer. At any time in history it is indeed comparatively few that Cross Over.

Few cross over

Edward Lear wrote a poem called "The Jumblies" which tells it very well—as he often did under the guise of nonsense verse. I am going to include the whole thing here for you to see what I mean. Even though much of it may not seem to apply to or be relevant to the search for liberation, it does, because those who seek Reality are even more strange and absurd than the Jumblies to the ants that run along the shore and never get anywhere, but like to say that one day they, too,

126

will cross over, yet somehow it does not happen. For "far and few, far and few" are the Jumblies who alone can do it.

The Jumblies

They went to sea in a Sieve, they did,
    In a Sieve they went to sea:
In spite of all their friends could say,
    On a winter's morn, on a stormy day,
In a Sieve they went to sea!
    And when the Sieve turned round and round,
And every one cried, "You'll all be drowned!"
    They called aloud, "Our Sieve ain't big,
But we don't care a button! we don't care a fig!
    In a Sieve we'll go to sea!"
        Far and few, far and few,
            Are the lands where the Jumblies live;
         Their heads are green, and their hands are blue,
            And they went to sea in a Sieve.

They sailed away in a Sieve, they did,
    In a Sieve they sailed so fast,
With only a beautiful pea-green veil
    Tied with a riband by way of a sail,
To a small tobacco-pipe mast;
    And every one said, who saw them go,
"Oh won't they be soon upset, you know!
    For the sky is dark, and the voyage is long,
And happen what may, it's extremely wrong
    In a Sieve to sail so fast!"
        Far and few, far and few,
            Are the lands where the Jumblies live;
         Their heads are green, and their hands are blue,
            And they went to sea in a Sieve.

The water it soon came in, it did,
　　The water it soon came in;
So to keep them dry, they wrapped their feet
　　In a pinky paper all folded neat,
And they fastened it down with a pin.
　　And they passed the night in a crockery-jar,
And each of them said, "How wise we are!
　　Though the sky be dark, and the voyage be long,
Yet we never can think we were rash or wrong,
　　While round in our Sieve we spin!"
　　　　Far and few, far and few,
　　　　　　Are the lands where the Jumblies live;
　　　　　Their heads are green, and their hands are blue,
　　　　　And they went to sea in a Sieve.

And all night long they sailed away;
　　And when the sun went down
They whistled and warbled a moony song
　　To the echoing sound of a coppery gong,
In the shade of the mountains brown.
　　"O Timballoo! How happy we are,
　　When we live in a sieve and a crockery-jar,
　　And all night long in the moonlight pale,
We sail away with a pea-green sail,
　　In the shade of the mountains brown!"
　　　　Far and few, far and few,
　　　　　　Are the lands where the Jumblies live;
　　　　　Their heads are green, and their hands are blue,
　　　　　And they went to sea in a Sieve.

They sailed to the Western Sea, they did,
　　To a land all covered with trees,
And they bought an Owl, and a useful Cart,
　　And a pound of Rice, and a Cranberry Tart,

128

And a hive of silvery Bees.
    And they bought a Pig, and some green Jackdaws,
    And a lovely Monkey with lollipop paws,
And forty bottles of Ring-Bo-Ree,
    And no end of Stilton Cheese.
        Far and few, far and few,
            Are the lands where the Jumblies live;
        Their heads are green, and their hands are blue,
            And they went to sea in a Sieve.

And in twenty years they all came back,
    In twenty years or more,
And every one said, "How tall they've grown!
    For they've been to the Lakes, and the Torrible Zone,
And the hills of the Chankly Bore;"
    And they drank their health, and gave them a feast
Of dumplings made of beautiful yeast;
    And everyone said, "If we only live,
We too will go to sea in a Sieve,
    To the hills of the Chankly Bore!"
        Far and few, far and few,
            Are the lands where the Jumblies live;
        Their heads are green, and their hands are blue,
            And they went to sea in a Sieve.

But some do

Buddha said that few cross over, but some do, and he tells us how they manage it.

However, those who follow the principles of the well-taught Truth will cross over to the other shore, out of the dominion of Death, hard though it is to escape (Dhammapada 86).

Thanissaro Bhikkhu: "But those who practice Dharma in line with the well-taught Dharma, will cross over the realm of Death so hard to transcend."

We must know dharma, but it must be well-taught—that is, it must be complete with nothing lacking, and nothing added that is not really a part of dharma. And certainly dharma is of little use unless it is well-learned as much as well-taught. There simply is no room here for cutting corners or slouching around. It will indeed be hard, and not an overnight matter, but if we follow all the principles of dharma we shall indeed transcend this realm of birth and death in which we are presently imprisoned. That is why study of scriptures such as the upanishads and the Gita are so important. Buddha was very conscious of his Aryan heritage, which is why he used the word so often, as well as other terms found in classical Indian scriptures. The idea that Buddha started a new religion is incorrect: he recovered Sanatana Dharma and restored it to humanity.

How to cross over

Buddha does not leave us unsure as to what the well-taught dharma will entail in our search for moksha (liberation). However, many (most) will like the hearers of Jesus say in response: "This is an hard saying; who can hear it?" (John 6:60). Nevertheless, here it is:

A wise man, abandoning the principle of darkness, should cultivate what is pure. Leaving home for the homeless life, let him seek his joy in the solitude which people find so hard to enjoy, and, abandoning sensual pleasures, let him cleanse himself of inner defilements, looking on nothing as his own (Dhammapada 87, 88).

Thanissaro Bhikkhu: "Forsaking dark practices, the wise person should develop the bright, having gone from home to no-home in seclusion, so hard to enjoy. There he should wish for delight, discarding sensuality—he who has nothing. He should cleanse himself—wise—of what defiles the mind."

Forsaking dark practices, the wise person should develop the bright. Here we have the only intelligent and viable basis for morality: we should avoid what darkens, limits and distorts the consciousness, and engage continually in that which brightens, expands, frees, and clarifies the consciousness. This is the only sensible way to find our way through the maze of this illusory world. Naturally, honesty, intelligence, and insight are needed to do this.

We are all familiar with people who do destructive things while insisting that they not only do no harm, they are actually beneficial to them. This is the horrible curse of addiction, and can also be an indication of a person who is so dead and gone that evil actions produce no perceptible change in him. Here is a real life example I gave in another commentary:

"One semi-renowned 'yogi' of twentieth century America used to tell about how when he attained Cosmic Consciousness he wanted to put it to the test. (No person in that state would need a test!) So he went right out to a restaurant and ate a big steak; and found it did not alter his consciousness (?!). Then he got a bottle of whiskey, drank the whole thing, and found his consciousness was unchanged. As a final test he went to a brothel and engaged in immoral conduct…and discovered that it made no difference in his state of awareness. Now, I believe him: he had a state of consciousness too low and inert to be changed by anything–it could not even be made more negative than it already was. Being truly negative, he saw everything backwards, mistaking the lowest state for the highest. People on the path to self-destruction continually make this mistake. They think they are growing and expanding when they are shrinking away. They boast of all the power they gain and wield when they are daily bleeding away their inner energies and becoming dead husks. A former Franciscan monk who had become engaged in 'magick' came to see me once and confided: 'I always feel like I am dying somewhere deep inside.' And he was. This is the cruel delusion of Maya."

However it may be for others, the wise person turns from darkening actions and turns toward those that enlighten him.

Leaving home for the homeless life, let him seek his joy in the solitude which people find so hard to enjoy. "Leaving home for the homeless life" means to formally take up monastic life. There is no place here for the absurd ideas of "a monk in the world," "a monastery without walls, " or–worst of all–"ordinary people as monks and mystics." Buddha says get to out of the house and into the monastery, that monastic life is the necessary prerequisite for even beginning the path to Bodhi (Enlightenment).

What more can be said? This is Buddha's view: monastic life is an absolute *sine qua non* in seeking true knowledge. That is why the Pali sutras almost always begin with the single word "Bhikkhus," indicating that teaching was for monks. Someone once complained to Buddha about the fact that he only lived and taught in the forest with the monks and never taught in the towns where most of the people lived. Buddha made no defense, but asked him to go into the nearby city and ask every single person he met what they most wanted in life. He did so, and it took a very long time. When he returned, Buddha asked: "How many people wanted enlightenment?" "None!" answered the man in disgust. "They wanted all kinds of things—all material and all selfish. No one wanted real knowledge." "Why, then, do you blame me for not forcing on them what they do not want?" was Buddha's response. The man got the idea, and so do the wise that seek joy in that inner solitude which the worldly so dislike.

The bhikkhus were a great multitude externally, but inwardly each one dwelt alone in his consciousness. The word "monk" comes from the Greek *monochos*, which means "one who lives alone." It has been applied for thousands of years to those who physically lived with dozens, hundreds, and even thousands of other monks, because it is a psychological term. By the practice of meditation we are solitary even in the midst of other seekers. And we find joy in that inward solitude which most people find so tedious and even maddening.

Abandoning sensual pleasures, let him cleanse himself of inner defilements. This can only be done by renunciation and meditation, for renunciation clears away the external obstacles, and meditation eliminates the inner obstacles.

Looking on nothing as his own, for nothing—no object in this world—really is ours, not even our body. Also, the wise does not say anything is "mine" because that which claims ownership is the illusory ego which ultimately does not even exist, much less have the ability to possess something. It is a ghost, a vapor that means and is nothing. This is why the monastics have a chance to follow these ideals of Buddha. The world of human illusions cannot exist without ego, and no one can live in it without being centered in ego. The very nature of worldly life not only demands ego-involvement, it produces and fosters the ego. That is why worldly people resent monastics so much and constantly assure themselves that they do not need to be like them. No wonder Buddha was not interested in talking to them. They set themselves to be increasingly entangled in samsara, and only pull in and drown those that reach out a hand to them.

Jesus gives a very clear picture of this situation, saying: "Then shall the kingdom of heaven be likened unto ten virgins, which took their lamps, and went forth to meet the bridegroom. And five of them were wise, and five were foolish. They that were foolish took their lamps, and took no oil with them: but the wise took oil in their vessels with their lamps. While the bridegroom tarried, they all slumbered and slept. And at midnight there was a cry made, Behold, the bridegroom cometh; go ye out to meet him. Then all those virgins arose, and trimmed their lamps. And the foolish said unto the wise, Give us of your oil; for our lamps are gone out. But the wise answered, saying, Not so; lest there be not enough for us and you: but go ye rather to them that sell, and buy for yourselves. And while they went to buy, the bridegroom came; and they that were ready went in with him to the marriage: and the door was shut. Afterward came also the other virgins, saying, Lord, Lord, open to us. But he answered and said, Verily I say unto you, I know you not" (Matthew 25:1-12).

Many are those that visit monasteries and "go on retreat" there and make friends with the monks, and even seek their advice. They want to get the oil of spiritual knowledge and experience that they have never bothered to obtain by living that life themselves. Many monastics waste their oil and their time with them. Rare are those honest (and courageous) enough to say: "Come, join us and produce your own oil," even though they know that Jesus said: "The kingdom of heaven is like unto treasure hid in a field; the which when a man hath found, he hideth, and for joy thereof goeth and selleth all that he hath, and buyeth that field" (Matthew 13:44). And: "Whosoever he be of you that forsaketh not all that he hath, he cannot be my disciple" (Luke 14:33). And further: "Verily I say unto you, There is no man that hath left house, or parents, or brethren, or wife, or children, for the kingdom of God's sake, who shall not receive manifold more in this present time, and in the world to come life everlasting" (Luke 18:29, 30).

The implication is that those who do not so renounce shall not so receive. Jesus had spent a great deal of time in Buddhist monasteries in India, and had learned the Buddha Way: to "seek his joy in the solitude which people find so hard to enjoy…looking on nothing as his own."

The wise

Those whose minds are thoroughly practiced in the factors of enlightenment, who find delight in freedom from attachment in the renunciation of clinging, free from the inflow of thoughts, they are like shining lights, having reached final liberation in the world (Dhammapada 89).

A ripe fruit falls off the tree effortlessly after having hung there and equally effortlessly matured. That is the right way for fruit, but not for human beings. Unfortunately, in the West nearly all yogis think that all they need do is allot some time for yoga practice, and they will automatically attain higher consciousness with little or no rearrangement of life, thought, or deed. This is because they are usually students of teachers or organizations that intensely hype their particular kind of meditation, assuring them that all they need do is add it to their life like salt and pepper to a soup pot. Not so, according to Buddha. Those that attain Nirvana in this very life:

1) *Are thoroughly practiced in the factors of enlightenment.* First, they know what the factors are, and second, they observe them diligently until they are proficient in them. This is because enlightenment is as precise a science as the physical sciences. Nothing is hit-or-miss or happenstance, nor is it a reward for sincerity or simple goodness, or bestowed by another, even a deity. Rather, enlightenment comes from specific practices, internal and external. And it

is attained in exact steps or stages, each of which is characterized by psychological factors that are often outwardly evident. In his discourses found in the Pali sutras, Buddha is very clear about them, as Krishna and Patanjali were earlier in the Bhagavad Gita and Yoga Sutras.

2) *Find delight in freedom from attachment in the renunciation of clinging.* Narada Thera renders this: "Who, without clinging, delight in 'the giving up of grasping.'" Renunciation is not just the path to freedom, it is the path to peace and joy. As Sri Yukteswar often said: "Finding God will mean the funeral of all sorrows." We must give up the unreal before we can attain the Real–a great bargain, indeed. When suffering comes to an end, joy (ananda) begins. So renunciation is not some grim exercise in dedication and sacrifice, it is the way of freedom. Those who understand this follow it with great contentment and happiness. They rejoice in the letting go that precedes the Great Attainment. Free from the compulsion of clinging or grasping, they know Peace Profound.

3) *Are free from the inflow of thoughts.* This cannot be faked. Yes, someone can act in an idiotic way and pretend that he is in that state, but he knows the truth of the matter. I know of a man in India whom any sensible person can see is in the final stage of Alzheimer's, but people flock around for "darshan" of someone who supposedly has gone beyond all thought or perception and rests in the Self. The man was never a yogi, he just went ga-ga. One of the silliest things I ever saw was Alan Watts on television pretending to be in the no-mind state. Considering he was an alcoholic and ultimately a suicide, we can safely conclude that he never came near it. It is tragic the number of "mystics" and "enlightened" who end up alcoholics or drug addicts, sometimes also committing suicide.

But Buddha is telling us about the real thing. No impression can touch the truly enlightened. This does not mean that liberated beings are living in a void without perception of what is going on in the world, it means that nothing changes their interior condition, no more than a reflection in a mirror really touches or affects the mirror. Nothing invades the mind of a perfect yogi, and the perfect yogi's mind never responds in the slightest to any stimulus. As Krishna says in the Gita: "Water flows continually into the ocean but the ocean is never disturbed" (2:70). This is the real meaning of *yogash chitta vritti nirodhah*—"yoga is the inhibition of modifications of the mind" (Yoga Sutras 1:2). It is not absence of thought, otherwise there would be a lot of enlightened people in the world! Rather, it is the non-response of the mind (chitta) to external impulses or perceptions. Those in that condition truly are "shining lights, having reached final liberation in the world."

Chapter 7

THE ENLIGHTENED

Journey over, sorrowless, freed in every way, and with all bonds broken–for such a man there is no more distress (Dhammapada 90).

(Other translators have either "fever" or "the fever of passion" rather than "distress.")

Here Buddha gives us four fundamental traits of the one who has realized the third and fourth Aryan truths that suffering can be ended and there is a way to bring about that end. They merit a good, careful look.

Journey over. There is an evolutionary path to be traversed which no amount of philosophizing and denial will abrogate. In his discourses Buddha tells about the great deal of time in his previous lives, as well as that one, which was spent in spiritual practice and meditation. Although our goal is transcendence, presently we and all other aspirants must move from the beginning point to the ending point. The universe is not haphazard, but a precision instrument of evolution which will enable us to reclaim our lost awareness and be so established therein that we can never again lose it. This is Nirvana. Although each one's journey is quite individual, at the same time there are points that will be common to each person. It is rather like the multitude of people that every day drive the same route from one city to another. Their vehicles will be different, and so will be their style of driving, as well as the number of stops they make, and where and why. So each trip is markedly personal and at the same absolutely the same. It is the same with the spiritual journey Buddha is speaking about. That is why upon attaining enlightenment he said: "Birth is ended, the holy life fulfilled, the task done. There is nothing further for this world." And others will say the same when they attain Nirvana. "The holy life fulfilled, the task done" is the journey that must be completed for all delusion and bondage to be ended forever.

Sorrowless. All inner pain is ended permanently for those that have attained perfect freedom in Spirit.

Freed in every way. No kind of limitation, inhibition, or binding remains for them. If in someone we see even the shadow of bondage or limitation, we should recognize the the goal has not yet been reached by them.

With all bonds broken. Nirvana literally means "no bonds." Again, ALL bonds are broken for the truly enlightened.

All these are the symptoms of a consciousness freed forever from all compulsion, stress, and pain.

The Swans

In India from time immemorial swans have been symbols of the liberated spirits. They fly easily through the boundless sky, and upon earth they can extract milk from a mixture of milk and water. They do this by means of an acid in their mouths which they expel into the water. The acid makes the milk coagulate, and the swans eat the solidified milk, leaving the water behind. Both the jivatman and the Paramatman are referred to as "Hansa"–swan–in the scriptures. This was well known to Buddha, so he said:

The recollected go forth to lives of renunciation. They take no pleasure in a fixed abode. Like wild swans abandoning a pool, they leave one resting place after another (Dhammapada 91).

Translators render this verse in differing ways. Two of the most authoritative, and which we should keep in mind are: Narada Thera: "The mindful [satimanto] exert themselves. To no abode are they attached. Like swans that quit their pools, home after home they abandon [and go]." Thannissaro Bhikkhu: "The mindful keep active, don't delight in settling back. They renounce every home, every home, like swans taking off from a lake."

The recollected go forth to lives of renunciation. Those who are inwardly perceptive are the most capable of understanding what is happening around them and the nature of the world in general. Consequently they know that without a total, life-consuming endeavor it will be impossible for them to attain any significant or lasting spiritual progress. Therefore they "go forth to lives of renunciation." This is not a mere formal taking up of an external ascetic life, but as Narada Thera puts it, they "exert themselves" continually, like good soldiers intending to fight on until the last breath. As Thanissaro Bhikkhu rendered it: "The mindful keep active, don't delight in settling back."

A lot of people experience some kind of awakening or opening, and then settle right back into the spot where they were before. A tremendous amount of people do this, even if they keep a few external marks accumulated during their awake period: they still have some trappings of dharma—maybe even a seldom-entered meditation room or area—and they may still retain some kind of affiliation to a spiritually-oriented group (some even become fervent and life-long cult members as a substitute for real progress). But inwardly they are right where they were before it all began.

They take no pleasure in a fixed abode. On the obvious level this means they no longer want a personal, ego-expressive environment, and leave such for an ashram-type situation. But a person can go to seed spiritually as easily in an ashram as in a private home. What is needed is to not settle down into any spiritual outlook or condition, but to keep moving onward, developing, and expanding their horizons. They should be always ready to revise, overhaul, and completely change their outlook and approach to the ways of dharma, for their understanding should continually expand and their spiritual vision should continually attain new horizons. This is one of the reasons why in Mahayana Buddhism aspirants say: "There are eighty-four-thousand dharma doors; I vow to enter them all." (Eighty-four thousand is a number symbolizing infinity.)

Like wild swans abandoning a pool, they leave one resting place after another. This is because true spiritual life is a matter of continual growth, and growth means change. If a person is seen to remain the same year after year he is not stable or established in spiritual life, he is sterile and static—he is dead, and very likely artificial. You cannot keep going forward and not be moving at the same time, passing from one place to another. "Home after home they abandon," as Narada Thera translates it. "They renounce every home, every home," in the version of Thanissaro Bhikkhu.

"Jesus saith unto him, The foxes have holes, and the birds of the air have nests; but the Son of man hath not where to lay his head" (Matthew 8:20). At first glance this just seems to mean that Jesus had no fixed abode and was a wanderer, but there is a much deeper meaning here. The awakened human being can rest his "head" nowhere upon earth, nor in inner ideas and contentments. Only in God-realization can he truly find rest. "O Lord, Thou hast created man to be immortal, and made him to be an image of Thine own eternity; yet often we forget the glory of our heritage, and wander from the path which leads to righteousness. But Thou, O Lord, hast made us for Thyself, and our hearts are ever restless till they find their rest in Thee." So says the Confiteor of the Liberal Catholic Mass. Those of lesser evolution easily and happily dwell in holes and nests, but those who have attained true human status which includes self-awareness and insight into the necessity for continual traversing of the path from relative to Absolute, but finite to Infinite.

The Prodigal Son (Luke 15:11-32) hired himself out to a pig farmer, and was so hungry he wanted to eat the garbage fed to the pigs, but he could not. It is the same with the awakened; they can no longer eat the swill in which those of lower evolution revel, but must find other sustenance. Just as the developing human being continually outgrows one status for another, so does the worthy aspirant. People often cluck their tongues and wag their heads over those who keep changing, moving from point to point in their spiritual journey, but Buddha commends them, likening them to "swans taking off from a lake"—ever growing, ever moving, ever free.

Neither things nor thoughts

Those for whom there is no more acquisition, who are fully aware of the nature of food, whose dwelling place is an empty and imageless release–the way of such people is hard to follow, like the path of birds through the sky (Dhammapada 92).

Those for whom there is no more acquisition. Having attained the Absolute, nothing remains to be attained.

Who are fully aware of the nature of food. No matter how much you eat, after a while you will need to eat again or you will die. Buddha is speaking here of the awareness of the impermanence of all material things, an impermanence that reveals their fundamental non-existence. So the wise have ceased to find anything real in material objects. Also the impermanence of any material satisfaction.

Whose dwelling place is an empty and imageless release. They dwell in that Being which is beyond all thingness–not nothing but No Thing. Such a condition beyond name and form and all objective consciousness is Release, Nirvana.

The way of such people is hard to follow, like the path of birds through the sky. The liberated pass through this world often without leaving a mark. As Jesus said: "The wind bloweth where it listeth, and thou hearest the sound thereof, but canst not tell whence it cometh, and whither it goeth: so is every one that is born of the Spirit" (John 3:8).

He whose inflowing thoughts are dried up, who is unattached to food, whose dwelling place is an empty and imageless release–the way of such a person is hard to follow, like the path of birds through the sky (Dhammapada 93).

This is very like the previous verse. The two additional points are important.

He whose inflowing thoughts are dried up. "Impressions" is a better translation than "thoughts," for thoughts proceed outward, not inward. From all sides impressions originating outside of us flow into our minds like breezes blowing over a lake causing ripples and thus disturbing the surface and distorting its reflecting power. These are the waves in the mind substance (chitta) whose cessation Patanjali defines as Yoga. The liberated yogi is not unaware of external phenomena, but they do not touch him—they make no impression whatsoever on his consciousness in the form of evoking a change or a response. He sees and knows, but is unaffected and unconditioned by those experiences. "Water flows continually into the ocean but the ocean is never disturbed," says the Gita (2:70).

Unattached to food—freed from all involvement or desire for externalities of any kind upon which the ego-mind can "feed."

He the gods hold dear

When a man's senses have come to peace, like horses well broken by the trainer, when he is rid of conceit and without inflowing thoughts—even devas envy such a well set man (Dhammapada 94).

Narada Thera renders it better: "He whose senses are subdued, like steeds well-trained by a charioteer, he whose pride is destroyed and is free from the corruptions—such a steadfast one even the gods hold dear."

He whose senses are subdued, like steeds well-trained by a charioteer. "Senses also have joy in their marriage with things of the senses, sweet at first but at last how bitter: that pleasure is poison" (Bhagavad Gita 18:38). "When senses touch objects the pleasures therefrom are like wombs that bear sorrow" (Bhagavad Gita 5:22). This is true of every sentient being, but for human beings there is a much worse effect: "The wind turns a ship from its course upon the waters: the wandering winds of the senses cast man's mind adrift and turn his better judgment from its course" (Bhagavad Gita 2:67).

The way out of this dilemma is also given by the Gita: "The senses are said to be higher than the sense-objects. The mind is higher than the senses. The intelligent will is higher than the mind. What is higher than the intelligent will? The Atman Itself" (Bhagavad Gita 3:42). Therefore: "The truly admirable man controls his senses by the power of his will" (Bhagavad Gita 3:7). Both the Gita and Buddha tell us that the man of wisdom has gained mastery over his senses by intense effort; that such control does not come about spontaneously, but only through will, which is the highest faculty we possess.

He whose pride is destroyed. The only way to destroy pride is to destroy its source: the ego. And the only way to destroy the ego, the not-self, is to dispel it by the light of the true Self.

Free from the corruptions. Actually, "corruptions" is not a very good term. "Inflows" (or influences) is better, for it means external stimuli that provoke a response from the individual, as contrasted with the perfect stability of one whose mind cannot be affected in any manner by the outside world.

Such a steadfast one even the gods hold dear. Such a person not only has harmonized himself, he brings harmony to the world around him. That is why Patanjali says that in the presence of someone perfected in non-violence no violence can arise. Buddha was a perfect example of this. Since the devas' whole intent is the harmonious movement of the cosmos, such a one is greatly valued by them, especially a yogi.

Like the earth

Like the earth he is not disturbed, like a great pillar he is firmly set and reliable, like a lake he is free from defilement. There are no more rebirths for such a well set man (Dhammapada 95).

Like the earth he is not disturbed. The earth is often cited in Indian writings as an example of patience.

Like a great pillar he is firmly set and reliable. The man of wisdom is established and profoundly stable–and therefore reliable. Jesus spoke of "a man which built an house, and digged deep, and laid the foundation on a rock: and when the flood arose, the stream beat vehemently upon that house, and could not shake it: for it was founded upon a rock" (Luke 6:48). Those who dig deep and establish themselves firmly upon the bedrock of Self-knowledge remain unshaken by any outer conditions.

Like a lake he is free from defilement. This was written before the days of chemical pollution, and refers to the fact that dirt thrown into a lake settles to the bottom and the water does not become dirty at all.

As long as we live in this world, dirt will be flying around, but even if it touches the wise, it is purified by the fires of wisdom and his mind remains as unclouded as before.

There are no more rebirths for such a well set man. It is when we can live in this world and be totally unaffected by it that we are ready to graduate to a higher level of existence and be freed from rebirth.

At peace

Freed by full realization and at peace, the mind of such a man is at peace, and his speech and action peaceful (Dhammapada 96).

No need for comment.

The ultimate man

He has no need for faith who knows the uncreated, who has cut off rebirth, who has destroyed any opportunity for good or evil, and cast away all desire. He is indeed the ultimate man (Dhammapada 97).

He has no need for faith who knows the uncreated. Obviously faith, however positive a force it may be, is not the desired end. Rather, *knowing* supersedes believing, "when faith is lost in sight." But it is not just just any kind of knowing that Buddha is speaking about. He means knowledge of "the Uncreated"–knowledge of Brahman which is attained only by the merging of consciousness in Consciousness, the union of the finite with the Infinite. Buddha also referred to this principle of enlightenment as "the Birthless" and "the Deathless." In other words, he is quite unequivocally proclaiming the existence of the jivatman (individual Self) and the Paramatman (Supreme Self). Further, he is making it clear that they can be known by those that reach the end of the evolutionary process in which we are all presently engaged–some consciously, but most unconsciously. All sentient beings are involved in this process and shall eventually realize its ultimate aim: Nirvana.

Who has cut off rebirth. Until the Absolute is known: "Death is certain for the born. Rebirth is certain for the dead" (Bhagavad Gita 2:27). But once perfect Knowing arises, rebirth is permanently ended.

Who has destroyed any opportunity for good or evil. The enlightened act in perfect accordance with their divine nature; they do nothing because it is "good" and avoid nothing because it is "evil." They have no compulsion to either, nor are they in any way influenced by those concepts. Instead, they see things in terms of Real and Unreal. They look upon themselves as neither good nor evil. They simply ARE. When the first person who met Buddha after his enlightenment asked him who he was, he replied: "I am awake." So it is.

And cast away all desire. Nirvana being total fulfillment, desire is completely impossible to the Knower.

He is indeed the ultimate man. He is the end, the pinnacle, the zenith of Being Itself.

A happy place

Whether in the village or the forest, whether on high ground or low [mountain or valley], wherever the enlightened live, that is a delightful spot (Dhammapada 98).

This has two meanings, one internal and one external. Wherever the enlightened live is delightful to them, for their consciousness is not external, but internal—in the realm of boundless freedom. Also, wherever the enlightened live is a delight to those who meet them there. Even if it be in a desolate place devoid of outer comfort, those who encounter them there will always remember it fondly as a place of greatest happiness. Those of us who met him know very well how right it was for Swami Sivananda to name his little house by the Ganges "Ananda Kutir"—Abode of Bliss. In Bengal I met a saint at a train stop—not a station, just an ugly rectangle of crumbling cement. Even now in my mind's eye I see it and feel great joy, whereas the memory of great scenic beauty spots or architectural monuments evoke no response at all; they are only mental images devoid of life. They are past, but the saints are ever-present.

Delightful for them are the forests where men find no delight. The desire-free find delight there, for they seek no sensual joys (Dhammapada 99).

The psychology of the wise is vastly different from that of the worldly ignorant. As the Gita says: "The recollected mind is awake in the knowledge of the Atman which is dark night to the ignorant: the ignorant are awake in their sense-life which they think is daylight: to the seer it is darkness" (Bhagavad Gita 2:69).

Once I was taken by a prison psychologist to meet a holy Carmelite nun. She had never left the monastic enclosure for nearly forty years, except once when she and the mother superior attended a conference of Carmelite nuns. She spoke to us sitting behind a grill. Since egotists cannot stop talking about themselves no matter where they are, or with whom, the psychologist began recounting in great detail about all the electric doors that he had to hear banging behind him whenever he went to work in the prison. When he finally stopped, I looked at the sister and said: "That may seem terrible to people in the world, but think much how we would like it." She agreed, but he was miffed because we did not feel sorry for him and even envied him a bit. I was thinking vividly of how wonderful it had been when I sat in my tiny hut on the bank of the Ganges in holy Haridwar, happy in the thought that New Delhi with all its "stuff" was far away.

Chapter 8
THE THOUSANDS

We now come to a section called "the thousands," though that is not always the number cited; a lot of "hundreds" come in, too. The straightforward good sense of this section makes it invaluable.

Pointless versus peace

Better than a thousand pointless words is one saying to the point on hearing which one finds peace.

Better than a thousand pointless verses is one stanza on hearing which one finds peace.

Better than reciting a hundred pointless verses is one verse of the teaching [one dhammapada] on hearing which one finds peace (Dhammapada 100-102).

The essence of these verses is quite simple: anything that does not lead to the peace of enlightenment and Nirvana is ultimately pointless. This should be the test of all teaching: Does it help in attaining Nirvana? If not, it is pointless. This may be a drastic outlook, but it is certainly necessary.

The third of these verses reveals how far people can drift from the original teachings of the Master they think they follow. Sutra recitation is an obsession with many Mahayana Buddhists. Every day they spend hours in mechanical recitation, confident that the mere words will somehow benefit themselves and others, completely missing the point that it is the *following* of the Buddha's teaching that produces results–nothing else. They are nothing more than "pointless word" factories.

It is with this perspective that Jesus said: "Whosoever heareth these sayings of mine, and doeth them, I will liken him unto a wise man, which built his house upon a rock: and the rain descended, and the floods came, and the winds blew, and beat upon that house; and it fell not: for it was founded upon a rock. And every one that heareth these sayings of mine, and doeth them not, shall be likened unto a foolish man, which built his house upon the sand: and the rain descended, and the floods came, and the winds blew, and beat upon that house; and it fell: and great was the fall of it" (Matthew 7:24-27).

There is another implication to these three verses: the fact that the way to peace can be gotten from discourses and books. As I mentioned before, the Venerable Master Chen Kung says we can become the disciples of any Master whose words we study and apply, no matter how long ago that Master lived and taught. For the way to peace must be travelled, not just studied and discussed.

The great conqueror

Though one were to defeat thousands upon thousands of men in battle, if another were to overcome just one–himself–he is the supreme victor (Dhammapada 103).

Solomon said: "He that is slow to anger is better than the mighty; and he that ruleth his spirit than he that taketh a city" (Proverbs 16:32). "If a yogi has perfect control over his mind, and struggles continually in this way to unite himself with Brahman, he will come at last to the crowning peace of Nirvana, the peace that is in me" (Bhagavad Gita 6:15).

Victory over oneself is better than that over others. When a man has conquered himself and always acts with self-control, neither devas, spirits, Mara or Brahma can reverse the victory of a man like that (Dhammapada 104, 105).

No external force, however mighty can move the enlightened yogi from his perfected state. It is in the context of Buddha's teaching that we can understand what Saint John meant when he wrote: "Whosoever is born of God doth not commit sin; for his seed remaineth in him: and he cannot sin, because he is born of God" (I John 3:9).

Greater than all sacrifices

Though one were to perform sacrifices by the thousand month after month for a hundred years, if another were to pay homage to a single inwardly perfected man for just a moment, that homage is better than the hundred years of sacrifices.

Though one were to tend the sacrificial fire for a hundred years in the forest, if another were to pay homage to a single inwardly perfected man for just a moment, that homage is better than the hundred years of sacrifice.

All the sacrifices and offerings a man desiring merit could make in a year in the world are not worth a quarter of the better merit of homage to the righteous (Dhammapada 106-108).

Many things mark out the great difference between East and West, but one of the most obvious is the great facility the East has for recognizing superior merit and paying it respect. The West, on the other hand, is busy insisting that everyone is equal and "as good any anybody else"–a form of egotism which has no basis in reality whatsoever. When the West "worships" they do so with ramrod straight backs, sitting in padded seats, and watching intently to make sure they are getting their money's worth. The East on the other hand (and this includes the Christian East), bows, bows, bows, and prostrates. In all Eastern places of worship it is this humble reverence that pervades everything. Consequently I learned early on in encountering the East that only those who can show reverence are worthy of it, and that only those who can bow low are able to rise high.

In all the religions of the East it is considered the highest merit to seek out the pure and the wise to bow in homage before them. Buddha was squarely in this perspective, therefore he spoke the foregoing verses. But why would he consider this true? Because when we are in the presence of an illumined person we begin to vibrate in sympathy with his powerful aura, and ourselves become elevated, at least for the time we are in his presence. And for many that elevation is permanent, inspiring them to follow the path to liberation. In India great value is placed on *darshan*, which Yogananda defines as "the blessing which flows from the mere sight of a saint." Those who have spent time with the saints know the reality of this. Many mental and physical ills are cured just by entering the presence of the truly holy. This is my personal experience. You can read of the value of darshan in many parts of *Autobiography of a Yogi*.

Four principal things increase in the man who is respectful and always honors his [spiritual] elders–length of life, good looks, happiness and health (Dhammapada 109).

Narada Thera: "For one who is in the habit of constantly honoring and respecting the elders, four blessing increase–age, beauty, bliss, and strength." I have been witnessing this for nearly half a century and I know it is true. "Honour thy father and thy mother: that thy days may be long upon the land which the Lord thy God giveth thee" (Exodus 20:12).

Better is a single day...

It would be a blessed thing if we could indelibly impress the following six verses in our consciousness, for they give the only spiritually intelligent perspective on life itself and its sole purpose.

Though one were to live a hundred years immoral and with a mind unstilled by meditation, the life of a single day is better if one is moral and practices meditation.

Though one were to live a hundred years without wisdom and with a mind unstilled by meditation, the life of a single day is better if one is wise and practices meditation.

Though one were to live a hundred years idle and inactive, the life of a single day is better if one is wise and makes an intense effort.

Though one were to live a hundred years without seeing the rise and passing of things, the life of a single day is better if one sees the rise and passing of things.

Though one were to live a hundred years without seeing the deathless state, the life of a single day is better if one sees the deathless state.

Though one were to live a hundred years without seeing the supreme truth, the life of a single day is better if one sees the supreme truth (Dhammapada 110-115).

As the Declaration of Independence says: "We hold these truths to be self-evident."

Chapter 9
EVIL

When the mind delights in evil

These next thirteen verses are entitled "Evil" in the Dhammapada text. It is as important to know how to deal with evil as to cultivate the good, as Buddha reveals to us. First he is going to speak of laxity as personal evil, as the path downward away from the light.

Be urgent in good; hold your thoughts off evil. When one is slack in doing good the mind delights in evil (Dhammapada 116).

Narada Thera: "Make haste in doing good; check your mind from evil; for the mind of him who is slow in doing meritorious actions delights in evil."

Make haste in doing good. Check your mind from evil. Spiritual life is not moseying along the Path, all mellowed out and somnolent. Spiritual life is *urgent*; it is a sprinting toward the Goal before "the night cometh, when no man can work" (John 9:4), the night of sickness, old age, and death as well as the morass of moral turpitude into which even the best aspirant can fall if he is neglectful.

Very few seekers fail because they suddenly turn and pursue ignorance and evil. Rather, they slide into the downward spiral through laxity and lack of vigilance. No matter how well regulated our outer life may be, there is evil lurking around every corner of the subconscious mind in the form of negative samskaras and vasanas. For that reason we must always be in charge of our mind, restraining it from wandering into the dark corners and getting into trouble. For the undisciplined mind is sure to pursue evil.

Of course there are those who preach the gospel of spiritual laxity. They can sense when a person is striving to move higher in life and consciousness, and keep insisting: "You can be too religious." "You can have too much discipline." You can do too much, you know." "You can go too far if you aren't careful." "God could not expect for you to...." "God doesn't care about...." And always said with the implication that you are a fanatic and a fool, or they are afraid you may become one. Often these are really "foxes without tails" as in the old fable, embittered at the thought of someone not messing up their life the way they have theirs.

The aunt of Saint Teresa of the Andes waged a virtual war against her becoming a nun, so imagine her amazement when her mother told her: "You aunt very much wanted to be a nun when she was your age." But instead she had become a shallow, greedy worldling, caring for none but herself. Saint Teresa resisted her machinations and today is listed among the saints of Christ. We must be like her. Just before she left for the convent, an unsuccessfully aspiring boyfriend said to her: "I am sorry you did not find someone worthy of your love." "Oh, but I have!" she replied.

The mind of him who is slow in doing meritorious actions delights in evil. Now this is the outright truth. It is not a matter of laziness but of a corrupted and corrupting heart. I cannot count the number of times I have seen people setting themselves up to fail and crash in spiritual life. They would weave the flimsiest veils around their mind's eye in order to blind themselves to the truth of their intentions. Some would build great structures of specious reasoning to convince anyone who might question their folly. I will admit that for a time I did not realize their deceit and when they tried to convince me of the rightness of their evil, I would patiently point out the fallacies, assuming they were sincere. Then in a week or two they would be back with another set of fantasies. Finally I had enough sense to realize that it was not a question of whether or not they would abandon spiritual life, but only *when.* All I was doing was frustrating their desires and earning their resentment. So from then on I would make some inane remark about how each person had to find their individual way and let them go on to destruction. As God said through the prophet David: "I gave them up unto their own hearts' lust: and they walked in their own counsels" (Psalms 81:12).

"Let us not be weary in well doing: for in due season we shall reap, if we faint not" (Galatians 6:9).

Be not inclined to evil

If a man has done evil, let him not keep on doing it. Let him not create an inclination to it. The accumulation of evil means suffering (Dhammapada 117).

If a man has done evil, let him not keep on doing it. That seems pretty obvious, but the fact is that the negative ego habitually tricks people into repeating the wrong. "Why be a hypocrite? Be honest with yourself and quit all those impossible 'holy' ideas. After all, you are just a human like everybody else." Accusing the aspirant of being a hypocrite if he does not keep on doing the negative action is, of course ridiculous, but those in the grip of evil are often fooled by it. Yes, it is hypocritical to claim aspiration to higher life and yet willingly do wrong things, but why should it be the aspiration that gets dropped? Why not the wrongdoing? But people fall into the trap all the time. Evil people do the same: when they see aspirants weakening or giving in, they sneer and bully them, mocking their aspirations. That is why in the Bible the force of cosmic negativity or Satan "the adversary" is also called the Devil, *diabolos*, which means slanderer and accuser (see Revelation 12:10). Of course the real enemy is the ego itself, and since that lives within us (or seems to), it must be ruthlessly reckoned with and all its suggestions ignored–not argued with, for that way lies possible delusion.

Let him not create an inclination to it. Wrong actions can become a habit, therefore new ones should not be repeated, and old ones, even if they have been engaged in for years (and no doubt lifetimes) must be stopped–not slowed, but *stopped*. This can be done. As Yogananda said, if we don't have will power, we must develop *won't power*.

The accumulation of evil means suffering. Suffering comes from the accumulation of evil in the form of negative karma. As we cannot hold live coals in our bare hand and not be burned, in the same way the presence of evil karma produces inner and outer suffering, either right now or later on. That is its nature. Therefore we must avoid it by every means if we would escape suffering.

Be inclined to good

If a man has done good, let him keep on doing it. Let him create an inclination to it. The accumulation of good means happiness (Dhammapada 118).

Everything said above applies to this, but in the opposite manner.

Fruition of good and evil

An evil man encounters good so long as his evil behavior does not bear fruit, but when his evil behavior bears fruit, then the evil man encounters the evil consequences.

A good man encounters evil so long as his good behavior does not bear fruit, but when his good behavior bears fruit, then the good man encounters the good consequences (Dhammapada 119, 120).

Buddha warned people to be very cautious regarding the matter of cause and effect, saying that it was very easy to make a mistaken attribution. We see this even now: people living to be over a hundred supposedly because they drink whisky or smoke cigarettes every day. When I was a child I heard it said that some people were too mean or too evil to get sick or die, and it seemed to be the case, even though it was not. When wrongdoers are seen to be thriving or content, many feel that the law of cause and effect is not operative in their lives, but Buddha is explaining that at the moment they are reaping the effects of past good karma, but in time they will reap the evil, as well. By observing a person's present life we certainly can see what kind of karma they created some time previously, and can know what kind will be coming to them later on.

Do not think lightly of evil or good

Do not think lightly of evil that not the least consequence will come of it. A whole waterpot will fill up from dripping drops of water. A fool fills himself with evil, just a little at a time (Dhammapada 121).

I once read an essay on what constituted a genuinely evil person. One trait was the insistence that rules and laws did not apply to them, that they could break the rules and laws and suffer no negative reaction. Sociopaths and maniacs throughout history have claimed themselves to be above the law of cause and effect, but they have always been proven wrong.

Another form of sociopathy and mania does not claim to be above the wrong deeds, but insists that the deeds are not wrong. "Those little things don't matter," they say, and they often call them "little no-harms." But in time they catch up with them and have become big harms. "Little drops of water, little grains of sand, make the mighty ocean and the mighty strand." It has now been over sixty years since I sang those words in Sunday School, but they are as true as ever. "Yet a little sleep, a little slumber, a little folding of the hands to sleep: so shall thy poverty come as one that travelleth; and thy want as an armed man" (Proverbs 6:10, 24:33). Habitual "little evil" is the path to eventual great evil, both in deed and in consequence. "Little white lies" turn into large black falsehood eventually–and karmically.

Do not think lightly of good that not the least consequence will come of it. A whole waterpot will fill up from dripping drops of water. A wise man fills himself with good, just a little at a time (Dhammapada 122).

Just reverse what was said about evil and you get the message.

Avoiding evil

One should avoid evil like a merchant with much goods and only a small escort avoids a dangerous road, and like a man who loves life avoids poison (Dhammapada 123).

It is quite fashionable to kick at the Roman Catholic Church nowadays, but I was an adult before encountering in Catholic literature the idea that the wise avoid "the near occasion of sin." It was obvious good sense, but I had never heard of it before in my Fundamentalist "hallelujah, glory, glory" religion. (I learned a great deal more wisdom from the "Scarlet Woman," and am most grateful.) Buddha has the same view. Also implied here is a wise and positive sense of our susceptibility to evil and an avoidance of foolhardy confidence in our wisdom and strength to withstand or detect evil. There is a time to take evil very seriously, as seriously as we view good.

If there is no wound on one's hand, one can handle poison. Poison has no effect where there is no wound. There is no evil for the non-doer [of evil] (Dhammapada 124).

The main idea is that there can be no evil consequences for those that avoid evil, but equally important is the implication that evil is fundamentally internal. Evil karma is internal, not external. It is not the overt act that creates the karma, but the thinking and putting forth of will that creates it. That is why the thought can create the karma even if there is no external act (see Matthew 5:21, 22, 27, 28).

Beware...

Whoever does harm to an innocent man, a pure man and a faultless one, the evil comes back on that fool, like fine dust thrown into the wind (Dhammapada 125).

Narada Thera: "Whoever harms a harmless person, one pure and guiltless, upon that very fool the evil recoils like fine dust thrown against the wind."

This should seem obvious to anyone who looks into dharma, but I think Buddha included this statement because the good and the holy desire no vengeance and always forgive those who wrong them, and even refuse to reveal their identity. Often saints have said that they would leave a place if those who harmed them were punished. Naturally this could make people assume that their blessing would prevent any retribution, even metaphysical. But that is not so. It is the nature of saints to forgive and wish well to all, but it is the nature of karma to be eventually faced—both are part of the Cosmic Law.

Further, the weight of karma is determined partly by the character of the person wronged. It is much heavier karma to wrong a good or holy person than an evil one. This is not a value judgment on the part of the universe, but a matter of the strength of the very life force of the person wronged. I have witnessed this myself, having seen swift and intense reaction come upon those who wronged or even insulted those who were engaging in intense tapasya. Others have told me of instances in which death resulted from injuring a great yogi or master. I know of two situations in which the transgressors and their families died shortly after the offense. I studied one of them myself when I first became a yogi, doubting that what I had heard could be true. But it was, and it gave me a very healthy respect for the law of cause and effect.

Rebirth

Some are reborn in a human womb, evil-doers go to hell, the good go to heaven, and those without defilements achieve final liberation [Nirvana] (Dhammapada 126).

Some karmas are over quickly, but the most long-lasting are the karmas that result in rebirth. Those that have mixed–good and evil–karma are reborn on earth where both types of karma easily come to fruition. Those with evil karma go to the "hells"–those astral regions where intense karma can be undergone without the person dying from the effects. Those with positive karma go to the "heavens"–astral regions where their happiness will not be clouded by the possibility or presence of suffering. Those who wisely have dissolved their karma, enter Nirvana, for Nirvana can never be the effect of any cause–only the absence of cause and effect.

Inevitable reaction

Not in the sky, nor in the depths of the sea, nor hiding in the cleft of the rocks, there is no place on earth where one can take one's stand to escape from an evil deed (Dhammapada 127).

Nor is there any place in the subtle worlds to escape, as the preceding implies.

Not in the sky, nor in the depths of the sea, nor hiding in the cleft of the rocks, there is no place on earth where one can take one's stand to not be overcome by death (Dhammapada 128).

For death is the fundamental effect of negative karma. So it is not death we must seek to avoid, but karma, the cause of death.

Chapter 10

THE ROD

All fear pain, and therefore that which brings pain. Buddha now speaks of "the rod." The word he uses is *danda*, which simply means a stick or rod, usually wooden, which at his time was a symbol of authority and an instrument of coercion and punishment. Even today in India the lathi is used by the police as a weapon, and most people know about the highly-feared practice of caning in Singapore in which a bamboo rod is used, just as in Buddha's time and today in India. Since all that happens to us is the manifestation of karma, and that which is pain-bearing is the result of negative karma, "the rod" means the reaction produced by such negative karma.

All tremble at the rod. All fear death. Comparing others with oneself, one should neither strike nor cause to strike. All tremble at the rod, life is dear to all. Comparing others with oneself, one should neither strike nor cause to strike (Dhammapada 129, 130–Narada Thera).

The word "strike" here means to kill, not just injure. Our English word "homicide" literally means to strike another human being. *Cide*–strike–at the end of any word means to kill (suicide, infanticide, parricide, genocide, etc.). The meaning is quite clear: since we do not wish to die, but prize our life, we should not kill another or cause another to be killed, or even morally support the killing of another. If we do, then we shall be killed in the future. When Jesus said: "All they that take the sword shall perish with the sword" (Matthew 26:52), he was quoting Buddha, as he does several places in the gospels.

160

He who does violence to creatures seeking happiness like himself does not find happiness after death.

He who does no violence to creatures seeking happiness like himself does find happiness after death (Dhammapada 131, 132).

Not just in this world do we reap karma, but in the subtler worlds, the heavens and the hells. Further, these four verses apply to all sentient beings, not just human beings.

Do not speak harshly to anyone. If you do people will speak to you in the same way. Harsh words are painful and their retaliation will hurt you (Dhammapada 133).

This is very clear and needs no comment.

If, like a cracked gong, you silence yourself, you have already attained Nirvana: no vindictiveness will be found in you (Dhammapada 134–Narada Thera).

Both Narada Thera and Thanissaro Bhikkhu say that this verse does not mean we attain to perfect Nirvana by controlling our speech, but that a kind of "pre-Nirvana" tranquility is experienced.

Like a cowherd driving cows off to the fields [with a rod], so old age and death take away the years from the living (Dhammapada 135).

This is not capricious or bad "fortune," but the effect of the "rod" of karma.

Even when he is doing evil, the fool does not realize it. The idiot is punished by his own deeds, like one is scorched by fire (Dhammapada 136).

Buddha said that one of the signs of inner awakening is the ability to feel guilt and shame. It is remarkable how few people can see the nature of their actions, shrugging off any moral sense and justifying anything they wish to do or have done. I grew up hearing people say: "I don't see that" to any moral principle they did not like. But of course blind people do not see, do they? And when they experience the reaction for their deeds they complain about being unlucky and even challenge the existence of God with the old cliché about "how could a good God…?" They never think to ask: "How could a good person do what I do?" It is their moral intelligence they should doubt, for God has nothing to do with it. The morally stupid do not realize that their entire life is nothing but their own past deeds coming to fruition.

He who does violence to the peaceful and harmless soon encounters one of ten things–he may experience cruel pain, disaster, physical injury, severe illness, or insanity, or else trouble with the authorities, grave accusation, bereavement, or loss of property, or else destruction of his house by fire, and on the death of his body the fool goes to hell (Dhammapada 137-140).

Well, there you have it. How many Westerners who claim to be Buddhists are even aware of these teachings of the Buddha?

Neither naked asceticism, matted hair, dirt, fasting, sleeping on the ground, dust and mud, nor prolonged sitting on one's heels can purify a man who is not free of doubts (Dhammapada 141).

Most of us have seen photographs and even motion pictures of the psychotic, drug-addicted "sadhus" in India who revel in their sub-human way of life. They were around in Buddha's time, and just as meaningless. The only way to be free of doubt is to have true knowledge. And the first step to knowledge is the abandonment of all the nonsense listed in this verse.

Even if richly dressed, when a man behaves even-mindedly and is at peace, restrained and established in the right way, chaste and renouncing violence to all forms of life, then he is a brahmin, he is a holy man, he is a bhikkhu (Dhammapada 142), whatever his formal mode of life may be.

Who in the world is a man constrained by conscience, who awakens to censure like a fine stallion to the whip? (Dhammapada 143–Thanissaro Bhikkhu).

Who indeed is ruled by conscience, and who, when censured or rebuked by the wise–either through spoken words or those found in holy writings–responds not with excuses or resentment, but begins running along the way of dharma as a good horse responds to the whip? Such are rare indeed, as are buddhas in this world.

Like a thoroughbred horse touched by the whip, be strenuous and determined. Then you will be able to rid yourself of this great suffering by means of faith, morality, energetic behavior, stillness of mind and reflection on the teaching, after you have become full of wisdom, good habits and recollection (Dhammapada 144).

No need to comment, just to apply.

Navies [irrigators] channel water, fletchers fashion arrows, and carpenters work on wood, but the good discipline themselves (Dhammapada 145).

We all have personal definitions of what makes a person good, but Buddha's is the best. The good do not busy themselves with trying to order others around and change them; they change themselves through self-discipline. They do it all themselves. Buddhas point the way, and they walk it.

"Go, and do thou likewise" (Luke 10:37).

Chapter 11

OLD AGE

In this next section of the Dhammapada Buddha insists that we face the truth about the aging and mortality of the body and indeed of this whole world and all in it.

What?
What is this laughter, what is this delight, forever burning as you are? Enveloped in darkness as you are, will you not look for a lamp? (Dhammapada 146).

What is this laughter, what is this delight, forever burning as you are? We all have heard about Nero fiddling while Rome burned–having himself set the fire–and we do the same. Through desires and aversions, egotism and illusions, we have set ourself on fire and burn along with everyone else. Yet we claim to be happy and have a good life at the same time. It is amazing the number of obviously miserable people that insist everything is just great and could not be better. It makes me think of a dangerous psychotic who was asked by a friend of mine how he was doing. "Oh, I'm still thrilled with Christ!" he answered with a twisted, miserable face. There you have it.

This laughter...this delight is only a cover of the truth of people's devastated lives. And until they admit the truth, misery is going to continue through this life and into many future ones. At any price people keep saying they are happy, but it does not make it so.

Enveloped in darkness as you are, will you not look for a lamp? Not as long as we keep calling the darkness light and believing in it as the sole reality. As the Gita says: "The recollected mind is awake in the knowledge of the Atman which is dark night to the ignorant: the ignorant are awake in their sense-life which they think is daylight: to the seer it is darkness" (Bhagavad Gita 2:69).

The puppet

Look at the decorated puppet, a mass of wounds and of composite parts, full of disease and always in need of attention. It has no enduring stability (Dhammapada 147).

Harischandra Kaviratna: "Behold this illusory human image, embellished (by rich attire and jewels), full of corruptions, a structure of bones, liable to constant illness, full of countless hankerings, in which there is nothing permanent or stable."

It is essential for us to realize the real nature of this body and all it implies. So Buddha continues:

This body is worn out with age, a nest of diseases and falling apart. The mass of corruption disintegrates, and death is the end of life.

When these grey bones are cast aside like gourds in autumn, what pleasure will there be in looking at them?

It is a city built of bones, and daubed with flesh and blood, in which old age and death, pride and hypocrisy are the inhabitants (Dhammapada 148-150).

The unaging and enduring

Even kings' splendid carriages wear out, and the body is certainly bound to grow old, but the Truth found by the saints is not subject to aging. That is what the saints themselves proclaim (Dhammapada 151).

Harischandra Kaviratna: "The gaily decorated royal chariots wear out. So likewise does this body. But the truth of the righteous does not wear out with age. Thus do the enlightened proclaim it to the wise."

When Buddha speaks of truth he does not mean intellectual ideas, but principles of dharma which never change as long as we are in the human form. That is why the term Sanatana Dharma, the Eternal Dharma, was coined. Yet there is a bit more than that. The Immortal Dharma makes those who follow it immortal, so when the body breaks down, the real part of us lives on unharmed and unchanged by the dream of death, and is nevermore subject to birth and death in this material plane. So the enlightened tell the wise who are wise because they hear and act upon their words.

In ignorance

I grew up with the expression "dumb as an ox" and the shorter one "dumb ox." It must be as old as Buddha, for he says:

An ignorant man ages like an ox. His flesh may increase, but not his understanding (Dhammapada 152).

Out of ignorance

I have passed in ignorance through a cycle of many rebirths, seeking the builder of the house. Continuous rebirth is a painful thing. But now, housebuilder, I have found you out. You will not build me a house again. All your rafters are broken, your ridge-pole shattered. My mind is free from active thought, and has made an end of craving (Dhammapada 153, 154).

It is possible to spend lifetimes unaware of the fact of rebirth and what produces rebirth, and therefore be helpless in freeing ourselves from that truly vicious cycle. Karma is the force or material from which a seemingly endless chain of house-bodies are built for our habitation. Karma means action, but action is not the root cause. Rather, the root of action is desire (kama) or craving (tanha/trishna). This is a fundamental teaching of Sanatana Dharma, very thoroughly expounded in the Bhagavad Gita. It is so simple it is easy to miss it, but Buddha very dramatically expresses it in this verse. When the mind is free from running after outside objects and has been so transformed that desire is no longer possible, then freedom, Nirvana, is attained.

Without the holy life

Those who have not lived the holy life, and have not acquired wealth in their youth, grow old like withered cranes beside a fish-less pool (Dhammapada 155).

In this and the following verse, the word translated "holy life" is brahmacharya, which has the primary meaning of celibacy (and is so translated by the Venerable Thanissaro Bhikkhu), but can also mean the entire range of necessary ascetic disciplines. (Obviously chastity would mean little for a drunken, drug-addicted thief.) The idea is that those who do not from their early life strive for higher consciousness, for Nirvana, will not acquire the true, inner wealth and richness. Such people will grow old in perpetual torment, like desperately hungry cranes standing in a lake that has no fish. I can think of no more apt description of the material world than that of a fishless pool. Yet nearly all the human race is busy pecking away at the empty mud, hopelessly hoping to be satisfied. And this goes on life after life after life. It is a terrible prospect!

Those who have not lived the holy life, and have not acquired wealth in their youth, lie like spent arrows, grieving for times past (Dhammapada 156).

This is no better seen than in those pathetic old men who are utterly obsessed with sex, leering at women, speaking of sex all the day long, desperately trying to titillate themselves and get some sexual jolt, often turning to the molesting of children.

Even those not sexually obsessed are constantly going over their past and drawing no ease from it. As Solomon said: "Remember now thy Creator in the days of thy youth, while the evil days come not, nor the years draw nigh, when thou shalt say, I have no pleasure in them" (Ecclesiastes 12:1). I grew up listening to morally frustrated ministers gabbling on about when they were "a sinner boy," obviously yearning for a repetition of those days, yet unable to get any satisfaction from those memories.

There is a particular type of fundamentalist Protestant that loves to recount their peccadilloes as a testimony to show how "saved" they have become. Anyone can hear the nostalgia in their voices as they recount their past sins. There is a joke about an old lady who was beating a bass drum in a Salvation Army street-corner meeting. At one point she gave her testimony, saying: "Before I got saved I used to get drunk, lie, steal, commit adultery, brawl and live like a devil. But then I got saved, and now all I do is beat this G-D drum!"

Chapter 12

THE SELF (ATTA VAGGA)

Yes, Buddha believed in the existence of the Self, and now we will see what Buddha really taught about the Self.

Self-discipline

If one holds oneself dear, one should protect oneself well. During every one of the three watches the wise man should keep vigil (Dhammapada 157–Narada Thera).

If one holds oneself dear, one should protect oneself well. This sentence tells us two things: everyone living in this samsara is in danger from both outer and inner forces. While we should not be fearful, we should be cautious and never overconfident. Second, we must protect ourself, not depending on others to do so. Buddha is telling us that we are fully capable of protecting ourselves, but we must learn how. This is an essential part of dharma. But we must not protect ourselves in a slipshod or minimal way, we must protect ourself well: completely and perfectly. This is no simple matter, and this is no facile platitude we are considering.

During every one of the three watches the wise man should keep vigil. The translation of Thanissaro Bhikkhu says that the three watches are the three stages of life: childhood, adulthood, and old age. The habit of wisdom should be established even when we are young. If not, then we must be vigilant throughout the remaining two watches. Dharma is a lifelong activity.

First he should establish himself in what is right. Then if he teaches others, the wise man will not be corrupted (Dhammapada 158).

There are also two aspects to this. First is that a teacher should be absolutely firm in his observance of dharma before he presumes to teach another. Second is the implication that if he is not so established, then eventually he will be corrupted. This is seen over and over in every religion and especially in the case of so many contemporary "gurus." In fact, teaching itself is risky, for it is easy for the ego to sneak in and ruin everything. Once the teacher ego grips the individual, his doom is sealed. I have never seen even one person escape from that terrible predator of souls. Rare and blessed are those who teach without falling into that deep pit, and blessed are those who learn from them.

If one would only apply to oneself what one teaches others, when one was well disciplined oneself one could train others. It is oneself who is hard to train (Dhammapada 159).

Greater is he who is his own master than he who numbers his disciples in the thousands. The lives of true masters reveal that they spent many years in discipline and spiritual practice before even considering teaching others. Ideal examples of this are Sri Ramakrishna and his disciples, Lahiri Mahasaya and his disciples, as well as Bhagavan Nityananda, Sri Ramana Maharshi, and Swami Sivananda. When Paramhansa Yogananda came to America he was only twenty-seven, but he had behind him over twenty years of intense tapasya. If such great ones do not teach until well-established, then lesser teachers should beware.

One is one's own guardian. What other guardian could one have? With oneself well disciplined one obtains a rare guardian indeed (Dhammapada 160).

This needs no explanation, but merits a long and serious pondering. For we can look outward for nothing—only within.

The self-destructing fool

The evil he has done himself and which had its origin and being in himself breaks a fool, like a diamond breaks a precious stone (Dhammapada 161).

The greatest disciple of Paramhansa Yogananda was an elderly nun called Sister Gyanamata, Mother of Wisdom. One time another nun asked her for general spiritual advice, and she wrote her a short note in which she said: "Your own will always come to you. Indeed you can have nothing but your own." This is a perfect statement of the absolute law we call karma. The egotist tries to weasel out of such responsibility, blaming God, nature, human beings, genetics, society, and whatnot, but never himself. As the Pali verse says: "I have nothing but my actions. I shall never have anything but my actions" in the form of karma. This is bedrock truth.

Evil karma originates in the individual and eventually crushes him if he does not apply himself to wisdom. It is not an outside force at all, but his own misapplied will-power turning back on him. Those who take refuge in wisdom gain the ability to become stronger during such karmic onslaughts, and rise above them to greater wisdom. It is also possible to erase all evil karmas through self-purification and enlightenment. So it is not fatalistic, but a matter of our own good sense or our continuance in ignorance.

A man of immorality is like a creeper, suffocating the tree it is on. He does to himself just what an enemy would wish him (Dhammapada 162).

Truly, "the wages of sin is death" (Romans 6:23), death of the inner consciousness, death of conscience, death of wisdom-discrimination, and ultimate destruction-death of the body. The first time I read the Gita I was impressed by many passages, one of which was: "Thinking about sense-objects will attach you to sense-objects; grow attached, and you become addicted; thwart your addiction, it turns to anger; be angry, and you confuse your mind; confuse your mind, you forget the lesson of experience; forget experience, you lose discrimination; lose discrimination, and you miss life's only purpose" (Bhagavad Gita 2:62, 63). Buddha is saying the same. The immoral person is a spiritual and mental suicide—and often a physical one, too. He is his own enemy and works his own destruction.

Easy evil

Things which are wrong and to one's own disadvantage are easily enough done, while what is both good and advantageous is extremely hard to do (Dhammapada 163).

This is the terrible dilemma of the human being, rooted in millions (if not billions) of lives in subhuman forms and then untold lives in deluded human situations. Since the problem is not intellectual but instinctual, no amount of intellectual activity or even emotional attempts will dislodge these delusions. We have to directly dissolve them in their form as bundles or aggregates of subconscious impressions known as vasanas. We have to engage in hand-to-hand struggles with them by entering the subconscious through the practice of meditation and dispelling them. This is the only way, and is not as difficult or traumatic as it might be expected, for: "Greater is he that is in you, than he that is in the world" (I John 4:4), meaning that our true Self, our Atman, is far more powerful than the delusive ego-mind that is only in the world, only a mass of vibrating energy, in itself nothing at all.

Once the mind has become purified of these vasanas and positive qualities have been established in the mind, the opposite occurs. Then evil is hard, even impossible, and good is easy and natural. It is all a matter of energy constructs in the form of samskaras and vasanas. That is why the Gita says: "Even a wise man acts according to the tendencies of his own nature. All living creatures follow their tendencies. What use is any external restraint?" (Bhagavad Gita 3:33). This is very important truth. Our actions spring not from our true Self, but from the energy levels in which the Self is enwrapped. So it is not our Self we need to change, but those subtle life energies that have been trained by our own actions to behave in a negative and detrimental manner. It is a matter of re-education, and that is the purpose of yoga.

Without yoga any lasting reformation is virtually impossible. People often undergo certain psychological upheavals and for a while the mind seems changed. But in time, even in a future incarnation, the evil habits return. Jesus was talking about this, saying: "When the unclean spirit is gone out of a man, he walketh through dry places, seeking rest, and findeth none. Then he saith, I will return into my house from whence I came out; and when he is come, he findeth it empty, swept, and garnished. Then goeth he, and taketh with himself seven other spirits more wicked than himself, and they enter in and dwell there: and the last state of that man is worse than the first" (Matthew 12:43-45).

"Therefore, become a yogi" (Bhagavad Gita 6:46).

Those who speak ill of dharma

The fool, who out of attachment to a wrong view speaks ill of the religion of the enlightened and noble ones who live according to truth, brings forth fruit to his own downfall, like the offspring of the bamboo (Dhammapada 164).

Narada Thera is definitely more accurate: "The stupid man who, on account of false views, scorns the teaching of the Arahants, the Noble Ones [Ariyas], and the Righteous [Dharmic], ripens like the fruit of the kashta reed, only for his own destruction."

It is not impossible that some of us have been in this situation. I know that, being blinded by the idiocies of my birth religion, I said a lot of stupid things about reincarnation, though without dislike or malice. Later on a lot of people around me—and even some I met for one time only—spoke with hatred and contempt about Sanatana Dharma and Yoga when I began to realize their truth and value. I was threatened with being outcast from society (what a great idea!), being possessed by demons, and being put in a mental institution if I persisted in "this craziness." The viciousness with which this was done was shocking. Perhaps you, too, have experienced the same. I think it is a very reliable sign of being on the right track. As Jesus said to such people: "Ye shut up the kingdom of heaven against men: for ye neither go in yourselves, neither suffer ye them that are entering to go in" (Matthew 23:13).

There is an evil intuition operative in many negative people which is an accurate indication of good and evil. The thing to remember is that what they hate is good and what they like is evil. Some years before the explosions I have just described I had figured this out. So instead of doubt being instilled in me when I encountered opposition from such people, my resolve to pursue the teachings of the Bhagavad

Gita and Yoga was strengthened by confidence in the intuition of the foolish who loved untruth and unrighteousness. It helped that I moved halfway across the continent to study yoga, but even there I continued to occasionally meet with those about whom Sri Ramakrishna spoke in this way: "Worldly people say all kinds of things about the spiritually minded. But look here! When an elephant moves along the street, any number of curs and other small animals may bark and cry after it; but the elephant doesn't even look back at them." So in such situations we must be elephants!

Apparently the kashta reed flourishes until it bears fruit, and then it quickly dies. So Buddha tells us that those who mock and defame dharma do so to their own destruction—not because they are punished, but because the karma of rejection reacts to further darken their understanding. This is especially true if they are doing so under the impulse of inner negativity. If they do so in misguided sincerity without malice, in some instances it actually works to their benefit and in time they embrace the truth they once rejected. Saint Paul is a classic example. The aunt and uncle of a friend of mine went to China to save the heathen, but instead embraced Buddhism themselves and became advocates of dharma. It all depends upon the quality of the heart.

Sole responsibility

By oneself one does evil. By oneself one is defiled. By oneself one abstains from evil. By oneself one is purified. Purity and impurity are personal matters. No one can purify someone else (Dhammapada 165).

Next to the Four Aryan Truths and the Eightfold Aryan Path, this is perhaps the most important of Buddha's philosophical teachings. It is uncompromising truth: our life is in our hands and ours alone. Yes, we can be influenced by others and even have others affect our life—but it is our choice to do so and we determine to what degree we will be affected. Certainly we reach into the world around us and take to ourselves various elements, but we do that intentionally.

Those who wish to escape responsibility insist that something is beyond their control, that they could not help themselves in a certain situation. But even those situations and that susceptibility were determined by them previously. For example, if a person builds a brick wall incompetently and it falls on him and injures him, he certainly did not build it with that as his purpose, but his incompetence brought the injury about, so at the root it was all in his sphere, none else. What about those harmed or even killed in "natural disasters"? That was their karma which they themselves created, and on a subliminal level they understood all the implications when they created that karma.

Another example occurred to a healer friend of mind. It was his practice to tune in with the inner mind of a person before attempting to heal them (actually, he taught them to heal themselves). When he tuned into a little girl who was severely mentally retarded, to his shock a deep, male voice shouted: "Leave me alone, I know what I am doing!" He realized this was the voice of the child's former personality, and that the retardation was for a purpose, and she was retarded by her own choice. Occasionally he would tune in to her and ask: "Have you learned what you need, yet?" "No," would be the answer. Then one day her inner mind said: "Yes. You can help me now." And that girl became totally normal. So here we see that it is all our choice, even when another factor enters our life and changes it.

Buddha spoke these words to people who had already produced in themselves a significant degree of awakening. Yet they (yes, by their choice) still carried with them mistaken ideas from past religious experience, including the fundamental bane of most religion: the attribution of responsibility to forces other than themselves, especially the reflexive attribution of everything to God. But now they had chosen to approach Buddha to be freed from those childish beliefs, and he did not fail them. Those clinging to the errors of the past accused Buddha of being atheistic, but he was not. You might just as well call someone atheistic if they said God had nothing to do with their cooking failures. Being the Source of all, everything involves God. But there are certain areas in which human beings control everything, and their life is one of them. God has manifested all the worlds and the various forms in which we incarnate. God has also woven various laws into the fabric of relative existence which operate at all times without exception. The universe is a great interactive school of learning set up so the students can teach themselves—a kind of ultimate Montessori school. The use, misuse, or neglect of the school and the opportunities it offers are solely the choice of each student.

Morality

Buddha gave another not very popular teaching already mentioned: one of the signs of awakening is the ability to feel shame—yes, guilt. Morality is of prime concern in the dharma of Buddha, despite the fact that Westerners flock to Buddhism (or a deformation of it) to get away from "Judeo-Christian morality." Vain hope! All Eastern religions have moral principles far more complex and realistic than those of Western religions. The difference is, they are voluntary and are not forced on others. That is of course a better situation, but anyone who thinks they can shake their guilt by "turning East" are self-deluded.

The practical side to moral principles is the capacity of the individual for both defilement and purification. Therefore Buddha taught:

By oneself one does evil. No one else is involved in the final analysis, for we act solely from our own ever-free will. Even a bent or perverted will got that way by a person's own past choices. So their apparent bondage is the result of the exercise of free will. It is habitual with people to blame environment, other people, disadvantages, etc., but action is done only by each one of us. That is why in one of the Pali sutras there is a section which contains statements such as: "There shall be lying, but we shall not lie. There shall be killing, but we shall not kill. There shall be stealing, but we shall not steal." This is the way it must be understood. We are not herd animals, even though society is usually nothing more than a herd. We are individuals with our own minds and wills. If we choose to run with the herd, it is still all our doing. A sensible aspirant knows that all around him people will be engaging in adharmic actions, and that should not influence him in the least. Yes, there will be wrongdoing, but we shall not do wrong. Wrong actions condition the mind and will to wrongdoing, but that is our choice. We do not do wrong because our wills are weak, but because they are strong and we have pointed them in the wrong direction.

By oneself one is defiled. Much of this has just been covered. Eastern religion understands that wrongdoing does not anger God, but that it brings negative results in the form of karma into our lives, and even worse, it defiles our minds and hearts, darkening and distorting them. This latter is the worst part, because karma can be exhausted, but defilement stays on, inclining us to more of the same negative actions.

By oneself one abstains from evil. Again, this is not a group thing, it is totally individual, although we can certainly draw inspiration from others to apply our free will in the right direction. Still, it is a completely personal, private matter. People who cannot stand alone on their own simply will not succeed in the pursuit of higher life. It is not for weaklings, whiners, or cowards. That is why spiritual teachers often use examples from military life, and the Bhagavad Gita is set on a battlefield.

By oneself one is purified. Purification is possible, this is Buddha's message of hope, and it can be fully accomplished by us, by our free will. In *Parsifal,* Parsifal touches the spear to the wounded side of Amfortas, saying: "That which wounded alone can heal." The spear represents the will of the individual. Of course we must know the way to purify ourself, not just cover up the wounds. Meditation is the supreme healer through self-purification.

Purity and impurity are personal matters. No, we did not inherit a propensity to evil from Adam, ancestors, racial memory, collective unconscious, our parents or society. Many people try to blame traumatic experiences, but those experiences came about because they were their karma, results of their past deeds committed through free will. There are no victims, only reapers of personal karma. Good and evil, purity and impurity, are our choice alone.

No one can purify someone else. How important this is! False religion and false gurus pretend to be able to purify us and forgive our sins.

NOT AT ALL. It is a destructive mythology, no matter how sincere it may be. No one takes away our sins, not even us. We must purify ourselves. Sometimes in yogic treatises it will be stated that a practice burns away or washes away impurities, but it is the individual's engaging in the practice that purifies. And that is a matter of will and action.

Actually we see this principle in the life of Jesus. Many times when people were healed by his touch he would assure them that their own faith was what healed them. This was not modesty, but honesty. Their faith and their effort in coming to him was a healing karma, and even more it was an opening, an allying of their will with his. So their healing was their doing, although Jesus was the instrument.

We are the answer to our own problems once we know the way to higher life and consciousness.

Right Priorities

One should not neglect one's own welfare for that of someone else, however great [the need]. When one has understood what one's own welfare really consists of, one should apply oneself to that welfare (Dhammapada 166).

Narada Thera: "For the sake of others' welfare, however great, let not one neglect one's own welfare. Clearly perceiving one's own welfare, let one be intent on one's own goal."

One should not neglect one's own welfare for that of someone else, however great. The idea that we should neglect our well-being for that of others is a very destructive and widespread delusion based solidly on ego. I knew a woman who told me that every time she sat to meditate either the phone or the doorbell would ring, and she would have to go help others. "My feeling is: 'Lord, it is you I am helping through all these forms,'" was her explanation to me. She was wrong. The help she gave was first of all superficial, no matter how emotionally charged it might have been and how desperately she was asked for it.

This is one of the tests that the sadhaka undergoes when beginning to make progress. It is one of Mara's (Maya's, Satan's) cleverest ploys, because falling for it makes us look good–compassionate–and refusing it makes us look bad—selfish and hardhearted. Ego chooses to "feel good about myself" every time. In Jesus' parable (Luke 18:9-14), the Pharisee who felt good about himself gained nothing, but the Publican who acknowledged his weakness was benefitted.

Another example from Jesus, who spent years in India studying Buddhism, is the parable of the wise and foolish virgins waiting for the bridegroom to escort him to the home of his bride (Matthew 25:1-12). The wise took extra oil for their lamps and the foolish did not, so when the groom was delayed the oil in their lamps was consumed. "And the foolish said unto the wise, Give us of your oil; for our lamps are gone out. But the wise answered, saying, Not so; lest there be not enough for us and you: but go ye rather to them that sell, and buy for yourselves." It is the same with the yogi: he dare not risk depleting his own spiritual resources for the (alleged) benefit of others, but they will have to tap their own inner power and act by it. Sri Ramakrishna often spoke of those who have not earned even a few rupees and yet want to give away thousands in charity. Even more, he said that a yogi could deplete all his spiritual power just to get someone on the spiritual path, and then they would come to nothing and so would he. Sadhaka, beware.

When one has understood what one's own welfare really consists of, one should apply oneself to that welfare. There we really have it all summed up. When we understand that liberation is our only real welfare—and therefore that of others—then we will strive for that single-mindedly and whole-heartedly, understanding that others will have to do the same, that each person gains his own welfare, no one else can do it for him or them. To know the truth of karma, rebirth, and the possibility of realization, and yet to do either nothing or very little about it is great folly—a waste of an entire lifetime and creation of the habit of spiritual neglect that will reach into future lives.

Chapter 13

THE WORLD

Now Buddha tells us the truth about the world.

Do not...
Do not practice an ignoble way of life, do not indulge in a careless attitude. Do not follow a wrong view, and do not be attached to the world (Dhammapada 167).

Do not practice an ignoble way of life. Just two verses back we read: "By oneself one does evil. By oneself one is defiled. By oneself one abstains from evil. By oneself one is purified. Purity and impurity are personal matters. No one can purify someone else." One of the most important teachings of Buddha is the truth that the purifying and ordering of our life is in our hands alone, that no one can do anything for us, we must do everything ourself. Certainly someone can give advice and even helpful teaching, but the following of it is entirely our choice and doing. This is why Buddha speaks of *practicing* an ignoble or unworthy way of life. It is willful action on our part, however much we may want to excuse ourselves and put the blame elsewhere. We must face up to this truth if our progress is to be real and lasting.

Harischandra Kaviratna renders it: "Let no one follow a degraded course of existence." All of us are born into a degraded environment, because ignorance rules the world, but it is up to us to resist and rise above it to lead the noble—aryan—life. A true aryan never "lets nature take its course," but takes charge and directs the course of his life according to his intelligent understanding.

Thanissaro Bhikkhu renders this clause: "Do not associate with lowly qualities" in ourselves or in others. "Touch not the unclean thing" (II Corinthians 6:17) is valuable advice. Associating with those who are of degraded character will in time influence and degrade us. When I was in college I had the stupid idea that it would be all right for me to accompany my friends to bars and dives, telling myself that I might be able to get them to drink less and get in less trouble. In two or three weeks I figured out how stupid this was, for only two things could happen: those places would become increasingly repulsive to me until I came to the point where I would refuse to go near them, or I would develop an affinity for them and what went on there until I myself became one of their customers. I chose to not let either one happen, so I spent a long time sitting in the car waiting for my friends to come out of the cesspools. Then I got wise to the fact that they were not my friends at all, that we walked on two separate ways. I stopped the association and never regretted it.

Do not indulge in a careless attitude. There are so many pitfalls for the beginner and the seasoned traveller on the path, and many of them seem of little importance, undramatic and easy to ignore. But they are as deadly as the obviously destructive ones. Simple carelessness is one of them—just not being vigilant or intent on following the disciplines and principles of spiritual life. I have known people who bragged about not bothering with this or that discipline or observance, thinking they were being sensible and sophisticated. But today their lives are devoid of spiritual content altogether. They have joined the ranks of the used-to-do and used-to-be people who have nothing but a sadly aborted past. If eternal vigilance is the price of political freedom according to Thomas Jefferson, so also is spiritual freedom and its pursuit.

Harischandra Kaviratna translates: "Nor live in indolence." Spiritual laziness is equally harmful.

Thanissaro Bhikkhu: "Do not consort with heedlessness." And that includes heedless people as well as leading a heedless life, especially one that blinds us to the dangers of samsaric existence. "I don't worry about that" is usually the seal of inner death.

You see, the spiritual demise of most people takes place through neglect of the details that so easily can be wrongly seen as unnecessary or too small to matter. And so they die "not with a bang but a whimper," as Eliot says.

Do not follow a wrong view. A wrong turn takes us off the path and makes us end up in a wrong place. It is the same with adopting a wrong idea about the way to higher consciousness: we will not reach it, and may have a great deal of damage to undo before we can try again. Error can never lead to truth, but it can certainly bog us down in delusion. The same is true of wrong types of meditation; they waste our time and can even harm us. I know of more than one meditation system in India that produces serious mental problems. Friends of mine in both India and America have had their lives and minds ruined by following them. And only a few were able to extricate themselves and be healed. I have seen people's mental troubles clear up in twenty minutes by just stopping the repetition of a harmful mantra. An Indian friend of mine suffered from suicidal tendencies produced by years of practicing a foolish yoga system. She constantly felt that God hated her. In a few hours after quitting that destructive practice all depression was gone and she came to me smiling. "I now know that God is always with me," she said. Many people in the East and West have their minds and lives damaged by dishonest and unqualified teachers.

Do not be attached to the world. Can it be more simple? We must cure ourselves of all worldly addictions.

Harischandra Kaviratna: "Nor be a person who prolongs his worldly existence." Right here and now the wise begin living in the spirit–not just inwardly but outwardly, too.

Thanissaro Bhikkhu: "Do not busy yourself with the world."

Wake up…

Wake up and do not be careless, but lead a life of well-doing. He who follows righteousness lives happily in this world and the next (Dhammapada 168).

This verse is all about dharma. No one can follow dharma who is not awakened to some degree. Unhappily, many people awaken to some degree but because they do not encounter dharma they fall back into the sleep of ignorance, losing another life in a chain of lost lives. We who have come into the orbit of dharma must not waste this most valuable asset, but follow it well. If we do so, then we shall live happily in this world and the next until Nirvana is reached.

Lead a life...

Lead a life of righteousness, and not a life of wrong-doing. He who follows righteousness lives happily in this world and the next (Dhammapada 169).

To do this we must learn the dharma well; then happiness will persist in this life and beyond.

See the bubble

Look on the world as a bubble, look on it as a mirage. The King of Death never finds him who views the world like that (Dhammapada 170).

First we realize that the world is like a bubble that quickly bursts and is gone. From the evanescent nature of the world we progress to realize that it is at all times only a mirage, a dream without real substance. Those who truly realize this through the cultivation of their inmost consciousness will never be touched by death, but will be forever immortal.

The gilded world

Come, look at the world as a gilded royal carriage, in which fools get bogged down, while men of understanding have no attachment to it (Dhammapada 171).

First we have to know what heavy and ponderous things chariots were at the time of Buddha, especially those of the wealthy that were covered with ornamentation—often of gold. They were miserably uncomfortable to ride in, but their ostentation suited the prideful who wished to overwhelm the ordinary people with their splendor and implied power. It reminds me of when the Indian Airlines planes would land in Khajuraho on the way to Benares. The rural people would be gathered to watch in wonder as the "great bird" came out of the sky and landed among them. Usually the captain would allow the braver of them to come up the entry stairs and peek inside with uncomprehending wonder. Perhaps to them the passengers were gods. I recall one very old and feeble sadhu struggling up the steps and coming further inside than the shy locals usually did. He carefully looked around without any expression, then turned and walked out and down. I had a feeling that he felt it was far from being a pushpaka—a magnificent flying machine of ancient India—as were the passengers certainly not like the great ones of old who flew in them. He definitely had seen enough of what little the twentieth century had to offer.

This world is an awkward, uncomfortable, gaudy vehicle carrying us along until it inevitably bogs down and we sink with it and suffocate in the swamp. Surely the wise care nothing for it.

The transformed man

Even if previously careless, when a man later stops being careless, he illuminates the world, like the moon breaking away from a cloud.

When a man's bad deeds are covered over by good ones, he illuminates the world, like the moon breaking away from a cloud (Dhammapada 172, 173).

Yes, the world is a swamp, but we can break the hypnosis of the world, turn around and start moving back to Reality. We can neutralize our negative actions by engaging in meritorious actions. When we do this we break free of the veils of illusion and shine, illumining the world around us. When the Buddha-Nature within us is revealed, once again the Buddha walks the earth and shows the way to lost humanity.

The Buddha in which we must take refuge is the Buddha within, not Gautama Buddha of history, though he continues to teach us through his recorded words. He points us to the inner Buddha, not to himself as an individual, and he assures us that Nirvana is our true nature, our true condition which we can recover. Jesus said: "I am the light of the world," but he also said to his disciples: "Ye are the light of the world....Let your light so shine before men, that they may see your good works" (Matthew 5:14, 16). They, too, were Christs, and we also are Buddhas and Christs. This is the true dharma.

Blind indeed

Blinded indeed is this world. Few are those who see the truth. Like a bird breaking out of the net, few are those who go to heaven (Dhammapada 174).

This is itself the plain truth. People are stumbling through this world completely blind to realities and even blind to themselves. "How hard to break through is this, my Maya," says the Bhagavad Gita (7:14), and rare are those who regain their sight and act upon it to break away from the orbit of this world and fly into the sky of freedom. For the heaven Buddha is speaking of is the limitless expanse of Infinite Consciousness.

The swans

Wild swans take the path of the sun. Men with powers travel through space, but the wise step right out of the world, by conquering Mara and his host (Dhammapada 175).

Strong birds such as wild swans fly from east to west, and those who possess the psychic powers known as siddhis can fly through the air at will, but the wise leave the world behind altogether by conquering Cosmic Delusion (Mara) and its attendant evils.

Unlimited evil

When a man has already violated one rule, when he is a liar and rejects the idea of a future world, there is no evil he is not capable of (Dhammapada 176).

Narada Thera: "There is no evil that cannot be done by the liar, who has transgressed the one law [of truthfulness] and who is indifferent to a world beyond."

In the Yoga Sutras of Patanjali truthfulness is a major factor in the yoga life, as it is in the teachings of the Buddha, being one of the Five Precepts. It is certainly interesting that Buddha uses this one transgression as the basis for many. Perhaps it is because a person lies purely from the basis of egotism and an attendant disrespect and even contempt for those he lies to, caring only for his own interests.

In defense of their evils, negative people almost always sneer at the karmic law which ensures they will reap the consequences of their evil deeds in the future: either in this life or another on the earth, or in the astral world. They deny it vigorously and mock those who accept it, considering them fools.

Having degraded themselves in these two ways, there is no longer any foulness that is not possible for them to commit, either through lack of conscience or defiance of dharma. They become capable of any wrongdoing, nothing whatsoever is beneath them. "Caught in the net of delusion, they fall into the filthy hell of their own evil minds....They sink down to the lowest possible condition of the soul" (Bhagavad Gita 16:16, 20).

Generosity

Miserly people certainly do not go to heaven. Fools for sure do not praise generosity, but the wise man who takes pleasure in giving is thereby happy hereafter (Dhammapada 177).

Narada Thera: "Verily, misers go not to the celestial realms. Fools do not indeed praise liberality. The wise man rejoices in giving and thereby becomes happy thereafter."

Devaloka, the world of the gods, is won only by many good deeds, for in that world a person is given all he desires and enjoys all beautiful and good things. He knows not a moment of discontent, but is always in a state of intense happiness.

Only kindness and generosity to others gain admission to that realm. Fools who are centered in their ego and preach the gospel of "Number One" have no use for generosity at all, but the wise delights in giving–not because it will win him merit, but because he truly is happy in the happiness of others. Generosity is also an indication that the person understands his oneness with all life, which is why in the East devout people feed and look after animals and even insects. Those who rejoice in helping others will certainly rise to the higher worlds of blessedness after death and reap far more blessings than they realized was possible on earth.

Entering the Stream

Better than being sole king of the whole earth, better than going to heaven or sovereignty over the whole universe is the fruit of becoming a stream-winner (Dhammapada 178).

At one point in our evolution we reach the point where the momentum of our spiritual aspiration and spiritual merit ensures that we shall indeed move onward to Nirvana without hindrance. Such a one is a stream-winner. Effort will still be required, and obstacles will yet have to be overcome, but the outcome is assured and we will from that time onward be moving in a direct line to liberation. This is certainly better than anything else we might be given, for all those things will be ultimately lost—that is the nature of relative existence. But to pass beyond all things is to gain Everything.

Chapter 14

THE BUDDHAS

The fundamental teaching of Gautama (Sakyamuni) Buddha is that all human beings can attain Buddhahood, that until they do they will be subject to continual birth and death with all their attendant suffering. So now he is going to describe the status of those who have attained Nirvana and become Buddhas just as he did.

Transcendent being

He whose victory is not relost, and whose victory no-one in the world can take away, that Buddha, whose home is in the infinite, pathless as he is, by what path will you lead him? (Dhammapada 179).

This is not easy to put in English, considering the vastly differing wording of translations. It might be best to look at Narada Thera's very literal rendering: "Whose conquest is not turned into defeat, no conquered of his in this world follows him–that Buddha of infinite range, by which way will you lead him?" The English is awkward, but a phrase by phrase analysis will give us the meaning.

Whose conquest is not turned into defeat. The attainment of a Buddha is irreversible. The victory he has won will never be undone, for his victory is over birth and death, and the kingdom he has won is Infinite Consciousness.

No conquered of his in this world follows him. That which the Buddha has vanquished is gone forever; it shall never arise again for him.

That Buddha of infinite range. The cosmos is but a mote in the sunlight of a Buddha's consciousness. Past, present, and future are one to him, as is relative and transcendent existence. And he dwells beyond even them.

By which way will you lead him? Having transcended all "ways" by gaining infinity, what path could he follow, even voluntarily? So the idea of anyone leading or influencing a Buddha is absurd. He has passed far beyond all the possibilities of relative existence.

Freedom from desire

He who has no entrapping, clinging desire to lead him in any direction, that Buddha, whose home is in the infinite, pathless as he is, by what path will you lead him? (Dhammapada 180).

Desirelessness is freedom from all compulsion and release into boundless Being.

Envy of the gods

Those wise men, who are much given to meditation and find pleasure in the peace of a spiritual way of life, even the devas envy them, perfect Buddhas and recollected as they are (Dhammapada 181).

Harischandra Kaviratna: "Those wise ones who are absorbed in meditation, who take delight in the inner calm of renunciation, such mindful and perfectly awakened ones even the devas (gods) hold dear." Thanissaro Bhikkhu: "They, the enlightened, intent on jhana, delighting in stilling and renunciation, self-awakened & mindful: even the devas view them with envy."

Here we have a list of the traits of Buddhas.

1) They are wise, not in the sense of learned scholars or clever philosophers, but through enlightenment. They no longer think: they know.

2) Meditation is the keynote of their life. They do not think that they have passed beyond the need for meditation, but like

Gautama Buddha they meditate intensely until their last breath on earth. Their entire lives are the fruition of meditation.

3) They find enjoyment and fulfillment in the peace that comes from renunciation. None but they can realize the joy of the path of the absolute renunciate who has nothing to turn back to, but moves ever onward in the depths of the Infinite.

4) They are awakened, but not by external factors. They are *sambuddhanam*, self-awakened. That is, their long-buried, eternal Buddha Nature has emerged as the chick does from the egg, complete and independent. Their enlightenment has arisen from and depends on no factor but their own Buddha Nature.

No wonder the gods envy them, for the Buddhas have passed beyond all capacity for compulsion and suffering, whereas the gods will in time, when their positive karma is exhausted, fall right back into the world of human beings and once more be crucified on the cross of material consciousness.

Difficult

A human birth is hard to achieve. Difficult is the life of mortals. To hear the true teaching is difficult, and the achievement of Buddhahood is difficult (Dhammapada 182).

There is nothing that is not difficult. Those who seek an easy way are looking for dry water and cold fire—it is simply not in the nature of things.

It is difficult to get a human birth because our karma strands us in the astral world, sometimes for centuries. Also, many spirits are waiting for the right combination of earthly elements to be born, and those with similar needs literally scramble and struggle with one another to win the prize of conception. And then the trouble really begins, for "difficult is the life of mortals." It is difficult to hear the true dharma for there is so little of it in the world and so few true teachers of it. It is also difficult because our darkened minds render us deaf to dharma when we hear it. It is rare to hear the dharma, but much, much rarer to recognize and embrace it. I do not think anyone doubts the difficulty of becoming a Buddha, but since everything is difficult, why not spend the time struggling for Buddhahood? That will end all difficulties permanently.

The teaching of the Buddhas

To abstain from all evil, the practice of good, and the thorough purification of one's mind—this is the teaching of the Buddhas (Dhammapada 183).

This verse gets tossed off a lot in both East and West by Buddhists and non-Buddhists, perhaps because it sounds so simplistic and so non-invasive, simple, minimal, and noble. It reminds me of a British documentary about a man who traveled the world to acquaint himself with the various religions as they are really lived. In Japan he spoke with a real saint, the head of a sect of Amida Buddhists. The saint outlined the path of Amidism, and the man remarked that it sounded too simple to him. The saint laughed and said: "Just try it." So we must not take this verse as lightly as many do.

Who can abstain from all evil, physical, mental, and spiritual? *All* evil! Who can only do good? *Only* good! And this is not according to our ideas, but according to the ideas of the Buddhas, whose perfect purity is inconceivable. What a task—to thoroughly purify our mind. We have taken millions of years to get our mind into this defiled state, how long will it take to undefile it? Yet this is the teaching of the Buddhas, and there are no shortcuts or bargain days.

A few facts

Long-suffering patience is the supreme ascetic practice. Nirvana is supreme, say the Buddhas. He is certainly not an ascetic who hurts others, nor is he a man of religion who causes suffering to others (Dhammapada 184).

Long-suffering patience is the supreme ascetic practice. Endurance—cheerful endurance—is a necessity in spiritual practice, for the attempts at higher consciousness reveal our weakness, laziness, doubts, and just plain cussedness. Like any other endeavor we are sure to have some falls and failures, and then the ego arises and condemns us for not being able or ready to lead a serious spiritual life. But that is a lie and we must close our ears to it.

Someone wrote to me, telling of serious spiritual failures and expressing profound discouragement and depression. This is what I wrote in response, and I think it will be meaningful to you, mostly because it comes from conversations I have had with saints.

"Many mistakes—and even falls—can occur in spiritual life, but a person can always get up and keep journeying onward. As long as this is done there is always hope for eventual success. There is only one thing that can prevent this: discouragement. If the sadhaka becomes discouraged at his failures and begins to feel hopeless and gives up his efforts, then no improvement is possible. Because of this, discouragement is the worst thing that can happen to a sadhaka, for it will end all spiritual progress. Be sure that you never give into this most harmful thing, and you need never fear failure. If it occurs, arise and keep on moving. Then nothing will be able to stop you in reaching the Goal."

Nirvana is supreme, say the Buddhas. This has two meanings. First, that Nirvana is the Absolute State, that there is nothing whatsoever beyond it. In writings of the Thai Forest Tradition we find the teaching that Nirvana is not just a state, but Ultimate Reality Itself. Nirvana is equated with the Buddha Nature as expressed by Mahayana Buddhists. Second, the attainment of Nirvana is the supreme necessity and should be the highest priority in the lives of those who would follow Buddha Dharma, the Buddha Tao. ("Buddhism" is a word coined by Western scholars for the teaching of Buddha, but Buddha Tao was the name given to it for over two thousand years by its followers.) Nirvana should be the highest aim of our life, and our life should be lived in the context of Nirvana, for it is the ultimate realization and union of Buddha, Dharma, and Sangha.

He is certainly not an ascetic who hurts others. "Hurt" covers all forms of injury, and it is incredible that anyone claiming to be a Buddhist would eat meat.

Nor is he a man of religion who causes suffering to others. What I just said applies here, as well. However, it should be pointed out that there is a vast difference between harming someone and offending them. Certainly it is wrong to attack another in speech or to deliberately try to hurt them. But there are professional offendees who use this to make the supposed offender look bad and to even suppress the speech or action they do not like. This has become epidemic in the last few decades, and sometimes reaches the positively psychotic and vicious degree. Buddha was not saying that the virtuous have to please everybody. He certainly did not himself, and he spoke very plainly, though never with any intent other than the welfare of his hearers. Their response was totally their choice.

The way to live

Not to speak harshly and not to harm others, self restraint in accordance with the rules of the Order [Patimokkha], moderation in food, a secluded dwelling, and the cultivation of the higher levels of consciousness–this is the teaching of the Buddhas (Dhammapada 185).

Although mention is made of the Patimokkha, the rules for monastics, this verse really applies to all.

Not to speak harshly and not to harm others. This has already been covered.

Self restraint in accordance with the rules of the Order. The Patimokkha is for monastics, but the Five Precepts are to be followed by all, and non-monastics should be intent on them.

Moderation in food. Buddha recommended eating only one meal at day at mid-day. He said that if someone could not manage this, then they should eat breakfast, but definitely not eat in the evening. Liquids are not considered to violate the rule, so a person can eat liquids such as juices, milk, or strained broths in morning and evening. For many people this gives great benefit, and has been very effective in losing excess weight. Buddha said it was extremely healthy and could even prevent health problems. Naturally people with special dietary needs–especially those related to blood sugar levels–should consult their physician before trying this regimen.

A secluded dwelling. This is helpful for all if it can be managed. We just do not realize how much chatter and stress is created by urban living, especially noise, including traffic sounds.

The cultivation of the higher levels of consciousness. As said previously, this is the number one priority of those who seek Nirvana, whatever their state in life. Such cultivation is through meditation and constant mindfulness.

Enjoyment (pleasure)

There is no satisfying the senses, not even with a shower of money. "The senses are of slight pleasure and really suffering." When a wise man has realized this, he takes no pleasure, as a disciple of the Buddhas, even in the pleasures of heaven. Instead he takes pleasure in the elimination of craving (Dhammapada 186, 187).

There is no satisfying the senses, not even with a shower of money. Even if all of the wealth of the world was accessible to us, no matter how much we spent there would be no satisfaction, for the sense are like fires and pleasures are like gasoline. Throw it on the fires and you only get more fire, more desires and more enslavement. "Only that yogi whose joy is inward, inward his peace, and his vision inward shall come to Brahman and know Nirvana" (Bhagavad Gita 5:24).

The senses are of slight pleasure and really suffering. But as Ajahn Fuang Jotiko points out, only those who meditate can see this and act upon it. The others keep hoping that somehow they will escape suffering through the senses, like gamblers who waste their lives in anticipation of a change of luck. So addiction blinds and binds us.

When a wise man has realized this, he takes no pleasure, as a disciple of the Buddhas, even in the pleasures of heaven. Whether the senses are physical or astral, the bondage and inevitable pain are the same. The wise know this.

Instead he takes pleasure in the elimination of craving. He finds the greatest joy in the freedom that comes from the elimination of desire-cravings.

As Socrates said when in advanced age he was no longer interested in sex: "At last I am free of a harsh and cruel master." But the wise do not wait for the body to burn out to eliminate craving, for rebirth will be there to return us to sense-bondage.

The only refuge
Driven by fear, men take to many a refuge, in mountains, forests, parks, sacred groves and shrines, but these are not a secure kind of refuge. By taking to this sort of refuge one is not released from suffering. He who has gone to Buddha, Dharma and Sangha for refuge, though, and who with true wisdom understands the Four Noble Truths of Suffering, the Origin of Suffering, the End of Suffering and the Noble Eightfold Path, leading to the Elimination of Suffering, this is a secure refuge, this is the ultimate refuge; by taking to this refuge one is indeed released from all suffering (Dhammapada 188-192).

Driven by fear, men take to many a refuge, in mountains, forests, parks, sacred groves and shrines, but these are not a secure kind of refuge. By taking to this sort of refuge one is not released from suffering. All these things listed are subject to decay and total annihilation—even mountains are eventually worn down—so they offer no secure refuge.

He who has gone to Buddha, Dharma and Sangha for refuge...is indeed released from all suffering. The Buddha, the Dharma, and the Sangha are eternal for they are The Truth of Things. Nevertheless, mere verbal taking of refuge means nothing. Only by following the Four Aryan Truths and the Aryan Eightfold Path can we come into touch with the inner Buddha, Dharma, and Sangha and progress on to Buddhahood. For as the wise teachers explain, it is our inner Buddha, the inner Dharma, and the inner Sangha that we must seek. The exterior counterparts exist only to point to the inner ones.

I will be analyzing the Eightfold Path and the Four Truths later on in Section Twenty, The Way.

Hard to find

A truly thoroughbred man is hard to find. He is not born anywhere, but where that seer is born, the people prosper (Dhammapada 193).

Narada Thera: "Hard to find is a man of great wisdom: such a man is not born everywhere. Where such a wise man is born, that family thrives happily."

What is there to say? We must strive to ourselves become "of great wisdom" and not wait for the advent of a teacher before we take up the Buddha Way.

Happy

Happy is the attainment of Buddhahood, happy the teaching of the true Teaching, happy is the concord of the Sangha, happy the training of those in concord (Dhammapada 194).

So now we know the way to happiness.

Great merit

When a man venerates those worthy of veneration, be they Buddhas or their disciples, who have transcended all obstacles and passed beyond sorrow and tears—venerating such as these, whose passions are extinguished and for whom there is no further source for fear, no one can calculate how great his merit is (Dhammapada 195, 196).

This does not mean a pointless kind of groupyism, which is most of the "discipleship" in East and West, but a following of the Buddhas and Bodhisattvas so that in time we, too, shall become what they became before us, and thereby showed us the Way.

Chapter 15
HAPPINESS

From the first time I ever heard it until today, "everybody does it" seems to me one of the most moronic and irrelevant—not to say almost always untrue—things anyone can say, especially if it is meant to justify some thought or action. Running with the herd is not an option for those seeking higher consciousness.

Without hatred

Happy indeed we live who are free from hatred among those who still hate. In the midst of hate-filled men, we live free from hatred (Dhammapada 197).

Thanissaro Bhikkhu: "How very happily we live, free from hostility among those who are hostile. Among hostile people, free from hostility we dwell."

The world seems to run on hate and anger; all we need do is look at history and see that humanity is a bundle of conflicts. That is the way things are, and we should accept it but not approve of it. Rather than waiting for a better day when hatred will be abolished we should determine to live without hatred or hostility ourselves, even when encountering those who do hate, and who may hate us for not hating. It is foolish to wait for everyone to do it before doing it ourselves. Waiting for a more congenial time or environment to practice virtue is a great folly. After all, it may be our friendliness (metta) and peaceful response to others that will help them be the same. But do notice that Buddha does not say that we shall attempt to change others and get them not to hate, for they have to put forth their own will to change themselves, just as we are doing.

The principle set forth in this verse applies as well to the ultimate activity of hatred: war. Rather than engaging in futile peace efforts that are usually embittered and violent—not to speak of being impractical and unreasonable—we must settle our hearts in peace. I have met many good men and women of peace who were saddened at the prevalence of war, and who strove to live lives of peace themselves. But I have met no peaceniks that were not narrow, hateful, and devoid of peace in mind and heart, as well as politically uninformed and bigoted. Blaming others for war, they did not see that they were contributing to the universal vibrations of anger and spite.

Fundamentally, this and subsequent verses teach us that each person must determine to follow the path of right thought and action and let others alone. Over a hundred years ago a wise man wrote an article on spiritual life entitled: "Others May, You Cannot." That is a good rule to remember.

Inwardly healthy

Happy indeed we live who are free from disease among those still diseased. In the midst of diseased men, we live free from disease (Dhammapada 198).

Thanissaro Bhikkhu: "How very happily we live, free from misery among those who are miserable. Among miserable people, free from misery we dwell."

Narada Thera comments that the disease spoken of here is "the disease of passions." It is strange but true that a great many people continually stir themselves up, deliberately choosing to live in a state of constant ferment, upset, and misery. Oftentimes this is because nothing else goes on in their life. Many neighborhoods have their local grouch whose only purpose in life is complaining and making trouble for others. This often includes complaints to the police and other authorities for petty "crimes" on behalf of others, especially regarding parking in front of their property. Children and adults are equal targets for their frustration and malice. When growing up I knew three of these bitter people, all of whom were old, ill, and without family or friends. Their ways were inexplicable.

But one of them came out differently. She had done some nasty, spiteful thing to an aunt of mine, and her son retaliated with some prank. The old lady did not know who did it, but my cousin began to feel really bad about what he had done. So he went to her house and apologized and asked her forgiveness. The poor woman nearly passed out in shock, since for years everyone had despised her. She was so moved she hugged and kissed him and apologized for being such a grouch. The result was she became friends with my aunt's family and soon was friends with all the neighbors. This is the power of goodness, even if belated.

Living amongst the passion-ridden, we can be passion-free and at peace.

Without worry
Happy indeed we live who are free from worry among those who are still worried. In the midst of worried men, we live free from worry (Dhammapada 199).

This must be an ambiguous verse in the Pali original, for Harischandra Kaviratna renders it: "Blessed indeed are we who live among those who are yearning for sense delights, without yearning for such things; amidst those who are yearning for sense delights, let us dwell without yearning." Narada Thera agrees in his translation, but Thanissaro Bhikkhu has it: "How very happily we live, free from busyness among those who are busy. Among busy people, free from busyness we dwell."

Whichever it is, we can profitably resolve to put away, worry, desire, and obsession with externals from our minds and live at rest in our hearts.

Happy with nothing
Happy indeed we live who have nothing of our own. We shall feed on joy, just like the radiant devas (Dhammapada 200).

This can be followed in two ways. The first is the obvious one of living in blessed simplicity without the burden of many things. A friend of mine used to take stock of everything in her house about every six months, and get rid of everything she did not really need. She had realized that the habit of possession creeps up on all of us, and each time she made her inventory, sure enough her own weakness had begun tripping her up. The second way is to live happily in the realization that absolutely nothing is ever really ours, that everything, including our body, eventually dissolves away. And besides, it is all just a dream which must end in time. This is the key to really enjoying things, for they are not hanging around our necks demanding that we look after them, guard them, protect them, and identify with them. To be possessed by possessions is misery, but freedom from them is the happiness of the gods.

At peace

A victor only breeds hatred, while a defeated man lives in misery, but a man at peace within lives happily, abandoning up ideas of victory and defeat (Dhammapada 201).

Thanissaro Bhikkhu: "Winning gives birth to hostility. Losing, one lies down in pain. The calmed lie down with ease, having set winning and losing aside."

Humans have an awful drive to be in control, to be ahead of others. Alpha dogs are bad enough, but alpha people are really a source of unhappiness to themselves and others. *The Lion in Winter* gives a vivid picture of people who just have to be one up on others, everything being a competition in which someone outwits another. There are people who would rather make one dollar by fooling or cheating someone than make ten dollars by selling them something worthwhile at a just price. This is sometimes a cultural trait in which an entire society lives just to prove their cleverness by deception and dishonesty. How terrible to see everyone as either a victim or a potential victimizer. "It's a dog eat dog world" is their philosophy. But who wants to be a dog?

The wise never look at life in terms of "I win, you lose" or vice versa. They live their life as a serious opportunity to advance in understanding rather than a game to play "gotcha" all day along.

Supreme miseries

There is no fire like desire. There is no weakness like anger. There is no suffering like the khandhas. There is no happiness greater than peace (Dhammapada 202).

This is quite plain. The khandas (skandas) are the five components of human nature in which the individual is trapped. Since he mistakes them for himself, he suffers at their changes and damages and losses, feeling a pain than cannot possibly be his. This is a terrible illusion, indeed.

More troubles

Hunger is the supreme disease. Mental activity is the supreme suffering. When one has grasped this as it really is, Nirvana is the supreme happiness (Dhammapada 203).

Regarding hunger, Narada Thera says: "Ordinary diseases are usually curable by a suitable remedy, but hunger has to be appeased daily." By "mental activity" is meant the running around of an uncontrolled and unsteady mind. Nirvana is the only permanent ending of these sources of suffering. When we really grasp the way things are, we seek for Nirvana.

Supreme good

Health is the supreme possession. Contentment is the supreme wealth. A trustworthy friend is the supreme relation. Nirvana is the supreme happiness (Dhammapada 204).

Health is necessary for unimpeded spiritual practice.

Spiritual joy

After enjoying the taste of solitude and the taste of peace, one is freed from distress and evil, as one enjoys the taste of

spiritual joy. It is good to meet with the saints. Living with them is always sweet. By not meeting fools one can be happy all the time (Dhammapada 205, 206).

There are two forms of solitude and peace: outer and inner. The outer is a means to the inner, for it is the inner solitude and peace that is needed. Those who possess them are happy whatever the outer conditions of stress may be.

The word translated "saints" is really *ariya* (arya). So we need not wait to meet supremely great souls, but should seek out the company of those who, like us, are aspiring after a higher mode of life. In India this is called satsang–company with truth–for such persons are living truthfully. To live with other seekers is a great advantage, which is why Paramhansa Yogananda put such emphasis on the formation of spiritual communities. The company of other yogis can be the difference between success and failure, for Yogananda also said: "Company is greater than will power." One of his fellow disciples told me that whenever his guru, Swami Sri Yukteswar, gave instruction in yoga to someone he would ask if they knew anyone who also practiced that form of meditation. If they said they did, he would tell them: "Good. Then make them your only friends and meditate with them as much as possible."

Just as important as company with other aspirants is the avoidance of fools. Fools come in many flavors, but Yogananda defined a fool as one who is not seeking God. That pretty well covers it all. Buddha is not exaggerating: By not meeting fools one can be happy all the time. I know this by experience, living in a solitary ashram devoted solely to the purpose of the evolution of its members, and keeping the doors and gate closed to idlers and dabblers who have no interest in devoting their life totally to the quest for liberation. Blessed peace!

Fools: a great evil

A man who keeps company with a fool, will suffer for it a long time. It is always painful to live with fools, like with an enemy,

but a wise man is good to live with, like meeting up with relatives (Dhammapada 207).

Now here we have the right attitude. Fools are poison. Some kill slowly and some quickly, but they both kill. That is, by their presence they kill peace of mind and heart, and radiate destructive vibrations. This is especially true when they are not vegetarians, but radiate the vibrations of the dead bodies they have eaten and assimilated. They are ghouls, feasting on the dead, and their bodies are graveyards. If they also ingest alcohol and nicotine they are the embodiments of spiritual defilement. They are their own enemies as well as the enemies of others. Behaving like the animals they eat, they disrupt the life of human beings–those who seek liberation.

On the other hand, the wise are our true kin.

Seek him out

Now Buddha tells us the kind of people to associate with.

Therefore, if he is a man of understanding and penetration, learned and habitually moral, devout and noble, one should cultivate the company of that just and wise man, in the same way as the moon keeps to a path among the stars (Dhammapada 208).

Now we know the way to happiness and the way to avoid unhappiness. And it is very simple.

Chapter 16
PREFERENCE

The unknowing

He who applies himself to what is not really an appropriate subject for application, and fails to apply himself to what is, missing the real purpose to grasp after what appeals to him, may well envy the man who does apply himself (Dhammapada 209).

Narada Thera: "Applying oneself to that which should be avoided, not applying oneself to that which should be pursued, and giving up the quest, one who goes after pleasure envies them who exert themselves."

Here Buddha is speaking of those who knew the right way of life, but who either never tried it or who did for a while and then left it, "giving up the quest" for Nirvana and instead seeking after self-indulgence. They shall always envy those who entered the way and persevered. That envy may be cloaked with sour grapes mockery and bitter resentment, but nevertheless at heart they know the truth: they have turned from reality to the fever dream that can never satisfy, for it has no substance.

In the 1940's Monica Baldwin, a nun, left her convent and wrote *I Leap Over the Wall*, which became a bestseller, being avidly read by those who wished to assure themselves that they were wise in not being monastic. (I read it a dozen or so years later and was not convinced she had done the right thing, and I was a Protestant.) She told of her wonderful "freedom," and some time later wrote a fiction book about how awful it was to be in an enclosed, contemplative order. I read that book, too, and was so inspired to take up monastic life that

I would have written her a letter thanking her, but knew it would not be appreciated. This book thrilled me, despite her intentions. Then, six years after I read the book, she wrote an article for *Emmanuel* magazine entitled *The Crux of My Downfall.* Yes, she had at last wakened to find herself in prison, not freedom as she had thought for so long. She had fallen, not risen. She wrote the article after having read a book by a priest who had left the priesthood and gotten married, and was writing about how it was all God's wonderful plan for him. Miss Baldwin knew better because she had slept the same slumber and dreamed the same deadly dream. Here is the conclusion of her article.

"The newspaper photograph of Mr. Davis and the former Miss Henderson after their wedding shows two mature people in whom the 'natural' man has won the day. It saddened me; for behind them, in the background, one saw oneself. A dim figure labeled for ever as one of those who, having put their hand to the plough, looked back; came down from the cross, because one lacked the courage and generosity—but above all, the love—that would have kept one there; thief of the holocaust once handed over so utterly to God but which, taken back from its rightful owner, must, now and for-ever, be looked upon as stolen property.

"Mr. Davis tells us that in human love (and in the freedom that I too so enjoyed for a period) he has found peace and happiness. He has got what he wanted. But even if this should last, there is one moment (whether in this life or the next one cannot know) that I do not envy him. For I have lived through it. It is the moment when the scales at last fall from one's eyes and one realizes, in agony of heart, the more than shabby meanness of what one has done:

"'And the Lord turned and looked upon Peter…and he went out and wept, bitterly.'"

Likes and dislikes
Never have anything to do with likes and dislikes. The absence of what one likes is painful, as is the presence of what one dislikes (Dhammapada 210).

Buddha is not speaking of objects for which we have liking or disliking, but of the need to avoid creating such reactions to any things. There are people who decide to be annoyed at everything; others decide to be hurt by everything; and others decide to be let down, disappointed and disillusioned by everything, and of course many decide to be offended day and night. All four deliberately make themselves miserable by those reactions. In the same way those who habitually classify everything as liked or disliked are setting themselves up for constant emotional upset and anxiety.

Therefore do not take a liking to anything. To lose what one likes is hard, but there are no bonds for those who have no likes and dislikes (Dhammapada 211).

Again, Buddha is speaking of creating in our mind a reaction of desire and pleasure which must in time result in aversion and pain when the liked object is lost or is discovered to not be what we originally thought it was. ("Where is the man/woman I married?" is a common plaint.)

Buddha is not telling us to be indifferent and unreacting like zombies, but is telling us not to artificially create what are only bonds to loss and sorrow. We make those experiences inevitable if we keep on creating them. He sums it up with these words:

From preference arises sorrow, from preference arises fear, but he who is freed from preference has no sorrow and certainly no fear (Dhammapada 212).

Sorrow and fear

From affection arises sorrow, from affection arises fear, but he who is freed from affection has no sorrow and certainly no fear.

From pleasure arises sorrow, from pleasure arises fear, but he who is freed from pleasure has no sorrow and certainly no fear.

From sensuality arises sorrow, from sensuality arises fear, but he who is freed from sensuality has no sorrow and certainly no fear.

From craving arises sorrow, from craving arises fear, but he who is freed from craving has no sorrow and certainly no fear (Dhammapada 213-216).

Here we find our own follies named, for none of these things exist in our hearts until we create them.

The dear one

Well may people hold dear the man who is endowed with morality and insight, who is well established in righteousness, a seer of the truth, and applying himself to his own business [duty] (Dhammapada 217).

This is an excellent list of the qualities of one who is worthy of our esteem. We should look for them in anyone who claims to be seeking for higher awareness, and more importantly we should cultivate them in ourselves. But good as this description is, Buddha goes on to describe one who is not just right thinking and right acting, but who has caught the vision that impels the aspirant onward and upward to the Goal.

He whose longing has been aroused for the indescribable, whose mind has been quickened by it, and whose thought is not attached to sensuality is truly called one who is bound upstream (Dhammapada 218).

This is a description of one who has evolved to the point that internal realities are increasingly occupying his consciousness. As internal things become more real to him, external things become less and less real to him. A quiet and blessed revolution is taking place, not just in his thinking but in his consciousness. He is coming to know—not just assume or philosophize. As a piece of steel is drawn to the magnet, in the same way he is being drawn to the ultimate reality of Nirvana. His mind has become alive to Nirvana, for that is the sole Truth. He is not learning intellectually, but awakening spiritually. This being so, attachment to outer life is fading away in proportion to the emergence of inner experience gained through meditation. Such a one is a stream-enterer, one who is truly on the right path to Nirvana, and who will attain it if he continues without slacking or deviating.

Beyond this world

When a man who has been away a long time at last comes home safely from far away, his family, friends and acquaintances rejoice to see him back. In the same way, when a man who has done good goes from this world to the next, his good deeds receive him like relations welcoming a loved one back again (Dhammapada 219, 220).

In contrast to the childish egotism of "we will all be reunited with our loved ones over there," Buddha tells the truth: at death—just as at birth—we meet our actions, our karma. For that is all we ever have. The dear man is met by his good deeds and by their power lifted to higher regions beyond the compulsion of earthly rebirth. And from those pure abodes of which Buddha frequently spoke he is enabled to attain Nirvana through unbroken cultivation of consciousness.

Chapter 17

ANGER

Abandon anger, give up pride, and overcome all fetters. Suffering does not befall him who is without attachment to names and forms, and possesses nothing of his own (Dhammapada 221).

This is really quite clear. I assume this verse was chosen to begin this section since it first mentions anger, which is the theme.

Charioteer

When a man governs his rising anger like a chariot going out of control, that is what I call a charioteer. The rest are just holding the reins (Dhammapada 222).

This is not complicated. Buddha is saying that the person who reins in his rising anger and does not express it is a person of true control, even though it is preferred that the capacity for anger be completely extinguished in time. So Buddha is giving the striving aspirant encouragement and praise.

Overcome

Overcome anger with freedom from anger. Overcome evil with good. Overcome meanness with generosity, and overcome a liar with truthfulness (Dhammapada 223).

This is a very significant verse. Although Buddha commends the one who controls the passions, he says that we must overcome them–cancel them out. And in their place we must establish their opposites–the real virtues, not just an appearance. It is good to suppress evil impulses, but it is better to have only impulses toward the good. Only by cultivating these positive virtues can anger, evil, meanness, and false-speaking be eliminated completely.

The company of devas

Speak the truth, do not get angry, and always give, even if only a little, when you are asked. By these three principles you can come into the company of the devas (Dhammapada 224).

How beautifully simple and practical are the teachings of Buddha, completely devoid of tangled metaphysics and the citation of mythologies. These three principles can win us a place in world far beyond this world where falsehood, anger, and selfishness are systemic evils.

Harmlessness

Those sages who do harm to no one, and who are always physically restrained, go to the everlasting abode, reaching which they will face no more suffering (Dhammapada 225).

This is a reference to the Pure Abodes, called Pure Lands in Mahayana Buddhism, which are realms free from the necessity for rebirth. They are also written about in Hindu scriptures and in the Gospel of Saint John: "In my Father's house are many mansions: if it were not so, I would have told you. I go to prepare a place for you. And if I go and prepare a place for you, I will come again, and receive you unto myself; that where I am, there ye may be also" (John 14:2, 3). Those who reach such levels are able to continually practice meditation under the tutorship of great evolved souls and eventually attain Nirvana. This is very important information, for by unceasing discipline and meditation we can fit ourselves to ascend to a Pure Abode after death and never more have to return here or to a lesser world. There without interruption we can engage in sadhana and attain the Goal. This is the hope set forth for all sadhakas, even those coming to it late in life. Ahimsa and determined restraint are the way.

Attaining passionlesness

Inflowing thoughts come to an end in those who are ever alert of mind, training themselves night and day, and ever intent on nirvana (Dhammapada 226).

Harischandra Kaviratna: "The influxes of passion disappear in those who are ever vigilant, who are absorbed day and night in spiritual studies, and who are bent on realization of nirvana."

Extinguishing the passions is extremely difficult, especially since they can seem to be eliminated when the mind is either hiding them or they remain in the form of karmic seeds that will sprout in the future in the undisciplined mind. Therefore Buddha tells us that we must be forever vigilant night and day, filling our mind with spiritual knowledge, perpetually aspiring after Nirvana. If this is done, the passions will not arise, or if they do, they will be so weak that we can easily toss them out. For they are always extraneous to us and really cannot touch us. Yet, they fool us into thinking that they are somehow ingrained in us and inseparable from us. For if they get us to believe this, we will think we are powerless against them. But that is a lie, an illusion; they really do not even touch us. Sri Ramakrishna used to give the example of a washerman and his donkey. Not wanting the donkey to wander off in the night, he would pass a rope around its forelegs and make it feel like it was tied. Consequently the donkey would stand there the whole night, believing it was unable to move. It is the same with us and the passions. But those who follow Buddha's advice will come to see the truth of things and know this is not so. And the passions will melt away before their empowered will.

Criticism

It was so of old, it is not just so today. They criticize him who sits in silence, they criticize him who talks a lot. They even criticize him who speaks in moderation. There is not a man in the world who is not criticized. There never has been, there never will be, and there is not now any man exclusively criticized or exclusively praised (Dhammapada 227, 228).

No matter what a person does or does not do, there will be those who will criticize him, those who will praise him, and those who will ignore him. No one is always praised, and no one is always condemned. So what should we do? Ignore it all. It means nothing. People just talk and talk, usually with little thought and no insight behind it.

Peer pressure should not even exist for us. I mean this literally. No one can really put pressure on us unless we are susceptible to it. Regarding this Sri Ramakrishna said: "Worldly people say all kinds of things about the spiritually minded. But look here! When an elephant moves along the street, any number of curs and other small animals may bark and cry after it; but the elephant doesn't even look back at them....God dwells in all beings. But you may be intimate only with good people; you must keep away from the evil-minded."

This should always be kept in mind.

Beyond criticism

If a wise man of unblemished behavior and endowed with wisdom, morality and stillness of mind, is praised by the discriminating after day in day out acquaintance with him, like a pure gold coin, then who is fit to find fault with him? Even the King of the devas praises him (Dhammapada 229, 230).

Only the good will and approbation of the wise need matter to us in any way.

Body, mind, and speech

Guard against physical unruliness. Be restrained in body. Abandoning physical wrongdoing, lead a life of physical well doing. Guard against mental unruliness. Be restrained in mind. Abandoning mental wrongdoing, lead a life of mental well doing. Guard against verbal unruliness. Be restrained in speech. Abandoning verbal wrongdoing, lead a life of verbal well doing. The wise who are restrained in body, speech and mind–such are the well and truly restrained (Dhammapada 231-234).

It is not enough to be disciplined in only one of these three. There must be restraint in all, for thoughts and words can be as destructive as physical actions. For example, a brilliant friend of mine, a writer most skilled with words, once became angry at his brother-in-law, a weak and unadmirable person, who spoke very insultingly to my friend on the telephone. In reaction my friend spoke to him with great bitterness at some length, expounding his worthlessness and the impossibility of his ever improving. When he hung up, the brother-in-law went directly to his room and shot himself through the head. My friend killed that unfortunate man with words. So body, mind, and speech must be consistent with the principles of non-violence and all the other virtues. Actually, in these four verses we have returned to the subject of anger and injury.

Chapter 18

IMPURITIES (TAINTS)

One of the most saddening traits of Western religion is its pessimism about human beings. People are told how weak, foolish, ignorant and sinful they are and how likely it is they are going to stay that way–and be punished for it. Then comes the "message of hope"–*God will disregard what a poor excuse of a human you are if you belong to us; then you will get to go to heaven and be happy forever with him. But you will still be a dud, a "sinner saved by grace," no longer able to sin in heaven, but still not worth God's time if he were not so merciful. Trillions will be screaming eternally in hell-fire as you sit in heaven. They were no more clueless than you, but there is a difference: you Believed.*

Eastern religion on the other hand has a much better, fuller grasp of the human condition, because it has taken the time to study humanity, not just shrug and grimace. It sees that this is all an overlay that cannot last. That the reality of each human being is a divine Self that can be rescued from the swamp in which he finds himself. And even more wonderful: he can rescue himself by *being himself*, by turning from the unreal to the Real, from darkness to the Light, from death to Immortality. For it is his nature to do so. He both can and will.

So Eastern religion shows you what a mess your are *in*, but does not claim that mess is what you *are*. Just the opposite. It says: "This is not you; this is not where you belong. Come home and be free." This is the idea of Jesus' parable of the Prodigal Son, though you would not guess it if you read or heard what Western Christians say about it. (Eastern Christians, if they have not been influenced by the Westerns, say just what the rest of Eastern religions would say it means.)

Now Buddha is going to talk to us about the impurities or taints that darken consciousness, and show us the way to dispel them.

Diagnosis

You are now like a withered leaf. Death's messengers themselves are in your presence. You are standing in the jaws of your departure, and provisions for the road you have none (Dhammapada 235).

Buddha is saying this to everyone, even a new-born child. For the moment we are born we begin moving toward death. Degeneration begins in the body, however slightly. However, he is speaking to adults who should be aware that death can come to them at any moment. Within a few days of my high school graduation one of my classmates was killed in a traffic accident. One of Giuseppe Verdi's collar buttons fell on the floor. When he bent over to pick it up he had a severe stroke and died six days later. We live amidst more potential causes of death can we can number.

So we are all "withered" to some degree. The messengers–potential causes–of death are with us at every moment. In our own body we have microbes, bacteria, viruses, and parasites that will kill us if they gain the ascendency. In a sense, all of us are going to be killed by our body, even if only through its inability to preserve itself. So the body which we mistakenly think is what makes us alive, is the supreme agent of death. Again, even at birth we stand in the jaws of death, both in the form of our body and external factors than can kill us, including freak accidents.

The real stinger in the tail is the final part: "And provisions for the road you have none." This is the great tragedy of humanity: the ignoring of death and making no preparation for death. Now by preparation for death I do not mean praying: "If I should die before I wake, I pray the Lord my soul to take." We prepare for death by living our life in such a way that when death comes we will ascend to a higher world, hopefully beyond any more birth and death. That is only possible if our consciousness has permanently been elevated to correspond to such higher worlds.

When Panchanon Bhattacharya was grieving over the death of Yogiraj Shyama Charan Lahiri (Lahiri Mahasaya), the Master suddenly materialized before him and said: "Why are you sorrowing? *You do not live in this world. You live with me!*" What a blessed thought! Right now we can live beyond this world and say with Emily Dickinson: "Instead of getting to heaven at last, I'm going all along!" I know this is possible because I have lived with those that were always in another dimension. My maternal grandmother never lived on earth. Every day with her was to live at the door of eternity. After her departure from this world, through her blessing I came to meet those who not only lived in eternity, but had the power to transfer into Eternity—for at least a while—those who were capable of it. And they freely taught everyone how to do it on their own. That is what yogis do.

Cure

In such a case, build yourself an island. Make the effort quickly and become a wise man. Cleansed of your faults and now without blemish, you will go to the heavenly land of the saints (Dhammapada 236).

Build yourself an island. This is invaluable counsel for beginner and adept. Not just a fortress is needed, for that would be on the same land as invaders that may come. Rather, in the sea of samsara create a point of stability as solid and unshakable as an island. In essence, *make yourself an island.* Render yourself impenetrable to anything; and that includes society and the clone-dupes that inhabit it. As Yogananda often said: "Make your heart a hermitage." Only one person lives in a hermitage—a hermit. Do not be anti-social—that is a reaction to society. Be non-social—forget society altogether. Walk through the crowded streets completely alone. Be like the great Saint John of Kronstadt who was surrounded by thousands of people every day, yet who was always alone with God—so said another saint, Silouan of Athos, who received Saint John's blessing to become a monk.

We have already cited Emily Dickinson, and once again she presents the idea very well.

The soul selects her own society,
Then shuts the door;
On her divine majority
Obtrude no more.

Unmoved, she notes the chariot's pausing
At her low gate;
Unmoved, an emperor is kneeling
Upon her mat.

I've known her from an ample nation
Choose one;
Then close the valves of her attention
Like stone.

Poets—real poets—are mystics whether they think so or not. That is why Emily Bronte (very much the English counterpart of Emily Dickinson) could describe samadhi so well:

I'm happiest when most away
I can bear my soul from its home of clay
On a windy night when the moon is bright
And the eye can wander thru worlds of light

When I am not and none beside
Nor earth nor sea nor cloudless sky
But only spirit wandering wide
Thru infinite immensity.

She, too, loved solitude, and from that well drew forth the waters of profound spiritual realization though, as in the case of my maternal grandmother, no one guessed it.

Make the effort quickly and become a wise man. The matter is crucial and brooks no delay, so Buddha is telling us to make the effort quickly, not work up to it or wait until we think we are ready, but begin at full steam and keep it up from there. We are to become wise, not "devotees" or "serious seekers" and such sentimental identities. Wisdom alone will suffice, and everything else blocks it.

Cleansed of your faults and now without blemish, you will go to the heavenly land of the saints. If we do not manage Nirvana in this life, we can rise to the Pure Lands (Shuddhavasa) beyond rebirth. But only if we are cleansed of all faults and without blemish.

I cannot help but reflect on how in my childhood we used to sing in church:

> Heaven is a holy place,
> Filled with glory and with grace–
> Sin can never enter there;
> All within its gates are pure,
> From defilement kept secure–
> Sin can never enter there.

> If you hope to dwell at last,
> When your life on earth is past,
> In that home so bright and fair,
> You must here be cleansed from sin,
> Have the life of Christ within–
> Sin can never enter there.

This does not sound any different from what Buddha has just said, does it? Certainly the understanding of Buddha and the sincere piety of Charles W. Naylor–who, by the way was one of America's greatest hidden healers–were not to be compared, but the same fundamental truth was expressed by both. We must have the life of Buddha-Christ within; then we are assured of freedom from the prison of this world, "that, when ye fail, they may receive you into everlasting habitations" (Luke 16:9).

At the end of the journey

You are now at your life's conclusion. You are in the presence of the King of Death. There is no stopping off place on the way, and provisions for the road you have none. In such a case, build yourself an island. Make the effort quickly and become a wise man. Cleansed of your faults and now without blemish, you will come no more to birth and aging (Dhammapada 237, 238).

What was wisdom in life is still so when approaching death. There will be no halting-place, but every breath brings us nearer the great departure. We must keep on making the effort that we may "come no more to birth and aging" in a future incarnation in this world.

Moment by moment

Little by little, moment by moment, a wise man should cleanse himself of blemishes, like a smith purifying silver (Dhammapada 239).

Little by little. One time I was having a conversation with a teacher of anatomy at a medical school. Actually we were discussing spiritual things, and he said to me: "Any qualified anatomist will tell you that any drastic or rapid change or growth in the body is always pathological." I understood his spiritual implication, for I had grown up with lightning-strike conversion as the ideal. I heard many tell of their instant rebirth, of how deeply their hearts had been changed and how in an instant all their evil desires and habits were ended. Usually it would only be a matter of weeks or months until things were right back where they had been, and the "saved" were avoiding us to whom they had so earnestly testified. When I was a freshman in college our English teacher read us an article entitled "How Billy Graham Saved Scotland." It began: "Last Sunday only four people were in attendance at our village kirk [church]." Then followed a description of how a number people from that small town (including the village atheist who carried a thermos of martinis) got on a bus together and went to Edinburgh to attend a Billy Graham Crusade. A lot of them got "saved" and on the way home the author totted up the numbers. But the article ended with these words: "Last Sunday only four people were in attendance at our village kirk." Just so. Real change comes gradually. Lightning lights up a place brilliantly and is gone in a moment, but the light of day comes gradually and remains.

Moment by moment. Not fits and starts, not hours one day and hardly minutes another, and certainly not sluffing off after some years under the pretense of having come to some kind of plateau and no longer needing to be so disciplined. Every single breath must be a step onward toward the Goal. I mean this literally.

A wise man should cleanse himself of blemishes, like a smith purifying silver. There is only one way this is done: by intense heat and by skimming off and discarding the impurities that come to the surface of the molten silver. It is the same with us. Through intense tapasya in the form of meditation and ascetic discipline and the rejection and discarding of the defilements that will arise due to the heating process, we can cleanse ourselves just as thoroughly as did the Buddha. This, too, is gradual though continuous.

Sending ourselves to hell

Just as the rust which develops on iron, derives from it but then proceeds to eat it away, so a person of unrestrained behavior is drawn to hell by his own actions (Dhammapada 240).

I had the karma of being raised in a religion that claimed God would send me to hell forever if I did evil. This had the effect of making everyone around me afraid of God, but I had a different outlook. I realized that I had no need to be afraid of God, who loved me, but rather I must be afraid of myself, for it would be my deeds that would send me to hell, not God. Looking around at the people in general in my home town, I figured that they were already jumping into hell—no need for either Devil or God to do the job. Buddha supports those early conclusions.

An extremely important point here is the indication that it is our own makeup, our own human nature, that corrupts and then poisons or devours us. After a monk had left a monastery where I was living, the abbot said to me: "The demons never bothered him. They didn't need to. He was his own demon." This is true of just about everyone. We are the demon that drags us down to hell by our own "unrestrained behavior."

Both Narada Thera and Harischandra Kaviratna prefer "states of woe" to "hell," and Thanissaro Bhikkhu renders it "a bad destination." Whichever, the lesson is the same: we must avoid becoming our own destroying enemy.

Kinds of blight (rust)

Lack of repetition is the blight of scriptures. Lack of repairs is the blight of buildings. The blight of beauty is laziness, and carelessness is the blight of a guard. The blight of a woman is misconduct. The blight of a giver is meanness. Bad mental states are indeed blights in this world and the next. But the supreme blight, ignorance, is the blight of blights. Destroying this blight, be free of blights, bhikkhus (Dhammapada 241-243).

This very clear: ignorance is the evil of evils, the cause of all evil.

Easy life/hard life

Life is easy enough for the shameless, the crow-hero type of man, offensive, swaggering, impudent and depraved. But it is hard for the man of conscience, always striving after purity, alert, reserved, pure of behavior and discerning (Dhammapada 244, 245).

Narada Thera: "Easy is the life of a shameless one who is as impudent as a crow, back-biting, presumptuous, arrogant, and corrupt. Hard is the life of a modest one who ever seeks purity, is detached, humble, clean in life, and reflective."

It is easy to fall and wallow on the ground, especially if it is soft mud, but not so easy to remain upright or to rise after a fall and stay standing. The qualities listed here are not hard to comprehend. Those who want an easy life can follow the crow people, and those willing to put forth effort will go the way of the man of conscience.

Self-destruction

When a man takes life, tells lies, takes what he is not entitled to in the world, resorts to other men's wives and indulges in drinking wine and spirits—such a man is digging up his own roots here and now in this world (Dhammapada 246, 247).

Thanissaro Bhikkhu: "Whoever kills, lies, steals, goes to someone else's wife, and is addicted to intoxicants, digs himself up by the root right here in this world."

This is certainly easy to understand. I only want to point out that taking life includes the eating of meat, no matter how strongly some Buddhists wish to deny it, even claiming that Buddha died from eating spoiled pork. Such people are shameless in their self-indulgence, like those that want to prove that Jesus was married or at least had a girlfriend. Actually, Buddha is going to speak of them in this very next verse.

Evil unrestraint

So understand this, my man—Unrestrained men are evil. Do not let greed and wrongdoing subject you to lasting suffering (Dhammapada 248).

The unrestrained are evil, and if we join them in their folly, the suffering that results will be of long duration, for willful evil produces powerful karma, hard to erase, often lasting for more than one life.

Getting displeased

People give according to their faith, or as they feel well disposed. If one is put out for that reason with other people's food and drink, then one will not achieve stillness of mind in meditation, day or night. But he who has destroyed that sort of reaction, has rooted it out and done away with it—he will achieve stillness of mind in meditation, day and night (Dhammapada 249, 250).

Readiness to be offended, hurt, or upset by the deeds of others is a most virulent—and usually hypocritical—disease of mind and heart. Buddha speaks of giving in charity, including the giving of necessities to monks, but it represents all aspects of other people's actions, especially those that are intended to be virtuous. I have known people that would be envious if someone gave another person a bent pin. Those who knew him often joked that Al Jolson would be consumed with envy if he learned someone had started a successful laundromat. I have also known some who would say: "Well, they could have given it to me," if they heard about any kind of gift or assistance. It was the reflexive reaction of the consummately greedy and selfish. Such people cannot have steady meditation because their inner fires of greed and jealousy will not stop burning within them. But those who have freed themselves of all such egotism will always be at peace in and out of meditation.

The worst

There is no fire like desire. There is no hold like anger. There is no net like ignorance. There is no river like craving (Dhammapada 251).

There is no fire like desire. Harischandra Kaviratna: "There is no fire like passion." Narada Thera: "There is no fire like lust." This is the truth: desire is the real fire of hell, here-and-now. It not only torments the desirer, it destroys him and usually destroys others around him. Wars are the greatest proof of the destructive nature of desire. The word used here is *raga*, which means intense desire and attraction, greed and passion. Like fire it destroys, often beyond hope of restoration. There is another aspect to fire: the more you feed it the more it grows. A lot of people tell themselves that repression is bad, and that if they will just accept their desire and fulfill it that somehow they will be able to control it. That is the same as throwing gasoline on a fire to reduce and put it out. It is impossible. There are two ways to put out fire: suffocate it or deprive it of fuel. We must do both. Ruthlessly. Otherwise we will be supervising our own spiritual cremation.

There is no hold like anger. Harischandra Kaviratna: "There is no stranglehold like hatred." Narada Thera: "There is no grip like hate." Those who can break this hold are mighty indeed. But if it is not broken it will strangle our mind and heart and paralyze us.

There is no net like ignorance. Harischandra Kaviratna: "There is no snare like delusion." Narada Thera: "There is no net like delusion." Deluded people revel in their delusion and try to spread it around to others. They can never escape it because they like it and even call it clear-sighted wisdom. There is no way to escape when we do not know there is a need for it. Ignorance is blindness and deafness. It is total darkness. How can a person who knows nothing else decide to get away from it? Only our innate urge to spiritual transcendence can save us. Until then we are buried alive and call it living.

There is no river like craving. Harischandra Kaviratna: "There is no torrent like craving." It is impossible for a person to halt the flow of a river for even one second. It goes on and on with no end in sight. How long have the Mississippi and Amazon rivers been flowing without a single moment of interruption? And if we fall in the river it can sweep us away and the undertow can pull us down and drown us. Craving (tanha) is just the same. We must not go near it or think we can diminish it, much less eliminate it, except through meditation and an ordered spiritual life.

Crazy King Canute thought he could stop the tide from coming in. He could not, but he found out that he could drown–and did.

Easy perception

Other people's faults are easily seen. One can winnow out other people's faults like chaff. One hides one's own faults though, like a dishonest gambler hides an unlucky throw (Dhammapada 252).

I think this is the experience of us all. Jesus talked about how easy it was to see a tiny speck in someone else's eye, while not knowing that we have a big beam or plank in our own eye (Matthew 7:3-5). Yet we are ready to take that speck out of their eye, but defensive about our beam, which we try to hide or deny. Like the gambler we cover up our errors. Thanissaro Bhikkhu agrees with Richard's translation, but both Narada Thera and Harischandra Kaviratna translate it as covering up our faults like a bird trapper covers himself with leaves to escape detection. Either way, we are awfully honest about other's faults and very dishonest about our own. Consequently:

When one notices the mistakes of others and is always finding fault with them, the inflow of one's thoughts just increases and one is a long way from the cessation of this influx (Dhammapada 253).

We just make ourselves miserable and agitated, and even more tangled up in our own flaws.

It is all within

Just as there is no path in the sky, there is no man of religion [*samana*] outside. Other people take pleasure in multiplicity, but the Buddhas are free from it (Dhammapada 254).

A samana is a holy person who has followed dharma and purified himself. Such a one is living totally within as the Gita says: "Only that yogi whose joy is inward, inward his peace, and his vision inward shall come to Brahman and know Nirvana" (Bhagavad Gita 5:24). Thanissaro Bhikkhu's translation is: "There is no trail in space, no outside contemplative."

Jesus said: "Except your righteousness shall exceed the righteousness of the scribes and Pharisees, ye shall in no case enter into the kingdom of heaven" (Matthew 5:20). The scribes and Pharisees were so obsessed with externals that their religion was nothing but outer observances. Jesus warned that such obsession did not just hinder entrance into the kingdom of heaven–which, as he said (Luke 17:21) is totally interior–it prevented entry. That is why Buddha (whose teachings Jesus studied diligently in India and Ladakh) tell us that just as there is no such thing as a path in the sky, in the same way there is no true saint who is not an "interior soul," whose focus is inward and whose life is inward, his outer life being only a minimal token. Those who had the great good fortune to meet Swami Venkateshananda, a disciple of Swami Sivananda, will remember how Swamiji was so kind, full of humor, and a real teacher of dharma; yet at the same time when you were with him you realized that he was living in another dimension, that his real life was completely unseen.

As Buddha further says, while others are immersed in multiplicity, those with genuine realization are totally free in awareness of Unity.

Just as there is no path in the sky, there is no man of religion outside. There are no lasting functions of the mind, but there is no oscillation of mind for the Buddhas (Dhammapada 255).

We identify with thoughts and feelings that come from the mind (manas and buddhi), but that is a grave mistake, for the mind is nothing but a field of subtle energy that is constantly in flux. Mental states are like the weather, constantly subject to change. Therefore we should not take them seriously, neither the good states nor the bad ones, for they are nothing in themselves. If we take a piece of clay and make a beautiful image, is the clay itself beautiful? No; only the momentary appearance is beautiful. We can smash the clay into a lump and then make an ugly image, but the reality is the same: the clay has not become ugly, only the appearance. In the same way the mind just keeps shaping and reshaping itself without cessation. Those who identify with the shapes will keep changing all the time. These are the people that talk about how they have ups and downs, how sometimes they are on the mountaintop and sometimes in the valley, and they even try to glorify this condition, claiming that "faith" makes it all right. It does not, for our eternal Self is never changing. It remains the same under all conditions, exactly the opposite of the mind. And that alone should be identified with. The permanent condition of the Self is Nirvana. Those who have attained Nirvana have transmuted the mind into Nirvana itself, so the waverings and mutations of the mind are ended forever. Until then, nothing worthwhile is going on with the mind.

Yoga is the remedy for mood swings and botheration rising from the changes of the mind. Yogis of steady practice have steadiness of heart, so even when the mind is still unsteady, the mind does not influence or trouble them. This was one of the first symptoms that my yoga practice was really taking hold. After over twenty years I was no longer at the mercy of the idiot mind. I was amazed. Oh, yes, the rascal kept hopping about and changing its masks, but I was not impelled to react. I could laugh at what had been a cruel and capricious jailer in the prison of earthbound life. I learned to fool it like it had been fooling me. For example, after meditating a while my mind would say: "I want to quit meditating." So I would say: "That's right. I'm bored. I'm quitting." And then it would shut up for twenty minutes or more. Then it would whine again and I would say: "Yes. I am quitting right now." Then I would have twenty more minutes of peace. (I have no idea why it took twenty minutes for the pathetic mind to figure out I had not stopped meditating.) Happily, after just a few weeks of this the whole drama stopped, because meditation had eliminated the split in my mind and I no longer had to pacify it by tricking it. It was not Nirvana, but it was progress along the way. Step by step we get there.

Chapter 19

THE RIGHTEOUS (DHARMIC) ONE

The righteous judge

One is not righteous if one decides a case without due consideration, but the wise man who takes into account both for and against, and comes to his decision about others with due consideration—such a man of discrimination who keeps to the truth, he is to be called righteous (Dhammapada 256, 257).

Thanissaro Bhikkhu: "To pass judgment hurriedly does not mean you are a judge. The wise one, weighing both the right judgment and wrong, judges others impartially—unhurriedly, in line with the Dharma, guarding the Dharma, guarded by Dharma, intelligent: he is called a judge."

This might not seem a particularly spiritual subject, but that is because in the West we have been conditioned to think dualistically, and that includes separating the material from the spiritual rather than seeing them as a single thing: life. This has also given rise to the idea that a material person will be practical and a spiritual person will be impractical. But Sri Ramakrishna said: "If you can weigh salt, you can weigh sugar," and he insisted that his disciples first of all learn to be methodical and practical and to guard themselves against carelessness and indifference. He especially insisted that they never let themselves be cheated or taken advantage of, as that would be passive cooperation with dishonesty and would blunt their moral sense. In the same way

Buddha is saying that we must be careful in all our judgments, never being hasty and always seeing all aspects of a situation. Most important, all our valuations should be in line with dharma and an expression of dharma. Further, when we come to a decision we should abide by it and order all things in accordance with what we know to be the dharmic position. Moral rectitude is an absolute essential for those seeking liberation (nirvana).

The truly learned

One is not a learned man by virtue of much speaking. He who is patient, without anger and fearless, he is to be called learned (Dhammapada 258).

I always cringe when I hear the authority of scholars, theologians or experts invoked in any matter, because in modern times these are simply misinformed and mentally shallow people who think much of themselves and get others to do the same. It is much better for all of us to use our own heads and learn about things for ourself. Nevertheless, those who talk and write a lot become "experts" on subjects they know next to nothing about. They not only know little, that little is misunderstood by them and their conclusions are absurd and even harmful.

Buddha give us three traits of a learned person. He is not saying that possessing these three qualities make a person learned, but that a truly learned person will have these qualities, otherwise we should not trust what he says. A wise man is patient because he is calm and humble, and because he is aware of his own and others' limitations. He is without anger because he is a master of all passions and the ego from which they arise. He is fearless because he possesses a mental and spiritual integrity that cannot be shaken or compromised.

Maintainer of the dharma

One is not a bearer of the teaching [dharma] by virtue of much speaking, but he who, even if he has only studied a little, has experienced the truth in person, he is indeed a bearer of

the teaching, who has not forgotten the teaching (Dhammapada 259).

This is always the viewpoint of the yogi: only direct experience is true knowing (jnana), and those who never forget or lose that experience are the true bearers of dharma. This is because the purpose of dharma is jnana, not just intellectual ideas. Dharma is nothing if it does not lead to jnana.

An elder

One is not an elder [thera] by virtue of having white hair. One is just advanced in years, and called "grown old in vain." He in whom there is truthfulness, non-violence, restraint and self control, however–that wise and faultless sage is to be called an elder (Dhammapada 260, 261).

Respect for age is a hallmark of a worthy civilization, but we should not think that mere age is a sign of knowledge or even experience. Most people truly do "grow old in vain"–that is, they gain nothing through the years but continue as unheeding and unaware of higher things as when they were children. This was something I knew long before I went to school. Looking at those around me, including my parents, I realized that when they died they would have done nothing, learned nothing, been nowhere, and become nothing. And so it was. Not one did, learned, saw, or became anything. Their lives amounted to zero. "When they die it will be as though they never lived," was my conviction, which they themselves proved to be true. Consequently I had a real horror of being a "nothing." And so should everyone.

Truthful, non-violent, restrained, self-controlled, and purified by those qualities–such is the real "elder of wisdom."

The admirable one

It is not just by fine speech or by flower-like beauty that one is admirable, if one is envious, mean and deceitful, but when that sort of behavior has been eliminated, rooted out and destroyed,

that faultless sage is said to be admirable (Dhammapada 262, 263).

This is quite straightforward, but it is true that Westerners interested in Eastern thought are extremely susceptible to external appearance in those they regard as teachers. If the teacher looks impressive, they are impressed, if they speak in an inspirational manner they are inspired, if they speak with authority they are convinced. But it is all superficial impression without any actual basis. The unimpressive, self-effacing, and simply clothed and simply behaved teachers of righteousness who are worthy of great reverence–those who have long ago eliminated the egoistic impulses that motivate the flashy teachers–are ignored. "I was not impressed," is the verdict. It takes intelligence and intuition to recognize the worthy teachers, so they have few students in comparison with the glitter-gurus. In time the negative character of the glitterati is revealed, but the dupes keep right on adoring.

Great masters of the spiritual life have been coming and going for nearly a century here in America, but few–mostly Indians–even knew about them because they avoided publicity and were interested only in spiritually benefiting those they came into contact with. The kind of people that gathered around them had no interest in publicity and institutionalization. The glitter-gurus attracted just the opposite–those who understood that if they exalted the guru then they, too, would be exalted by association and eventually would have access to power and money. One group was making hundreds of thousands of dollars a year, and when their guru was caught out being immoral, they just kicked him out of the ashram and kept right on raking in the cash. He immediately went to the west coast and picked up another group of opportunists and parasites and kept right on. But it makes no difference; the real seekers find the real teachers, and the fakes find the frauds.

The real monk

A shaven head does not make one a man of religion, if one is irreligious and untruthful. How could a man full of desires and greed be a man of religion? But when a man has put aside all evil

deeds, both great and small, by that putting away of evil deeds he is indeed called a man of religion (Dhammapada 264, 265).

Harischandra Kaviratna: "Not by tonsure does one who is undisciplined and utters lies become a monk. How can he who is overcome by desire and greed become a monk? But he who constantly stills his evil tendencies, small or great, is called a true monk (samana), because he has quieted all these evils."

One of the great problems of the East is the way young men flood into monastic life simply because they know they will be assured of clothing, food, and shelter for the rest of their life without doing a thing to merit them. Criminals often join the monastic life hoping that their shaven head and monastic garb will disguise them from the police, who will not be looking for them in a holy place, anyway. Some become monks because they cannot get a job. Malcontents often get a fit of renunciation and become monks at least for a while so they can get away from their worldly obligations, including wife and children, and often debts. Sri Ramakrishna said: "There is a kind of renunciation, called *markatavairagya*, 'monkey renunciation.' A man, harrowed by distress at home, puts on an ochre robe and goes away to Benares. For many days he does not send home any news of himself. Then he writes to his people: 'Don't be worried about me. I have got a job here.'" Because of this people lose respect for monks and the worthy monks suffer because of it. Often a sincere young man finds himself surrounded by men whose morals and character are worse than any he had encountered before coming to the monastery. It was so in Buddha's time and before and since then. Many, if not most, of the present-day glitter gurus became monks solely because it will enhance their careers. And they make others monks to be their staff and promoters. For this reason monks should be carefully scrutinized before being accepted as such.

One is not a bhikkhu by virtue of taking alms from others. By taking up any old teaching, one is not a bhikkhu on that account. But he who has here and now ejected both good and evil, and in leading the holy life lives in accordance with reason—he is indeed called a bhikkhu (Dhammapada 266, 267).

Narada Thera: "He is not thereby a bhikkhu merely because he begs from others; by following the whole code (of morality) one certainly becomes a bhikkhu and not (merely) by such begging. Herein he who has transcended both good and evil, whose conduct is sublime, who lives with understanding in this world, he, indeed, is called a bhikkhu." Harischandra Kaviratna: "He is not a religious mendicant because he begs alms from others. He does not become a bhikkhu merely by outward observances of the Law. But he who has transcended both merit and demerit, who leads a life of purity and lives in this world in full realization of the Truth, he indeed is called a bhikkhu." Thanissaro Bhikkhu: "Begging from others does not mean one is a monk. As long as one follows householders' ways, one is no monk at all. But whoever puts aside both merit and evil and, living the chaste life, judiciously goes through the world: he's called a monk."

By looking at all four of these translations we can get a good idea of what Buddha intended to say. Two points strike me in reading them. One, a monastic must have a completely different mode of life, a completely different psychology, actually, from that of worldlings. Two, he must live in a thoroughly sensible and practical manner. There is no place for the fiction of "crazy wisdom" here, nor the pretense that a monastic of advanced spiritual realization is somehow beyond the rules of right conduct. A fool is a fool; a loony is a loony. No real monk is either of these. And he certainly is not a liar and a scoundrel.

The sage

Silence does not make a sage [muni] if he is stupid and ignorant, but when a man avoids evil as if he were choosing something of value on the scales–he is a sage. That indeed makes him a sage. He who discriminates in both worlds is for that reason called a sage (Dhammapada 268, 269).

Stupid and ignorant people do not attain anything in this world, and certainly not in the spiritual realm. That is a fact. One of the worst mistakes of religion is trying to accommodate everybody, including the stupid and ignorant, the indifferent and the unfit. That, too, is a fact.

A worthy person avoids evil because he sees that virtue is of great value, not because he wants people to have a good impression of him or fears punishment for sin—and that includes fear of bad karma. True morality is a positive character, a reaching out for the good, not just the avoidance of the bad.

Those who even now are at home in both the material and spiritual worlds, and who live intelligently in each one, aware of the innate laws of both, are sages, none other.

The aryan

One is not noble [arya] if one harms other living creatures. It is by non violence [ahimsa] to all forms of life that one is called noble (Dhammapada 270).

This is absolutely so. The Venerable Narada Thera includes the background-story of each verse of the Dhammapada. Regarding this one, the story is: "A man named Arya was fishing. The Buddha told him that one did not become an Arya by harming others." This should be taken seriously as an indication that Buddha advocated strict abstinence from the flesh of sentient beings. (It is a shame that such a point need even be made.) Further, this shows that vegetarianism was originally a tenet of Theravada Buddhism, just as does the fact that when Ashoka, Emperor of India, adopted the Theravada school personally he immediately outlawed animal slaughter and the eating of meat throughout India.

True peace

It is not just by means of morality and religious observances, not by great learning nor by attainments in meditation, nor by living alone, nor by thinking, "I am enjoying a spiritual happiness which ordinary people do not know" that a bhikkhu achieves peace if he has not achieved the elimination of inflowing thoughts (Dhammapada 271, 272).

This is a surprising verse, but nonetheless true. Only when a person's mind no longer is conditioned by or responds to external and internal stimuli does he have peace. This is why Patanjali defines yoga as the non-arising of modifications of the mind–that is, when the mind is in a state in which no response can be provoked in any way, but is completely under the control of the yogi's will as to response or non-response. "The enlightened, the Brahman-abiding, calm-hearted, unbewildered, is neither elated by the pleasant nor saddened by the unpleasant. His mind is dead to the touch of the external: it is alive to the bliss of the Atman. Because his heart knows Brahman his happiness is for ever" (Bhagavad Gita 5:20, 21).

Chapter 20

THE WAY

Of paths the Eightfold one is best, and of truths the Fourfold. Dispassion is the best of mental states, and of human beings the best is the seer (Dhammapada 273).

Thanissaro Bhikkhu: "Of paths, the eightfold is best. Of truths, the four sayings. Of qualities, dispassion. Of two-footed beings, the one with the eyes to see."

The Eightfold Path

The Eightfold Path was mentioned in verse one hundred ninety-one, but for some reason it did not occur to me to include it in the commentary. Now it should be, because many people may not have read an exposition of it or memorized it. (As a Buddhist nun once said: "If you like lists, then Buddhism is the religion for you.") It is very important, because in the next verse Buddha declares that this is the only path to the purification that enables us to attain Nirvana.

The Eightfold Path consists of: 1) Right View; 2) Right Intention; 3) Right Speech; 4) Right Action; 5) Right Livelihood; 6) Right Effort; 7) Right Mindfulness; 8) Right Concentration. All of these are inter-related to some extent.

1) Right View

View–drishti–literally means the faculty of sight, but also includes a person's view, opinion, or perception of something, and is right view of the right thing, namely the way to live so as to lead to

236

Nirvana. The trivia which occupy the minds of nearly every human being ultimately mean nothing, and Buddha is not concerned with that. Right view is the right evaluation of things as well as the right understanding of them. Right view is seeing things as they really are, and knowing which matter and which do not. Naturally this includes a right response to right view, including the right way to live. It is obviously a function of the buddhi, the intelligence, and not the sensory mind or the emotions. The mind is like a mirror, and if there is any distortion of the mirror then all perceptions will be distorted. So Right View presupposes right condition of the mind. Each of the eight parts of the path is psychological, even if some of them include external modes of behavior.

2) Right Intention

Sankalpa means resolution, will, determination, and intention. Obviously Right View is a prerequisite of Right Intention. Right intention, again, is focused on the right subjects, the ones that matter. It controls the direction of our life and the way we will live it. Certainly right intention includes a right understanding of the need to live and act in perfect accordance with the highest standards. This does not admit of superficiality, mere dabbling, or moseying along through life. Self-discipline is another requisite to carry out Right Intention. The intention to reach Nirvana—and for the right reasons—is the sum of Right Intention.

3) Right Speech

Vak is speech: the ability to speak, the intelligence to speak (the thought behind speech), and the speaking itself. It is the last two that are referred to by Buddha. The wellsprings of our speech must be right, both our understanding and intention in speaking. So must our inner speaking, our thinking. Right speech does not allow of disparity between thought and word. All speech must be beneficial, true, complete, useful, sincere, and an expression of friendliness (maitreya). Then it will be right in every aspect.

4) Right Action

Right Action (karmanta) can also be translated as Right Conduct. This is according to the codes established by the teachers of wisdom, including the five precepts of Buddhism: No lying, no stealing, no injury (of others or oneself), no immorality, and no intoxication. More complete is the yama-niyama of the Yoga Sutras. One thing is certain: the code of Right Conduct must be as broad, as all-inclusive, as possible, in contrast to the Western attempts to limit the principles of right action to only glaring misconduct or only the things specifically mentioned in scriptures or other authoritative texts. Rather, general principles must be applied as thoroughly as possible, making sure that no infractions of any kind or degree occur. This is the way of the East, the only way that really succeeds.

5) Right Livelihood

This is an exceedingly broad precept, based on many moral principles. It is not just that we must abstain from livelihood that breaks those principles, we must engage in livelihood that embodies them. Our livelihood must not only not harm others, it must genuinely benefit others. For example, we cannot be dishonest, but neither should we be persuading people to buy items or services that are unnecessary. There are many ways to cheat or steal and we must be sure our mode of livelihood is far from them, not skirting or just avoiding them narrowly. Scrupulous honesty on all levels is mandatory. Further, livelihood encompasses our relationships with others such as suppliers, employees, government regulations, promotion (advertising)–every single aspect of business. And it also includes the highest standards in all aspects, as well. As I say, the scope of this is so vast that it is impossible to spell it all out, and frankly a worthy aspirant can figure it out without having every detail set forth.

6) Right Effort

Right Effort (vyayama) can also be translated as Right Endeavor. It is both doing the right thing and doing it in the right way. Here, too, the determination of "right" must be exceedingly broad and scrupulous. This includes action and acting in the right and beneficial and dharmic way. Right Effort has Nirvana for its goal. This, too, does not admit of superficiality, mere dabbling, or moseying along through life.

7) Right Mindfulness

Smriti means memory in the sense of keeping in mind what should be remembered, in other words holding the right perspective on things in the context of the principles of dharma that have been learned or experienced for oneself. However, the Pali word *Sati* means awareness and attention, as well. This does not mean being totally absorbed in the present moment or in every tiny external activity. Such an interpretation is outright silly. Rather, this principle means that we must never for a moment permit the right perspective to slip from our minds, and we must also remain fully conscious of our inner being, not letting it be overshadowed by externals. Our attention must be mostly focused inwardly and only peripherally on outward things. However, our outer attention must be so perfectly clear that we do all outer activities well and carefully. Nevertheless, our hearts must be intent on the inner work of attaining Buddhahood. Right Mindfulness includes being aware of the character of everything around us and the implications of all situations. It also means evaluating and responding to them in exactly the right way. It also entails knowing what should be paid attention to and what should be ignored.

8) Right Concentration

Although in later times samadhi became a technical yogic term for an intense state of interior union and superconsciousness, at the time of Buddha it simply referred to the state of meditative concentration. Samadhi included all meditative states, from the least to the highest, and was a matter of degree of contemplation. So samadhi could be spoken of as weak or strong, but the main point is that it must be Right. Now what does that mean? It means that meditation must accomplish its sole purpose: Nirvana (Moksha). A lot of meditation practices can give a buzz, a high, and entertain and even give psychic experiences, but none of that has anything to do with liberation; in fact, very little contemporary yoga does. Right samadhi can only be produced by right practice, which includes both right methodology and the right way of doing it.

A summary

This concludes my analysis of the Eightfold Path, but I would like to include a summary taken from a Theravada Buddhist source as I think it has a value of its own.

Right view=understanding suffering; understanding its origin; understanding its cessation; understanding the way leading to its cessation.

Right intention=intention of renunciation; intention of good will; intention of harmlessness.

Right speech=abstaining from false speech; abstaining from slanderous speech; abstaining from harsh speech; abstaining from idle chatter.

Right action=abstaining from taking life; abstaining from stealing; abstaining from sexual misconduct.

Right livelihood=giving up wrong livelihood; earning one's living by a right form of livelihood.

Right effort=the effort to restrain defilements; the effort to abandon defilements; the effort to develop wholesome states; the effort to maintain wholesome states.

Right mindfulness=mindful contemplation of the body; mindful contemplation of feelings; mindful contemplation of the mind; mindful contemplation of phenomena.

Right concentration=the four stages of meditation (jhana) culminating in liberation.

The Four Truths

The Four Truths are: 1) There is suffering. 2) Suffering has a cause. 3) Suffering can be ended. 4) There is a way to end suffering. These are so incredibly simple that it seems equally incredible that they should need explaining, but Buddha said that the people of earth had dust in their eyes and were blinded to even the basics. So we should take a brief look at each one for they can bring about a veritable breakthrough in awareness for those who comprehend them fully.

1) *There is suffering.* Also incredible is the fact that many people in the West, especially those who consider themselves Buddhist, complain that this truth is negative. This is of course typical of the distorted, reverse thinking that is a trait of Western minds: that it is not negative to be something negative, only negative to recognize the fact and say it. This is demonic psychology and it prevails in today's New Age. Truth is never negative, nor is its acknowledgement. Illness may be a negative state, but its recognition is potentially positive because it can lead to seeking a cure. Anyone who cannot endure to acknowledge the fact that there is suffering in the world is spiritually psychotic. Of course there is suffering. Yet Buddha did not stop there, but went on to tell us one of the most positive facts in the universe:

2) *Suffering has a cause.* If we cannot understand our situation in life we will be unable to determine its character and know how to proceed. All suffering comes from past wrong action which created the force we call karma. There are different kinds of suffering, but if we understand that karma is a metaphysical version of the law that for every action there is an equal and opposite reaction, we can understand exactly what kind of action caused our present status. Then Buddha gives us an even more positive truth:

3) *Suffering can be ended.* Suffering need not be accepted fatalistically as an inexorable inevitability, but can be ended and a life free from suffering created for us. And the best thing is that we can end it ourselves without dependence on another. This is an extremely positive affirmation of the power and capability of each human being.

4) *There is a way to end suffering.* There is a specific, methodical way to end suffering, to wipe out karma and prevent its future rising in the form of more birth and death in the material world. The

Buddha Way, the Eightfold Path, diligently pursued does this. It is actually very simple.

The best mental state

While working our way through the Eightfold Path, what should our basic mental state be? Buddha says that it is Vairagya. *A Brief Sanskrit Glossary* defines vairagya in this way: "Non-attachment; detachment; dispassion; absence of desire; disinterest; or indifference. Indifference towards and disgust for all worldly things and enjoyments." That pretty well says it all. We have had enough of getting caught up in ego-involved action for lifetimes, and we do not need to fall into the same trap regarding our following of the Eightfold Path. Rather, our spiritual pursuit should be done in a cool-minded, level-headed manner without anxiety, obsession, attachment, or any kind of passion whatsoever. Vairagya is the way to tread the Eightfold Path so that it becomes an ever-increasing source of peace and happiness.

The one with eyes to see

The best kind of human being is one whose inner eyes of unity and truth are open and operating in an effective manner. Anyone can discuss philosophy, but only the "seeing" can live it and reap its benefits. The opening of the eyes is a matter of evolution–nothing else can produce it. There is no use trying to open the eyes of others, it cannot (and should not) be done. Everything happens at the right time and it is solely the business and concern of the individual, not anyone else. It is certainly possible to force plant growth, but not human evolution. It is like birth: until the child is ready to be born the mother will not go into labor. A friend of mine refused to have labor induced after nine months of pregnancy. When her baby was born after a full ten months he was completely healthy and all the better for being allowed to wait until he was ready for birth. It is the same in the matter of spiritual conception and birth. Each one of us should pay attention to our own development and let others alone until they spontaneously awaken and begin to move along the way of conscious growth.

Purification

This indeed is the Way–there is no other–for the purification of one's vision. Follow this way. It leads to Mara's confusion (Dhammapada 274).

Harischandra Kaviratna: "This is the path; there is no other path that leads to purity of insight. Follow this path, for this path bewilders the Evil One (Mara)." Thanissaro Bhikkhu: "Just this is the path–there is no other–to purify vision. Follow it, and that will be Mara's bewilderment."

When he says this is the only way, Buddha does not mean this in a narrow sense. Rather, he is saying that all the elements listed previously put together form the only way to Nirvana. Buddha never claimed to be unique and the only one to become enlightened. Actually, he was a very traditional Sankhya yogi who was reviving Arya Dharma in his age.

Purification is the purpose of the path, for we have nothing to attain, only to reclaim, to recover. We are ever the perfect Buddha-Self, but we have lost awareness of that and created a labyrinth of false identities from life to life, piling up mountains of karma beneath which we seem to suffocate. But it is only the false side of us that acts and creates and reaps karma. Once we clear that falsity away, nothing remains but the Truth, the eternal Dharmakaya. That alone is freedom.

Such an attainment eludes the force of cosmic ignorance or Mara, for it is impossible for darkness to perceive the light. We need not battle evil or even reject it. Rather, like Buddha we ignore it and stay intent on our path to Nirvana. Nothing more is needed. Mara is only part of the great dream, as unreal as anything else within it. Awakening is our business, and we must be about it.

Ending suffering

Following this Path you will put an end to suffering. I have taught you the Way after realizing the removal of the arrow myself (Dhammapada 275).

When we are purified, the darkness of ignorance will disappear and so will suffering, for suffering is an illusion, a mirage.

"I have taught you the Way after realizing the removal of the arrow myself" is one of the great statements of the Dhammapada, for no one is a worthy teacher who has not first practiced and come to know the way. A teacher need not be a Buddha, but he must be a "son of the Buddha" whose feet are well along on the path and who will not waver or regress. Even Buddha could not teach what he had not himself already come to know. He often used the simile of an arrow wound in speaking of the desperate condition of ignorant human beings. We cannot live with the arrow, we must remove it–not just philosophize about it or hope that someone comes along one day to remove it. Each one must remove his own arrow. Until he had done so, Buddha did not presume to teach others.

You must do it yourself

Making the effort is your affair. The Buddhas have pointed out the Way. Those who are on the way and practicing meditation will be freed from Mara's bonds (Dhammapada 276).

No one saves us but we ourselves. No one attains enlightenment except by his own effort, and it is that which must absorb our attention, not intellectualizing, philosophizing, discussing, and confusing others by teaching what we do not really know ourselves. It is not just Gautama Buddha who is Self-awakened and Self-enlightened, but everyone who attains the goal. A religion which propounds any savior beyond ourself is a destroyer, an enemy worse than any vice. Even the greatest teacher can do no more than show the way, the rest is up to us. Anyone who claims to be able to help us or do it for us is a liar, especially those who pretend to be able to take on or free us from our karma. Karma is only a dream, and no one can wake up for us; we must awaken ourselves. And meditation, which is purely individual, is the way to awakening

Impermanence

All processes are impermanent. When one sees this with understanding, then one is disillusioned with the things of suffering. This is the Path of Purification. All processes are painful. When one sees this with understanding, then one is disillusioned

with the things of suffering. **This is the Path of Purification (Dhammapada 277, 278).**

Narada Thera: "Transient are all conditioned [sankhara] things: when this, with wisdom, one discerns, then is one disgusted with ill; this is the path to purity. Sorrowful are all conditioned things: when this, with wisdom, one discerns, then is one disgusted with ill; this is the path to purity."

Narada Thera notes: "Sankhara is a multisignificant term. Here it is used in the sense of things conditioned by causes. Supramundane Nirvana is not included in sankhara as it is not conditioned by any cause. It is causeless and timeless." He defines "ill" as: "Suffering caused by attending to the five Aggregates."

When we realize that nothing is permanent and that all things are conditioned–limited and defined–by their component parts, we see they are not to be clung to by the wise. There really are no things in themselves, but just varying combinations of substances that are nothing more than differing configurations of the basic factors of relative manifestation. Even the physical elements are varying arrangements of atomic particles. So nothing ever really exists as itself and all things are destined to break apart and dissolve.

This inevitable change produces myriad shades of discontent and unhappiness, filling our life with countless modes of suffering and stress. This is the nature of life in all relative levels of existence, not just this world in which we now find ourselves. Holding on to anything is to doom ourselves to disappointment since all things eventually change, including our body which we mistakenly think possesses what we cling to. So if things do not "die" out of our life, we will certain die to them. Renunciation, then, is simple wisdom, the only realistic response to life in this or any other world.

All processes are out of my control. When one sees this with understanding, then one is disillusioned with the things of suffering. This is the Path of Purification (Dhammapada 279).

Harischandra Kaviratna: "All forms of existence are unreal [an-atta]; he who perceives the truth of this gets disgusted with this world of suffering. This is the path to purity." Thanissaro Bhikkhu: "When you see with discernment, 'All phenomena are not-self'–you grow disenchanted with stress. This is the path to purity."

Buddha did not at any time teach that there is no Self. Just the opposite, he continually exhorted his hearers to know the Unborn and the Deathless–and that is the Self. Being in the line of classical Sankhya philosophers and yogis, he taught the doctrine of anatma (anatta): "Not-Self." ("No Self" is niratma or niratta, a term he never used.) This was a major characteristic of the teaching of Swami Sivananda, as well.

Anatma is the exposition of that which must be realized as not being the Self, as that with which we must not identify or even consider as having the slightest connection with us. There are two ways to express anatma: "That is not me" and "I am not that." The most perfect expression of anatma is found in the *Stanzas on Nirvana* by Shankaracharya:

> I am not the mind, intellect, thought, or ego;
> Not hearing, not tasting, not smelling, not seeing;
> I am not the elements—ether, earth, fire, air:
> I am the form of Conscious Bliss: I am Shiva!

> I am neither Prana, nor the five vital airs;
> Nor the seven components of the gross body;
> Nor the subtle bodies; nor organs of action:
> I am the form of Conscious Bliss: I am Shiva!

> I have no aversion, clinging, greed, delusion;
> No envy or pride, and no duty or purpose;
> I have no desire, and I have no freedom:
> I am the form of Conscious Bliss: I am Shiva!

> I have no merit or sin, nor pleasure or pain;
> No mantra, pilgrimage, Veda or sacrifice;

Not enjoying, enjoyable, or enjoyer:
I am the form of Conscious Bliss: I am Shiva!

I have no death or fear, no distinction of caste;
Neither father, nor mother, nor do I have birth;
No friend or relation, guru or disciple:
I am the form of Conscious Bliss: I am Shiva!

I am without attributes; I am without form;
I am all-pervading, I am omnipresent;
By senses untouched, neither free, nor knowable:
I am the form of Conscious Bliss: I am Shiva!

When we realize that nothing is ours and we have no relationship with anything, then we cultivate indifference (vairagya) to all things. Again, this is just being realistic. And it is the path to the end of suffering.

Laziness

Since he will not exert himself at the time for exertion, and although young and strong is full of indolence and irresolution and idleness, the lazy man is incapable of recognizing the way of wisdom (Dhammapada 280).

Harischandra Kaviratna: "He who does not get up when it is time to do so; who, although youthful and strong, is yet given to indolence, is weak in resolution and thought–such an idle and lazy person does not find the path to wisdom."

Laziness is a profound psychological flaw for it indicates weakness of will and intellect. The lazy will simply never find the path of wisdom. Spiritual indolence is the curse of the day. People not only do not want to put forth any effort at all (witness the man from India who emailed a few days ago telling us to provide him with a visa and the money for travel to America so he could live in our ashram), their minds are so debilitated that they cannot sustain any attention or act of will for more than a few minutes. The satirical book, *How To Become*

A Modern Guru, says that the attention span of the average "seeker" is about one-half second. That is an exaggeration for humor, but I have observed for nearly fifty years that it is rarely more than twenty minutes, unless strongly motivated by greed or fear. Then it may last a day or two. For that reason I never reply to a silly email because I know that by the time it was opened the writer had forgotten all about it and will not write again.

Three ways of wisdom

Be guarded in speech, restrained of mind and not doing anything wrong physically. Perfect these three forms of action, and fulfill the way taught by the sages (Dhammapada 281).

Many of the things required of the seeker for higher awareness are esoteric, abstract, or outright difficult. But some are quite easy—at least in principle—and these three are, though they entail the restraining and breaking of bad habits. Although they make take time to perfect, nevertheless they are simple to grasp and work at.

To be careful of speech entails always being truthful, not babbling on about trivia or pointless subjects, and never to be careless in speech and harm anyone in any way. I think we all know lots of people that are unthinkingly rude and embarrassing day and night. So this rule includes being aware of the effect of our words on other people. This implies recognizing the value of others and caring about them, though some people are so narcissistic that they do not even know others exist except as props in their private life-drama.

Besides controlling speech we must control the mind and not let it chatter on and on to no purpose. Some people seem incapable of shutting up mentally, and are always talking and fantasizing to themselves. For such people, who are usually incorrigible, meditation and any significant degree of spiritual life is simply impossible. So it is crucial that we do not become one of them. Also the mind must not be allowed to run after memories, fantasies, and emotional tangles.

When speech and mind are reined in it should not be very hard to no longer do any wrong physically, through the body, for all good and evil originate in the mind. Unfortunately there are people who pretend that they can do evil physically but it does not harm their spirit or mind. There are Fundamentalist Protestants who believe–or say they believe–that the body can sin independently of the individual. Anyone with good sense can see that is an impossibility, but morally degraded people do not have good sense, do they? Anyhow, Buddha says this lest there be those of such perverted intellect that they would claim to be self-disciplined in speech and thought while doing wrong through the body.

The important point is that those who follow these three precepts will then be able to "fulfill the way taught by the sages."

The source of wisdom

From meditation springs wisdom. From lack of meditation, loss of wisdom. Recognizing these alternative roads of progress and decline, one should so direct oneself so that one's wisdom will increase (Dhammapada 282).

From meditation springs wisdom. Although meditation is surely meant in this and the next sentence, the word used is *yoga*. The ancient Hindu and Buddhist texts spoke very alike and even used identical terminology. And that was because they were the same religion, really.

Anyhow, wisdom comes from meditation, from the opening of spiritual intuition by means of which the yogi comes to know far more than can be found written in books, and also to understand levels of truth that mere scholars do not even dream exist. The implication is also that without yoga there is no true wisdom, only unproved and indemonstrable ideas.

From lack of meditation, loss of wisdom. This is very interesting, for it means that those who do not meditate will lose even what wisdom they have, for there will be no stability in their minds to hold on to what they do know. It also implies that meditators who abandon their practice will lose that which they gained through it.

Recognizing these alternative roads of progress and decline, one should so direct oneself so that one's wisdom will increase. Yoga is the upward path, and life without yoga is the downward path. It is up to us to choose which we will take.

Cut it down and clear it away

Cut down the forest, not just a tree. Out of the forest of desire springs danger. By cutting down both the forest of desire and the brushwood of longing, be rid of the forest, bhikkhus (Dhammapada 283).

Thanissaro Bhikkhu: "Cut down the forest of desire, not the forest of trees. From the forest of desire come danger and fear. Having cut down this forest and its underbrush, monks, be deforested."

You can see that the translators do not agree on the first sentence. It is the same with others who are certainly reliable scholars, so we should consider both, as there is a good lesson in each mode of translation.

Cut down the forest, not just a tree. This is great wisdom. Those who set about to improve themselves just one trait or one mental aspect at a time will never manage, because the mind is seemingly infinite and they will just not have the time to completely change themselves. Plus all the aspects of the mind, like the trees of the forest, are interrelated. In his commentary on the Yoga Sutras Shankara uses the simile of a forest to point out that right meditation does not cut down one tree—one mental flaw—at a time, but it mows down the whole forest. It will take time, but not an eternity, to straighten out the mind.

Another fallacy is being warned against here. Some people think that if they do one good thing or conquer one negative trait it renders them a very good and worthy person. Certainly it shows their ability to correct themselves, but just changing a few undesirable habits is not sufficient. For example, in today's climate of shameless immorality there are people who try to cloak their evil by doing good deeds. They live in a hellish manner most of the time and then do volunteer work in a homeless shelter or drive handicapped people around the town, and make a point of letting everyone know they are doing it. But "doing good" does not make a person good. Swami Sivananda had a huge sign made and put up in the ashram: "BE good. DO good." First we must be good, otherwise it is only an appearance, a sham. More than one Nazi war criminal made the defense that they were good family men, as was the colossally evil Joseph Goebbels. Believe it or not, some people tried to defend the monster Klaus Barbie by saying that he played the piano beautifully and was kind to his grandchildren! And Joseph Mengele lived in a Christian commune to hide himself from the world's eye. It does not work.

Cut down the forest of desire, not the forest of trees. Actually this fits in with the foregoing, for Buddha is saying that making nice externally and obsessing on outer behavior and environment is not what we need. Rather, we must clear out the forest of the mind–specifically the forest of desire. Real change is inner change. Then the outer will automatically improve.

Out of the forest of desire springs danger. ("From the forest of desire come danger and fear.") Desire torments us with the fear that we may not be able to fulfill it, and the danger of possibly losing what we have already desired and gained. Further, it addicts us to more and more desire. Like any addiction it grows and grows until it completely devours us and we become mere shadow-slaves of desire. People become driven and tortured by desire, but like drunks who believe they are sober they do not realize the hell in which they live–in fact they are indignant if the truth of their situation is pointed out to them. Here is part of the commentary on the sixty-sixth verse of the Dhammapada that reveals this:

"Human beings are astonishing, even in their foolishness. One of the most astonishing follies is their insistence on doing things which bring them nothing but bitterness inwardly and outwardly. 'Aren't we having a good time?' they ask their fellow-fools, shuffling through their little dreary lives that are crammed with activity that is really doing nothing in the end result.

"I have already referred to the camel that chews on thorns that pierce its mouth and make it bleed, but keeps on chewing. People are the same. Over and over they do what makes them suffer, often resolving to never do it again, but just as often repeating their folly. Many more people are destroying themselves without any idea they are doing so. They are bewildered as to what the problem is, and keep on piling up the pain. Others have somehow anesthetized themselves so they do not even know they are suffering. That is why Buddha said the first step we must take is the acknowledgment of the fact of our suffering."

By cutting down both the forest of desire and the brushwood of longing, be rid of the forest, bhikkhus. ("Having cut down this forest and its underbrush, monks, be deforested.") We must not control or suppress desire, we must destroy its very roots and ensure that it cannot grow back and oppress us again. This is why Paramhansa Nityananda praised desirelessness and declared the desireless person to be liberated while living.

Buddha does not just mention the trees of the forest, but the underbrush, as well. This is so we will realize that the little things, the petty ways of human life, as just as dangerous and misery-producing as the trees of big delusions and desires. Many people think that if they eliminate the big, obviously destructive, faults they can keep the small ones and keep entertaining themselves by indulging them. Not so. Everything has to go under the axe of discipline and wisdom.

The condition of bondage

So long as the least desire of a man for women has not been eradicated, he is fettered in mind, like a sucking calf to its mother (Dhammapada 284).

Thanissaro Bhikkhu: "For as long as the least bit of underbrush of a man for women is not cleared away, the heart is fixated like a suckling calf on its mother."

Since he was speaking to monks, Buddha mentions the "desire of a man for women," but really what he is speaking about is the delusive sexual drive in any form. No matter how attenuated that attachment-addiction may be, if it is not totally eradicated the person is hopelessly bound and subject to rebirth and its attendant sufferings. Again, the underbrush is mentioned because it is easy to detect the intense, physical aspects of sex, but there are subtle sexual ties that are either unsuspected or seem to be harmless, even nobly romantic, or love that is "pure" or "spiritual."

What is wrong is desire and dependency in any form. Therefore:

Pluck out your desire, like one does an autumn lotus with one's hand. Devote yourself to the path of peace, the nirvana proclaimed by the Blessed One (Dhammapada 285).

Death

"Here I will spend the rainy season, and here the hot season." This is the way a fool thinks. It does not occur to him what may happen in between (Dhammapada 286).

According to commentators, Buddha is speaking of death, and is urging us to ever be aware that nothing of earthly life is sure, especially life itself. We should realize that all things planned are only tentative, and that the only sure thing is death.

This is not to be taken in a fearful or pessimistic sense, but should stimulate us to a constant awareness of the impermanence of all things, an awareness that will keep impelling us forward in the search for the Birthless and Deathless that alone is real and abiding. Otherwise:

Death comes and snatches away the man infatuated with children and livestock, while his mind is still full of desire, like a great flood sweeping away a sleeping village (Dhammapada 287).

For at that time:

There are no children to take refuge in then, no father or any other relative. When a man is seized by that terminator, Death, there is no taking refuge in family (Dhammapada 288).

Again, this is not negative or gloomy, but positive. For:

When he has seen the implications of this, a wise man, restrained by morality, should quickly develop the path leading to nirvana (Dhammapada 289).

Buddha thus shows us that awareness of the emptiness of earthly life and the practice of morality are the two basic ingredients of the attitude need to "quickly develop the path leading to nirvana."

How simple and how sure is the wisdom of Buddha.

Chapter 21
MISCELLANEOUS

Happiness for happiness
If he sees that by sacrificing a slight happiness he can obtain a greater happiness, then a wise man should sacrifice the lesser happiness with a view to the greater happiness (Dhammapada 290).

Perhaps the greatest obstacle to progress in spiritual life is our clinging to the pitiful things of earth which give only a fleeting and illusory happiness that usually results in some form of pain. Infinite joy (ananda) awaits us in the higher states of consciousness that culminate in the realization of God, yet we cling to the petty and unsure pleasures of relative existence, and thereby miss the everlasting abundance of Divine Bliss. Rare is the person who understands that by letting go of the tiny joys of earth it becomes possible to lay hold of eternal happiness that is boundless in its abundance and scope. Rarer still is the person who gladly and wisely tosses aside the attractions of this world to ascend to those of Divinity Itself.

This verse gives the perspective that all sadhakas should hold in relation to the necessary disciplines and sacrifices of the yogic path. Rather than grudgingly letting go of the tinsel of earth they gladly drop them in confidence of gaining joys presently inconceivable to the ordinary human beings. The Bhagavad Gita describes such a person in this way: "His mind is dead to the touch of the external: it is alive to the bliss of the Atman. Because his heart knows Brahman his happiness is for ever" (Bhagavad Gita 5:21). "Utterly quiet, made clean of passion, the mind of the yogi knows that Brahman: his bliss is the highest. Released from evil his mind is constant in contemplation: the way is easy, Brahman has touched him, that bliss is boundless" (Bhagavad Gita 6:27, 28).

The wrong path

He who seeks his own happiness by inflicting suffering on others, does not reach freedom from hatred, caught as he is in the toils of hatred (Dhammapada 291).

Venerable Thanissaro Bhikkhu: "He wants his own ease by giving others dis-ease. Intertwined in the interaction of hostility, from hostility he's not set free."

This unhappy mode of living is seen all around us, from the petty selfishness of individuals to the outrageous disregard of humanity by greedy business and government. Often it is cloaked in a pretense of seeking a higher good or even setting things in order. The Nazis specialized in this insane evil.

Here Buddha tells us the unerring principle that if our happiness or welfare involves the suffering or deprivation of others–including the taking of their life–then we are embodiments of hatred, of enmity for humanity. "These are deluded, sunk low among mortals. Their judgment is lost in the maze of Maya, until the heart is human no longer: changed within to the heart of a devil" (Bhagavad Gita 7:15). The Gita further describes such people in these words: "There is no truth in them, or purity, or right conduct....In the darkness of their little minds, these degraded creatures do horrible deeds, attempting to destroy the world. They are enemies of mankind. Their lust can never be appeased. They are arrogant, and vain, and drunk with pride. They run blindly after what is evil. The ends they work for are unclean. They are sure that life has only one purpose: gratification of the senses. And so they are plagued by innumerable cares, from which death alone can release them. Anxiety binds them with a hundred chains, delivering them over to lust and wrath. They are ceaselessly busy, piling up dishonest gains to satisfy their cravings. 'I wanted this and today I got it. I want that: I shall get it tomorrow. All these riches are now mine: soon I shall have more. I have killed this enemy. I will kill all the rest. I am a ruler of men. I enjoy the things of this world. I am successful, strong and happy. Who is my equal? I am so wealthy and so nobly born. I will sacrifice to the gods. I will give alms. I will make merry.' That is what they say to themselves, in the blindness of their ignorance. They are addicts of sensual pleasure, made restless by their many desires, and caught in the net of delusion. They fall into the filthy hell of their own evil minds....These malignant creatures are full of egoism, vanity, lust, wrath, and consciousness of power. They loathe me, and deny my presence both in themselves and in others. They are enemies of all men and of myself; cruel, despicable and vile. I cast them back, again and again, into the wombs of degraded parents, subjecting them to the wheel of birth and death. And so they are constantly reborn, in degradation and delusion. They do not reach me, but sink down to the lowest possible condition of the soul" (Bhagavad Gita 16:7, 9-16, 18-20). I know I cited this when commenting on verses fifteen and sixteen, but it is also relevant here.

Wrong priorities

What IS their affair is put aside. What is NOT their affair gets done. The inflow of thoughts in such brazen and careless people just goes on increasing (Dhammapada 292).

Harischandra Kaviratna: "If what ought to be done is neglected, and what ought not to be done is done, then the sensuous influxes of the arrogant and the heedless increase."

This is a thumbnail sketch of the human race in general: arrogant and heedless of realities, they despise and refuse to do what is right, and insist on loving and doing the wrong. That is the simple fact. So naturally the inflow of desires and aversions and foolish aspirations just keep on flowing in, drowning their spiritual consciousness and turning them into morally insane delusionals–hopelessly so, in most instances. Their heart-prayer is: "Lead us from the Real to the unreal; from Light to darkness; from Immortality to death." And their prayer is abundantly answered from life to life. As I just quoted: "The evil-doers turn not toward me: these are deluded, sunk low among mortals. Their judgment is lost in the maze of Maya, until the heart is human no longer: changed within to the heart of a devil" (Bhagavad Gita 7:15).

Right Priorities

They whose recollection of the body is always well established, however, have nothing to do with what is not their affair, always persevering in what IS their affair. The inflow of thoughts in such recollected and aware people simply dies away (Dhammapada 293).

Harischandra Kaviratna: "Those who are constantly watchful as to the nature of the body, who abstain from doing what ought not to be done, who strive to perform the deeds that ought to be done, who are mindful and self-restrained—in such men the sensuous influxes are extinguished."

Those who understand what is mortal and what is immortal, avoid wrong and gravitate toward the right, their innate goodness finally rising to the surface and bringing hope of their further emergence into the Light of Reality. To those who continually seek the Good and the True, impulses opposing their upward movement become weakened and then altogether annihilated.

Inner warfare

After killing mother, father and two warrior kings, and destroying the kingdom along with its subjects, the brahmin goes on his way unperturbed (Dhammapada 294).

Buddha, born a member of the warrior caste, here exhorts us to inner warfare. It it pretty well agreed that "mother" is desire and "father" is egotism, but the rest is not so sure. Basically, kings and kingdom—distracting powers and that upon which they so effectively act—should be destroyed along with all they imply and which are their side-effects. Only when this is done can the Brahmin, the Knower of Brahman, walk through life unperturbed. For this reason the Gita says:

"Smoke hides fire, dust hides a mirror, the womb hides the embryo: by lust the Atman is hidden. Lust hides the Atman in its hungry flames, the wise man's faithful foe. Intellect, senses and mind are fuel to its fire: thus it deludes the dweller in the body, bewildering his judgment. Therefore, Arjuna, you must first control your senses, then kill this evil thing which obstructs discriminative knowledge and realization of the Atman....Get control of the mind through spiritual discrimination. Then destroy your elusive enemy, who wears the form of lust" (Bhagavad Gita 3:38-41, 43).

When we realize that as an Essene Jesus was brought up on the spiritual traditions of the East, including Buddhism, and that he lived in Buddhist centers in India, we can understand what he really meant when he said: "If any man come to me, and hate not his father, and mother, and wife, and children, and brethren, and sisters, yea, and his own life also, he cannot be my disciple" (Luke 14:26). He is speaking of inner forces, not our families. Without an understanding of Indian religion (including Buddhism and Jainism as well as Hinduism) we cannot understand Jesus and his teachings. Buddha continues the theme, saying:

After killing mother, father and two priestly kings, and killed a tiger as his fifth victim, the brahmin goes on his way unperturbed (Dhammapada 295).

First he spoke of warrior kings—forces for personal gain and satisfaction—and now he speaks of priestly kings: forces of externalized philosophy and religion that really lead away from the reality of the aspirant's true nature. Whether the tiger is ego, desire, delusion, or suchlike, everything that is not real must be destroyed out of our consciousness. Then we can go on our way in peace toward Nirvana.

Well awakened

The next six verses in the translation of Venerable Narada Thera begin with the words "well awakened the disciples of Gautama ever arise...." There are many kinds of awakening that come to human beings, most of them negative such as awakening to the possibilities of ego and evil in its many forms. That is wrong awakening in contrast to the rare and wondrous awakening of which Buddha is going to speak.

As a student of Buddhist wisdom, Jesus was quite aware of these verses, and spoke of the two kinds of awakening, which he called "rising up" even though the English translations usually say "resurrection." He said: "Marvel not at this: for the hour is coming, in the which all that are in the graves shall hear his voice, and shall come forth; they that have done good, unto the resurrection of life; and they that have done evil, unto the resurrection of damnation [*krisis*–accusation or condemnation]" (John 5:28, 29). This has nothing to do with a mythological Last Day or end of the world, but is speaking of the effect and response that occurs when people hear the teaching of Eternal Wisdom. Some rise to life, and others rise to willful death of the the spirit-consciousness. No longer unaware of the laws of spiritual life (and death), their subsequent actions will determine their expansion or contraction of consciousness. So Buddha says:

Well awakened the disciples of Gautama ever arise–they who by day and night always contemplate the Buddha.

Well awakened the disciples of Gautama ever arise–they who by day and night always contemplate the Dharma.

Well awakened the disciples of Gautama ever arise–they who by day and night always contemplate the Sangha (Dhammapada 296-298).

These are of course the Three Refuges of those who ascribe to Buddhism. They are interpreted both externally and internally. The internal principles are the Buddha Nature of each sentient being, the Dharma that is the personal practice that will lead to Buddhahood, and the Sangha is gathering inward of the individual's powers in order to orient and impel them toward the attainment of Nirvana. (Sometimes the third element is said to be spiritual association with Buddhas and Bodhisattwas that can be invoked by the aspirant to be of assistance on the path to Nirvana.)

Well awakened the disciples of Gautama ever arise–they who by day and night always contemplate the body (Dhammapada 299).

Those who remain ever aware of the temporary and unreliable nature of the body–including the "body" of the material universe–will retain the correct perspective on their momentary life in this world and will develop the requisite attitudes toward them, especially intense disinterest and detachment.

Well awakened the disciples of Gautama ever arise–they who by day and night always delight in harmlessness (Dhammapada 300).

Ahimsa, nonviolence, is an absolute requisite for following the Buddha Way. And it is to be delighted in, not acted upon grudgingly or with dragging feet. Without a perfect–total–observance of ahimsa there no possibility of enlightenment.

Well awakened the disciples of Gautama ever arise–they who by day and night always delight in meditation (Dhammapada 301).

What I said just now about ahimsa applies to meditation as well.

The causes of difficulty in life

Hard is the life gone forth, hard to delight in. Hard is the miserable householder's life. It is painful to stay with dissonant people, painful to travel the road. So be neither traveler nor pained (Dhammapada 302–Thanissaro Bhikkhu).

"The life gone forth" is the usual term for monastic life. Here Buddha tells us that both the monastic and non-monastic life in this world are difficult and not easy to delight in. This is because both of them involve immersion in relative consciousness and intense awareness of this world. "The miserable householder's life" means that the householder life is miserable right across the board without exception. The "happily married" are simply unconscious of their perilous status, as are many monastics. In other words, life in this world is problematic whatever its external modes may be. The monastic must not be proud of his life and think he is superior to others, for if he is clear-sighted he will see that he is in the same boat as everyone else. As someone once remarked: "If you are on the Titanic it does not matter if you are booked in first class or steerage." The wise are ever aware of this and seek Nirvana whatever the external conditions of their life.

Everyone knows that living with discordant people is painful, and the world is composed of little else. All translators agree that a "traveller" is one enmeshed in the cycle of birth and death, whether in or out of the body (between incarnations). So we must become inwardly calm amidst the dissonant and eventually extricate ourselves altogether from "traveling" in any form.

Receiving honor

When a man has faith, is endowed with virtue, and possessed of fame and wealth, wherever he lives he will be honored (Dhammapada 303).

However, there is a great difference between those endowed with faith and virtue and those who are famous and wealthy. Usually those with fame and wealth are valueless in association, whereas the faithful and virtuous are of of great value when met with. One kind gains the honor of the deluded world and the other has the honor of the wise and those who seek to become wise.

The good are conspicuous a long way off, like a Himalayan peak, while the bad are just not noticed, like arrows shot into the dark (Dhammapada 303, 304).

This is the viewpoint of the seekers after enlightenment and those that are enlightened. The good are seen and the bad are unseen. The good exist in the world of wisdom and the bad and ignorant simply are ghosts to those pursuing the True. The good are real and the others are unreal. And it should be so for us. We should have no negative reactions to the negative, but expend our attention and energies on associating with and honoring the good.

Living alone in the forest

Living alone, sleeping alone, traveling alone, and resolute, alone and self disciplined, one should take pleasure in living in the forest (Dhammapada 305).

Buddha loved the forest life and permitted no other life for the monks, but some authoritative translators say that "the forest" is this world of desires and delusions. Kaivalya, independence, is a term for liberation used from ancient times. Even if surrounded by many others, the seeker is by the nature of his search always alone in the sense of isolation and independence. It is interesting that "monk" (*monachos*) means "one who lives alone" even though some monasteries have contained hundreds and even thousands of monks. (The monastery of Saint Pachomius in Egypt once had over thirty thousand monks.) A contemporary book on monastic life was aptly entitled *Living Together Alone*. Those who wish to live in a herd and have "community" are not fit for the monastic life, nor are monastic foundations that are herds or "families" true monasteries.

Chapter 22
A WOEFUL STATE

The Pali title of this section is *Niraya Vagga*. Some translate it "hell" and others translate it "a woeful state." Some verses can only mean an after-death state, but others can certainly apply to the future in this life or in another incarnation, as well. This should be kept in mind.

Perhaps more important is the need to face the fact that Buddha talked about hell—not in the way of Western religion, but certainly as a reality of which we should be aware. As I have mentioned before, in the West many people think that they can hide in Buddhism from "Judeo-Christian" moral principles and the belief in heaven and hell as consequences of keeping or breaking those rules. They fool no one but themselves. Morality, heaven, and hell are facts understood by all religions, however differently their presentation or attitude regarding them may be. A true disciple of Buddha will not try to blind himself to any part of Buddha's teaching. So here we go.

Untruth

He who speaks untruth goes to hell, as does he who, having done something, says, "I didn't do it." Men of ignoble behavior, they both end up the same in the next world (Dhammapada 306).

Thanissaro Bhikkhu: "He goes to hell, the one who asserts what didn't take place, as does the one who, having done, says, 'I didn't.' Both—low-acting people—there become equal: after death, in the world beyond."

Basically, lying in any form leads to hell or a miserable rebirth. This is the severest injunction against lying that I have found in any scripture, East or West. The yogis of India believe that speaking the truth literally strengthens and develops the subtle bodies, including that of the mind and the life force in general. Speaking untruth does the opposite, so a liar weakens both mind and body. A habitual liar is actually destroying his body and mind in this life and in future ones.

Buddha does not speak so forcefully because he hates lying, but out of mercy for the ignorant who do not realize the terrible effects of falsehood. This is what marks out the morality of East and West. The East enunciates moral principles to warn people and spare them suffering. The West thunders at them thinking to echo God and His anger and sure punishment of sinners. The motives are directly opposite and based on opposing concepts of both man and God. I cast my lot with the East, but again affirm that there is no way to avoid karmic retribution, whether we think we are being punished or merely experiencing the law of action and reaction. The behavior must be the same, even if for different reasons. As the song says: "There's no hiding place down there." Only Up There, away from it all.

Hypocrites

Many of those dressed in the yellow robe are evil and unrestrained, and the evil end up in hell because of their evil deeds (Dhammapada 307).

This is extremely clear, but I am afraid that many monastics in the various religions do not realize the truth of it. In Eastern Christianity they say: "Lower than a demon is a fallen monk"–but what if they had nothing to fall from to begin with? So many take up monastic life for personal advantage and material gain–it cannot be denied.

Only a few hours before coming to this verse for comment I was vividly remembering two truly unsavory Buddhist monastics, one a man and the other a woman, whom I saw at a Buddhist vegetarian restaurant. They came in ushered by fawning groupies who began running around making sure everything was perfect for them, and as usual with that sort, just making confusion and disorder. Nevertheless, the "jewels in the lotus" were gratified to see how anxious their dupes were to serve them. The outfits of both were a combination of Buddhist monastic dress and "designer" accessories of varying degrees of pretentious uselessness. They began divesting themselves of these accretions as they stared hostilely at me and the monks I was with. I assumed they were used to being the only monastics and claiming all the attention. Fortunately, a few minutes' scrutiny convinced them that we were just a rag-tag bunch without enough sense or savvy to be competition. So they settled back to ordering regally and quietly bullying their groupies over this and that. The groupies were in apprehensive delight at such attention.

Buddha had just such in mind when he spoke this verse. There is a spiritual Mafia, and he meant them.

It is better to swallow a red-hot, flaming iron ball than for an unrestrained and immoral person to eat the alms food of the land (Dhammapada 308).

One thing that has deeply impressed me about authentic Buddhist monastics is their extreme care in spending the money given to them by the laity. They never spend a mite on something not needed, and they are scrupulous custodians of material objects given to them. This noble behavior puts to shame those who are not so conscientious. Even worse, of course, are the immoral and undisciplined who by wearing the robes insult and dishonor the Buddha and the Sangha. Them I have seen, too.

Buddha shows us the severity of the karma of those hypocrites who plunder the well-meaning and pure-hearted who trust them. Certainly, the merit of those good people is as great as though they gave to the Buddha himself, but the demerit of those false monastics is colossal.

The adulterous

The thoughtless man who consorts with another man's wife encounters four things: accumulation of demerit, disturbed sleep, thirdly disgrace, and hell fourth.

Accumulation of demerit, a bad rebirth and the slight pleasure of a frightened man and a frightened woman–while the

authorities impose a severe penalty too. Therefore a man should not consort with another man's wife (Dhammapada 309, 310).

What more is to be said? An evil present begets an evil future.

Unworthy monasticism

In the same way that a wrongly handled blade of grass will cut one's hand, so a badly fulfilled life in religion will drag one down to hell (Dhammapada 311).

Narada Thera: "Just as kusha grass, wrongly grasped, cuts the hand, even so the monkhood wrongly handled drags one to a woeful state."

Having cut myself with kusha grass (it feels like the worst possible paper cut), I understand the simile. You must handle kusha grass just right–or else. Kusha grass is extremely valuable because it insulates from cold and damp. This benefits both the meditator and the sleeper. I have slept on damp ground in the Indian winter and been warm and dry because I was lying on kusha mats. But the yogi must be careful how he handles his treasure. In the same way monastic life is a great boon, a protection, and a fortress of peace if lived rightly. If not, it becomes the opposite, and the destruction of the unworthy.

Worthless behavior

Lax behavior, broken observances and dubious chastity– these are of no great benefit (Dhammapada 312).

Buddha was aware that many would be half-hearted in their spiritual life–not outright transgressing but always being borderline and iffy in all they did. Not bad people, but not good, either. Jesus, having studied the words of Buddha, perhaps had this verse in mind when he said: "I know thy works, that thou art neither cold nor hot: I would thou wert cold or hot. So then because thou art lukewarm, and neither cold nor hot, I will spew thee out of my mouth" (Revelation 3:15, 16). Not an appealing prospect.

Such people are so mediocre and meaningless in their life that they do not incur the terrible karmic consequences Buddha has been warning about. Instead they muddle through this life and their future ones, just being nothing much at all.

Do worthy deeds in a worthy manner

If it ought to be done, then do it; apply yourself to it strenuously. A lax man of religion just spreads even more dust (Dhammapada 313).

Here Buddha goes directly to the heart of most aspirant's problems: laxity. If we grasp how crucial it is to seek enlightenment, we should devote our entire life to it, making it the prime purpose of our whole life. Those who just mosey along the path, careful that they take no risks and incur no inconvenience, will never amount to anything. Worse, they will have created the habit of carelessness and neglect that may reach into future lives and retard their progress—or stop it altogether.

If you ever find yourself saying about any aspect of spiritual life: "That is for monks," know that you are in danger. I have never heard those words spoken in honesty. They are a tragic denial of spiritual realities and the kind of lie that Buddha says in verse three hundred six leads to hell. It is as harmful to say: "I don't need to do it" when we should, as it is to say: "I didn't do it," when we did. The Buddha Way is the same for all.

Avoid the bad, do the good

A bad action is best left undone. One is punished later for a bad action. But a good deed is best done, for which one will not be punished for doing it (Dhammapada 314).

Narada Thera: "An evil deed is better not done: a misdeed torments one hereafter. Better it is to do a good deed, after doing which one does not grieve."

Karma is the law—pure and simple.

Guard yourself

Guard yourself like a frontier town, guarded inside and out. Do not let a moment slip you by. Those who have missed their

opportunity grieve for it when they end up in hell (Dhammapada 315).

Harischandra Kaviratna: "As a frontier city, well-guarded within and without, so guard yourself. Do not lose a single moment, for those who let opportunity slip away do indeed grieve when they are born in the woeful state (hell)."

This is an excellent simile. A frontier town is in danger of being invaded by foreign forces. In our true nature we are Buddhas, but we have been invaded and occupied for so long by worldly ways and attitudes that we think to seek Buddhahood is some kind of astounding and impossible thing, that it goes against nature when just the opposite is true.

We must be guarded inwardly and outwardly against all that is not compatible with who we really are, which in any way dims our awareness of the upanishadic dictum: Tat Twam Asi–"That Thou art." Unless we are vigilant against alien invasion (and continued occupation), we render our aspirations completely useless. That is why there are so many Buddhists and so few Buddhas, so many Christians and so few Christs.

Swami Sivananda wrote a song that said: "It is difficult to get a human birth; so do your very best to realize in this birth…." Every moment, literally every waking breath, is an opportunity not to be missed if we would not live in regret later on, whether in this world or another.

Bad rebirth

Ashamed of what is not a matter for shame, and not ashamed of what is, by holding to wrong views people go to a bad rebirth.

Seeing danger where there is no danger, and not seeing danger where there is, by holding to wrong views people go to a bad rebirth.

Seeing a fault in what is not a fault, and not seeing a fault in what is, by holding to wrong views people go to a bad rebirth (Dhammapada 316-318).

Elsewhere Buddha has said that the ability to feel shame is a sign of awakening. But the feeling must be appropriate. We must know what is laudable and what is reprehensible–in the perspective of a Buddha, not a bound and ignorant samsarin. Consider how may people think that taking up spiritual life and discipline will be a danger ("you can go crazy, you know…people will think you are a kook… what if it's all a fantasy…"), but that living in a heedless and degraded state will be safe. And how many see all kinds of faults in "organized religion" and its members, but none in worldly endeavors and associations or the deluded people whose company they cultivate and value. Turning from the medicine of immortality they frantically gulp down the poison of false identity and foolish action. They are "inclusive" and "non-judgmental"–but only in relation to evil. The good they shun and denigrate. What, then, can await them in this or any world?

Good rebirth

Recognizing a fault as a fault, and what is not a fault as not one, by holding to right views people go to a good rebirth (Dhammapada 319).

This is why Buddha avoided abstruse metaphysics and advocated simple, good, common sense. To know the good as good and the evil as evil is a sure path to the Good and the True.

Chapter 23

THE ELEPHANT

In India the elephant is King of Beasts because of its intelligence. Although elephants are often used in forestry, they can be taught amazing skills. Only recently I reread *Mooltiki and Other Stories,* a collection of true stories by Rumer Godden. The last story was about Mooltiki, an elephant that showed amazing intelligence and had a very definite (sometimes difficult) personality. Mooltiki was living in a hunting camp on the border of Bhutan. It was essential that a fire be kept burning all night to keep away the many tigers and leopards that lived in the area. Mooltiki was the fire tender. Three times a night she brought small tree trunks, made a pyramid shape of them on top of the low-burning fire, and got them to blaze up, even moving the hot coals around with her foot. In the day she gathered the fuel, but if it ran out she went into the jungle in the deep of night and got more. She never ripped leafy branches off trees and waved them about the way other elephants do. Rather, when she saw a particularly beautiful flower she would delicately pick it and carry it in her trunk. When she crossed a river she loved to put her trunk under the water and blow bubbles–another thing elephants do not usually do. Though Mooltiki was cantankerous and often unkind to Rumer Godden, still she liked going for jungle walks with Mooltiki because she knew she was with a real person, not a "beast" at all.

Buddha takes the good qualities of elephants and uses them to teach us how to live.

Patient endurance

I will bear criticism like an elephant in battle bears an arrow from a bow. Most people are bad in behavior (Dhammapada 320).

Narada Thera: "As an elephant in the battlefield withstands the arrows shot from a bow, even so will I endure abuse; verily most people are undisciplined." Thanissaro Bhikkhu: "I–like an elephant in battle, enduring an arrow shot from a bow–will endure a false accusation, for the mass of people have no principles."

People in difficult situations are often advised to be thick-skinned like an elephant and not get pierced with the arrows of negative speech and acts directed toward them. Sri Ramakrishna often said that when an elephant walks down the street all the little dogs bark, but the elephant pays no attention and just keeps on walking. So must the sadhaka be.

The continual straightforwardness of Buddha's speech in the Pali Sutras is a welcome break from the mindless, false "positivity" of popular metaphysical philosophers. Everybody is not just wonderful, wonderful. Plenty of people are real stinkers. So Buddha counsels us to be aware that most people are uncontrolled and unprincipled, that we should just accept the fact without negative reaction and go on with our life just like Sri Ramakrishna's elephant.

The best of men

One can take a trained elephant even into a crowd. The king himself will ride a trained elephant. He who is disciplined is the best of men, since he can bear criticism (Dhammapada 321).

This verse continues the theme of the previous one, but it contains a valuable implication. Many people undergo all types of ascetic disciplines, especially in the matter of diet, living frugally and even uncomfortably. Yet when confronted with negativity from others they explode and are more abusive and violent than ordinary people. One of my friends in India, a remarkable yoga-siddha, told me one of his disciples ate nothing but sal leaves (the kind that are usually stitched together and used as leaf plates), that she gave him some she had cooked up and he could not bear to eat it. She slept very little and lived in a bare room with almost nothing. Yet all his other disciples detested her because she was so nasty and contemptuous of everybody. In his autobiography, *In the Vision of God*, Swami Ramdas tells of several ascetics who were colossally egotistical and incredibly rude to others. According to Buddha such people are not truly disciplined at all, so we should not be impressed with external disciplines that the great Thai master, Ajaan Lee, said is usually nothing but an expression of self-loathing.

Reaching the Unattainable

Trained mules are excellent, and so are thoroughbred horses from the Sindh, and so are great battle elephants, but more excellent than them all is a disciplined man.

There is no reaching the Unattainable with mounts like these, but with himself well under control a disciplined man can get there (Dhammapada 322, 323).

Narada Thera: "Excellent are trained mules, so are thoroughbred horses of Sindh and noble tusked elephants; but far better is he who has trained himself. Surely never by those vehicles would one go to the untrodden land (Nirvana), as does one who is controlled through his subdued and well-trained self."

Nirvana is unattainable, is untrodden, by earthbound consciousness, but it is attained by one who has cut off the sensual and egoistic life and risen above them. The necessity for this is given by Buddha next, when he says:

Dhammapalo, the elephant, is hard to control in rut. Even when tied up, he refuses his food. The great tusker is thinking of the elephant forest (Dhammapada 324).

This is a perfect picture of the human being whose mind has been seized by moha (delusive attachment/attraction) and addiction to both senses and the ego. It cannot think of anything but what it wants, or thinks it wants. It refuses even food, for nothing can distract it from its passionate desire. The desire may be for things material or abstract but the root–delusion–is the same. At such times we experience the incredible ability of the mind to focus on a single thing and direct all its energies toward it. The ability is a great virtue, but it is directed to vice. Buddha is hinting to us that we must discipline the mind before it gets into the Dhammapalo state. There is more regarding this:

When a man is a lie-abed and over-eats, a lazy person who wallows in sleep like a great over-fed hog, a fool [dullard] like that will be reborn time after time (Dhammapada 325).

Some people are like this physically, and some are like this mentally (quite a few are both), but the result is the same: continual rebirth. Such a one does not even merit hell.

The needed resolve

My mind used formerly to go off wandering wherever it felt like, following its own inclination, but today I shall control it carefully, like a mahout does a rutting elephant (Dhammapada 326).

This is a most wise and necessary resolve. Just because the mind has roamed about for lifetimes does not mean that it cannot stand still. How does a mahout control an elephant? First, by sitting atop it, being above it. This is accomplished by simple attention, strange as that may seem. By calmly observing the mind, it also becomes calm. However, at times a sharp prick with a goad is required. The goad we need is discipline, however little the mind may like that. It may be unpleasant, but it saves us from much greater pain. As Krishna says in the Gita: "Patiently, little by little, a man must free himself from all mental distractions, with the aid of the intelligent will....No matter where the restless and the unquiet mind wanders, it must be drawn back" (Bhagavad Gita 6:25, 26). "The truly admirable man controls his senses by the power of his will" (Bhagavad Gita 3:7).

Meditation is essential. As Krishna further says: "Make a habit of practicing meditation, and do not let your mind be distracted" (Bhagavad Gita 8:8). "In this yoga, the will is directed singly toward one ideal. When a man lacks this discrimination, his will wanders in all directions, after innumerable aims" (Bhagavad Gita 2:41). Buddha did not gain enlightenment through philosophy or austerity, but through meditation.

Intelligence and will

Take pleasure in being careful. Guard your mind well. Extricate yourself from the mire, like a great tusker sunk in the mud (Dhammapada 327).

Narada Thera: "Take delight in heedfulness. Guard your mind well. Draw yourselves out of the evil way as did the elephant sunk in the mire."

True heedfulness, or sati, is not a dose of bitter medicine, but actually brings happiness and delight. It only needs to be carefully attended to, and we soon discover the great peace and relief it brings. When we are intelligently aware, by our own will we can lift ourselves out of the aeons-old muck of ignorance that has been blinding and tormenting us for so long. We need not depend on any other than ourselves. This is a cardinal teaching of Buddha.

All religions (including popular Buddhism) cater to human laziness and lack of will by recommending good deeds and calling on external powers such as devas and ancestral spirits. Taking refuge in Buddha, Dharma, and Sangha is made into a fetish in modern Buddhism, even though enlightened teachers such as Ajahn Lee of the Thai Forest Tradition have explained that these three Gems are really internal, part of each one of us, and taking refuge is purely psychological. In Mahayana Buddhism people become obsessed with going from teacher to teacher and holy place to holy place, "taking the refuges" and "taking the precepts," as if there will be a magical effect, that suddenly everything will straighten out for them without their doing anything but hitting on the right person or place to make it all work. What could be further from Buddha's teaching?

Good company

If you find an intelligent companion, a wise and well-behaved person going the same way as yourself, then go along with him, overcoming all dangers, pleased at heart and mindful (Dhammapada 328).

Good company is a valuable factor in spiritual life. In Hinduism it is called satsang, company with Truth or company with the True (Real), because a good and wise person who diligently cultivates The Way brings us into contract with liberating reality by his mere presence. Notice that Buddha does not tell us to grovel before a guru and consider ourselves helpless without him. Rather, he tells us to find a fellow-seeker (not someone who claims enlightenment) and travel along with him to the Goal. As I point out before, when Swami Sri Yukteswar Giri, the guru of Paramhansa Yogananda, instructed someone in yoga he would ask them if they knew anyone else who did the same practice. If they did, he would advise them to make that person their only friend and to meditate and associate with them as much as possible. The value of real spiritual companionship can hardly be overestimated.

But...

But if you do not find an intelligent companion, a wise and well-behaved person going the same way as yourself, then go on your way alone, like a king abandoning a conquered kingdom, or like a great elephant in the deep forest (Dhammapada 329).

Valuable as a spiritual companion is, next best is striking out on your own, completely independent and moving silently through the world like a silent elephant deep in the inner forest of your own cultivated awareness. Certainly we would like some kind of spiritual company–that is understandable,. But we must not settle for association with the half-sighted, those that do not understand the goal or the means of the Buddha Way. For the company of those who do not comprehend higher truth–and especially those who have no effective cultivation practices–will only acclimatize us to a half-way status and perhaps halt our progress. No matter how sincere and good-hearted and well-meaning people may be, ignorance is still ignorance and is a mark of the bound, not the free. Their company is not better than nothing, it is worse than nothing. Therefore Buddha continues:

It is better to travel alone. There is no companionship with a fool. Go on your way alone and commit no evil, without cares like a great elephant in the deep forest (Dhammapada 330).

This implies that the company of the ignorant exposes us to evil and care, which it most certainly does. Go on alone.

Good

There are many definitions of good, and now Buddha lists some factors of life that both are good and bring good to ourselves and others.

It is good to have companions when occasion arises, and it is good to be contented with whatever comes. Merit is good at the close of life, and the elimination of all suffering is good.

Good is filial devotion to one's mother in the world, and devotion to one's father is good. It is good to be a sannyasi in the world and to be a brahmin too.

Good is good behavior up to old age, good is firmly established faith, good is the acquisition of understanding, and abstention from evil is good (Dhammapada 331-333).

It is good to have companions when occasion arises. Lest we think from what has just been said that Buddha wants us to become anti-social recluses, he tells us that on occasion we will meet worthy people, and that when we do it is good to be with them for however long they will be in the orbit of our life. And of course, if one or more begin living right near us, permanent association will be a great good.

It is good to be contented with whatever comes. Easily said, not so easily done. Meditation is the key.

Merit is good at the close of life. Indeed so, for accumulated merit can ensure that we will leave this world "in knowing, not in unknowing" (Maha Rahulovada Sutra). At the time of death everything distills and the state of mind that most arose during our lifetime will be that at the time of our death. So also Buddha is warning us that waiting till the end of life to follow dharma may have very little effect. It does become a matter of: "He that is unjust, let him be unjust still: and he which is filthy, let him be filthy still: and he that is righteous, let him be righteous still: and he that is holy, let him be holy still" (Revelation 22:1). As another Buddhist texts says: "I have nothing but my actions; I shall have nothing but my actions." So the wise begin accumulating merit right now and keep on doing so. Merit can also guarantee an easy transition from this plane to another.

The elimination of all suffering is good. I should say so! But easier said than done. Cultivation is the only way to eliminate suffering, and the only way to rid ourselves of all (actual or potential) suffering is to free ourselves from the bonds of rebirth. Here, too, Buddha is reminding us that it is a lifetime project.

Good is filial devotion to one's mother in the world, and devotion to one's father is good. Sad to say, there are people who think that rejection or neglect of their family is spiritual. Buddha tells us otherwise. Even though parents may not be the best, still a great debt is owed them, for without this human birth there would be no way to strive for liberation. Often parents do not earn respect from their children, but respectful attitude and behavior is a must—even if done from a distance if the parents are incorrigible. This is not always easy, but it is a mark of progress and lessening of ego when we can manage.

It is good to be a sannyasi in the world and to be a brahmin too. It is good to be a renouncer of the artificial world of deluded humanity, but mere renunciation does not guarantee true wisdom. Many monastics are mental and moral ruins because they have no real insight or knowledge. They must also be "brahmins"–knowers of Brahman.

Good is good behavior up to old age. Lifetime goodness is a good investment.

Good is firmly established faith. Such faith produces positive confidence in dharma and in our following of dharma. It also ensures steadiness of practice and focus of will.

Good is the acquisition of understanding. That is why the Bhagavad Gita says: "Lose discrimination, and you miss life's only purpose.... The blazing fire turns wood to ashes: the fire of knowledge turns all karmas to ashes. On earth there is no purifier as great as this knowledge, when a man is made perfect in yoga, he knows its truth within his heart. (Bhagavad Gita 2:63, 4:37, 38)

Abstention from evil is good. No one is good who engages in evil, no life that has even a taint of evil can be called a good life. Absolute purity is a requisite for enlightenment. No one rises above this law.

Chapter 24

CRAVING

The Pali word translated "craving" is *tanha*, which is the exact equivalent of the Sanskrit word *trishna* which means internal or external thirst, craving, or desire. Since this is the cause of so much activity and eventual suffering, and its elimination brings peace, an entire section of the Dhammapada is devoted to the subject.

Increase of craving
The desire of a thoughtlessly living man grows like a creeper. He drifts from one life to another like a monkey looking for fruit in the forest (Dhammapada 334).

Thanissaro Bhikkhu: "When a person lives heedlessly, his craving grows like a creeping vine. He runs now here and now there, as if looking for fruit: a monkey in the forest."

Heedless living is the order of the day. Narada Thera renders it "addicted to careless living," reminiscent of Judge Robert Bork's book title: *Slouching Toward Gomorrah*. In the main people dress, act, speak, and think like slouches. Cheapness and heedlessness are the marks of contemporary society. Some might call it casual, but only a fool lives casually, and Buddha explains why. Beneath the pretence of the easy-going mellowness of the "no sweat" slouchers intense craving festers. But since they are so indolent they crave the easily attained, especially turning to drugs to achieve mental and emotional states they are too lazy to pursue legitimately. Their recreation is equally banal and pointless, as are their lives in every aspect. Those who can afford it

280

sometimes become hyper-active Beautiful People, but their cheapness and shallowness just costs a lot more.

Although those in the grip of desire do go from life to life, that is an interpretive translation. Thanissaro Bhikkhu renders it literally, "He runs now here and now there," which makes more sense. People run here and there, "channel surfing" their life, living like a restless monkey in the forest of desire.

Increase of sorrow

When one is overcome by this wretched, clinging desire in the world, one's sorrows increase like grass growing up after a lot of rain.

But when one masters this wretched desire, which is so hard to overcome, then one's sorrows just drop off, like a drop of water off a lotus (Dhammapada 335, 336).

We are surrounded by a deluge of books, articles, talks, and seminars on peace, but there is no peace. Yoga is touted as a way to peace, "getting saved" is a supposed way to peace, and of course there are the hostile endeavors of peace activism and the futility of peace conferences and peace negotiations. "They have seduced my people, saying, Peace; and there was no peace" (Ezekiel 13:10). It is all totally without value or effect. Why? Because craving increases sorrow like grass growing after rain. There is only one way out: the overcoming of desire. It is hard to do, but there is no other way. When desire is gone, sorrow is gone. The lotus is not touched by the water; its oily surface repels it. And wisdom repels desire.

The way to peace

This is what I say to you—Good luck be with you, gathered here. Dig up the root of craving, as one does a weed for its fragrant root. Do not let Mara destroy you again and again, like a stream does its reeds (Dhammapada 337).

Buddha truly wishes us well ("good luck be with you"), so he tells us the straight truth. Craving must not just be suppressed, made dormant, or lessened, it must be dug totally out of our minds and heart. Otherwise we will be drowned in the river of ignorance and negativity again and again, even from life to life. Let us face it: life in this world kills us; and the root of worldly life is desire. Otherwise:

In the same way that even a felled tree will grow again if its root is strong and undamaged, so if latent desire has not been rooted out, then suffering shoots up again and again (Dhammapada 338).

Streams of craving

When the thirty six pleasure-bound streams of craving are strong in a man, then numerous desire-based thoughts pull the deluded man along.

The streams (of craving) flow everywhere, and the creeper shoots up and establishes itself, so when you see the creeper shooting up, cut away its root with your understanding (Dhammapada 339, 340).

It is insight alone, true intuitional wisdom, that can cut away craving.

Seekers of enjoyment

The recollection and attraction of pleasures occur to a man, and those who are attached to the agreeable and seeking enjoyment, they are the people subject to birth and aging (Dhammapada 341).

"Are you happy?" is the mindless cant of "those who are attached to the agreeable and seeking enjoyment." "The pursuit of happiness" is a pathetic exercise in futility when it is out-turned, for happiness (sukha) and joy (ananda) are found only within. "It tastes like 'more'" is a kind of southern pleasantry when eating something good, but it unfortunately becomes a philosophy of life: "If it feels good, do it." What insanity. It reminds me of the radio adaption of *Arsenic and Old Lace*. One of the poisoners fondly remembers that one of the old men they poisoned "lived long enough to say it tasted good." Saint Ignatius of Antioch, a disciple of the Apostle John, wrote of people who ingest spiritual poison and "sweetly drink in their death." Birth and decay are the bitterness within the "good things of life," as they experience, but yet do not learn.

Trapped

People beset by desire run here and there, like a snared rabbit, and those trapped in the bonds of attachments keep returning for a long time to suffering.

People beset by desire run here and there, like a snared rabbit, so one should get rid of one's craving if it is freedom from desire that one wants (Dhammapada 342, 343).

Hamsters run and run in their wheel and get absolutely nowhere; in the same way people rush here and there, busy and distracted, not knowing that they are really tied down. As Sri Ramakrishna said, a human's supposed free will is nothing more than the length of the rope an animal is tied to. It moves about freely in that area, but no more. Everyone is tied to the stake of death and does not know it. They are awaiting slaughter all unaware. One time in South India I saw a herd of ducks obsessively and fearfully clustering around their owner as he went to market. When he got there, they crowded up to him and stood completely still. Every so often someone would approach and point out a duck they wanted to buy. He would reach down, pick up the duck, and deftly break its neck in one swift movement. And that duck had felt so secure, so safe, being near him—as the others still did. Freedom from desire in the only real freedom and safety.

Return to bondage

When a man out of the forest of desire is drawn back into the forest, then free from the forest as he is, he runs back into it. Look at him—free, he is running back to chains (Dhammapada 344).

A lot of people manage a momentary escape from the bonds of earthly life and then turn and run right back into the prison. In the same way people temporarily are free of desire, especially when great sorrow comes to them or death is witnessed. But it is only a momentary distraction, and in a little while they are again gripped and driven by craving. Someone's spouse dies and they swear they will never marry anyone else, but often in a matter of months "the old ball and chain" gets welded on again. People are grieved at the death of a beloved pet and declare that they will never get another one, but after a bit they get not one, but two. If freedom is not permanent it is not freedom at all.

The fetters

The wise say that it is not an iron, wooden or fiber fetter which is a strong one, but the besotted hankering after trinkets, children and wives, that, say the wise, is the strong fetter. It drags one down, and loose as it feels, it is hard to break. Breaking this fetter, people renounce the world, free from longing and abandoning sensuality (Dhammapada 345, 346).

The wise say that it is not an iron, wooden or fiber fetter which is a strong one. No external bonds, even though forged of steel, are strong when compared with our mental bonds, for intense and powerful as the outer world is, the inner world is much more so. The result is that mental bonds are the strongest, but it also means that we have the inner power to shatter those bonds. So the message is also optimistic and should be kept in mind as we consider the rest of the verse.

But the besotted hankering after trinkets, children and wives, that, say the wise, is the strong fetter. What is to be said? Yearning for possessions, including possessing a family of one's own, is the strong fetter. Buddha was speaking to monks, so naturally he spoke of wives, but his words apply equally to women who feel a dependent need for husbands. "Man must have his mate" is denied by Buddha, and he ought to know, because he had a wife and child along with great wealth, but freed himself by cutting the outer and inner bonds, and so can we. The bound do not like it, but the saying that a woman needs a man like a fish needs a bicycle is certainly true, and it applies equally to a man needing a woman.

Actually, it applies to any "need" whatsoever. Freedom is a wonderful thing, and wonderful are those who seek and attain it.

It drags one down. Those who are in bondage often deny it. An acquaintance of mine was a psychologist in a federal prison. He had a patient who vehemently denied being a prisoner and insisted that she was a resident employee. He could not speak with her at all of her real situation or she would get hysterical. She was highly intelligent and capable, but unable to accept reality. In the same way, the slaves are insulted when their status is accurately named and analyzed. But Buddha is speaking to those who can face the facts: material life and material relationships drag us down and degrade us. From childhood I watched people being subjected and degraded by their wives and husbands. I saw the life crushed out of people so their personalities and ideas would not get in the way of a selfish and manipulative spouse's wishes and ambitions. Many of them were completely unaware of it, and others were resigned to it like the prisoners they were. "The old ball and chain" is no joke. And when the horror is compounded by greedy, demanding and disrespectful children, it is inexpressible misery.

And loose as it feels, it is hard to break. Sri Ramakrishna often spoke of the way a washerman would pass a rope around the legs of his donkey at night. Thinking he was bound, the donkey would not move the entire night. That is the way of the bound: their bondage is false, only in their mind. In the same way, as Buddha points out here, the bound often feel free–after all, they chose to be bound and exerted their utmost power to win their "mate" and be tied to them. (Pathetic are those who think that if they do not get married to their "partner" they will not be bound. It is a case of self-delusion.)

Few things are more tragic than the ideal spouse who is loving, sacrificing, forgiving, generous and totally faithful to a worthless, undeserving, and often abusive mate. I have seen those, too. Their love and caring were also terrible bonds. One of my aunts was such a wife, married to an infantile, selfish and cold-hearted man who was never overtly abusive only because he was so indifferent to her. "I would not want to live if George died," she told me with complete sincerity. But when he died she found what it was to live, and for nearly twenty years enjoyed herself as she had never done during the time she was his house-slave. (He would not wear clothes that were not warm from just being ironed. She would have to set up an ironing board outside the bathroom when he took a shower and hand the clothes in to him the moment they were ironed.) I will never forget the panic and outright fear displayed by a beautiful and intelligent friend of mine when she saw by her watch that she might not get home in time for her husband to see her bringing food to the table when he opened the house door at the end of his work day. (I do not exaggerate. He demanded that upon opening the door she should literally be bringing the food to the table.) She seemed to think it not at all unreasonable of him. How tight that "loose" bond was around her neck. For most people it is impossible to break. Some remain slaves even when the spouse has died. A cousin of mine was a genuine hellion. Although she died, for the rest of his life (decades) her husband would do things, saying: "Amy would want me to," and would refuse to do other things, saying: "Amy wouldn't like it."

As Marley's ghost told Scrooge: "I wear the chain I forged in life. I made it link by link, and yard by yard; I girded it on of my own free will, and of my own free will I wore it."

Breaking this fetter, people renounce the world, free from longing and abandoning sensuality. This is the only way, however much the slaves, slave traders and slave owners may screech and deny it. Freedom has a price: a blessed casting aside of bonds and binders. It can be done.

Those on fire

Those on fire with desire follow the stream of their desires, like a spider follows the strands of its self-made web. Breaking the bond, the wise walk on free from longing, and leaving all suffering behind (Dhammapada 347).

Desire is not an external force, it is completely internal, as is temptation and the other passions. In other words, desire is totally self-created, just as is the web of the spider. As the spider roams around in its web, in the same way we roam around in the desires and passions we have created and are working to maintain and increase. We are the only Satan we have to fear and the only Savior in which we can hope. As Buddha points out, we can break the bond and be free from suffering.

Let go

Let go the past, let go the future, and let go what is in between, transcending the things of time. With your mind free in every direction, you will not return to birth and aging (Dhammapada 348).

We must let go of our obsessions, pleasant or painful, with past, present and future, and we must expunge the conditionings of all three as well. For in the present we are forming conditionings, part of which is expectation for the future. Though the future is theoretical, nevertheless our ideas and emotions about it color our present and will carry on into the actual future. Time itself must be transcended by entering into the Transcendent Reality that is beyond time. Buddha called this the Birthless and Deathless where birth, aging and death cannot exist.

How it works

When a man is stimulated by his own thoughts, full of desire and dwelling on what is attractive, his craving increases even more. He is making the fetter even stronger. But he who takes pleasure in stilling his thoughts, practicing the contemplation of what is repulsive, and remaining recollected, now he will make an end of craving, he will snap the bonds of Mara. His aim is accomplished, he is without fear, rid of craving and without stain. He has removed the arrows of changing existence. This is his last body. Rid of craving and without clinging, an expert in the study of texts, and understanding the right sequence of the words, he may indeed be called "In his last body," "Great in wisdom" and a "Great man" (Dhammapada 349-352).

This is completely clear. The only thing I want to point out is the fact that this is all done by us. We bind ourselves and we free ourselves, and the way we do it is right here in this verse. Buddha indicates that such a freed person is conversant with the teachings of the wise, studying and applying them correctly. Such a one may truly be called great.

The free man speaks

"**All-conquering and all-knowing am I. Amidst all states of mind, unaffected am I. By abandoning everything, I am liberated by the cessation of desire. Having achieved Realization by myself, who should I point to as my teacher?" (Dhammapada 353).**

These are the words of one who has truly attained. Once again Buddha shows us that it is all a matter of our doing: discipline, practice, understanding, and liberation. Certainly we all have temporary teachers—including Buddha through his recorded teachings—but ultimately it is our own application and our own experience and insight that free us. Teachers are like highway signs; they point out the way to go, but do not take us a single inch; we go on our own. We are self-taught in the sense that we made the effort on our own and therefore reap the effects on our own. Spiritual self-sufficiency is an absolute requirement, for dependence is delusion and destruction.

Truth

The gift of Truth (dhamma) excels all other gifts; the flavor of Truth excels all other flavors; the delight in Truth surpasses all delights. The destruction of craving overcomes all suffering (Dhammapada 354–Harischandra Kaviratna).

Thanissaro Bhikkhu: "The gift of Dharma conquers all gifts; the taste of Dharma [conquers], all tastes; a delight in Dharma [conquers], all delights; the ending of craving, all suffering and stress."

When Truth (sabba/satya) comes to us and is assimilated fully by us, only truth remains; all other gifts, tastes, and delights are vanquished from our minds and hearts along with the craving, suffering, and stress they bring.

Riches

Riches destroy a fool, but not those who are seeking the other shore. The fool destroys himself by his craving for riches, as he destroys others too (Dhammapada 355).

Those who seek "the other shore" of Nirvana cannot be harmed by materiality, for they do not let it enter their heart. But those who crave material gain destroy themselves and others associated with them in this pursuit, whether supporters and adversaries. It is poison all around.

Offerings to the wise

Fields have the blight of weeds; mankind has the blight of passion; therefore, offerings given to those devoid of passion bring forth abundant fruit.

Fields have the blight of weeds; mankind has the blight of hatred; therefore, offerings given to those devoid of hatred bring forth abundant fruit.

Fields have the blight of weeds; mankind has the blight of delusion; therefore, offerings given to those devoid of delusion bring forth abundant fruit.

Fields have the blight of weeds; mankind has the blight of desire; therefore, offerings given to those devoid of desire bring forth abundant fruit (Dhammapada 356-359—Harischandra Kaviratna).

It is good to give alms to those in need, but Buddha is saying that there is no greater merit in alms than giving to those monks who are free from passion, hatred, delusion, and desire, or who genuinely seek to be free from them.

Chapter 25

THE BHIKKHU

Since the last verses of the previous section pertained to monks, this section will deal them them in depth. "Bhikkhu" literally means "one who lives on alms," but of course that includes anyone who lives on the charity of another, including beggars. So lest monks should pride themselves on their poverty and non-possession—something they have in common with many unfortunate people, though theirs is voluntary—Buddha will describe what a real, worthy bhikkhu is.

Restraint

Restraint of the eyes is good. So is restraint of the ears. Restraint of the nose is good, and so is restraint of the palate.

Restraint of the body is good. So is restraint of speech. Restraint of mind is good, and so is restraint in everything. The bhikkhu who is restrained in everything, is freed from all suffering (Dhammapada 360, 361).

This is very clear and needs no comment.

Restrained

Restrained of hand, restrained of foot, restrained of speech and restrained in his highest faculty [the mind], with his joy turned inwards, his mind still, alone and contented—that is what they call a bhikkhu (Dhammapada 362).

"Restrained of foot" means one who does not wander around aimlessly impelled by a restless and idle mind. As the Gita says: "Only that yogi whose joy is inward, inward his peace, and his vision inward shall come to Brahman and know Nirvana" (Bhagavad Gita 5:24). The true monk is a self-contained person, not a "swell guy" or a "good mixer" with "a great personality." Unhappily, these "personality kids" abound in every monastic tradition, but they are parasites, not monks. Non-monastic spiritual parasites love them, however. Venerable in every sense of the word, the genuine monk lives away from "society" and is contented—for it is discontent that drives a monk out of his retirement into "the swim of things" and turns him into a performing monkey for the delight of the ignorant and anti-spiritual. As the Gita also says: "Turn all your thought toward solitude, spurning the noise of the crowd, its fruitless commotion" (Bhagavad Gita 13:10). There is no other way to true contentment (santosha).

Good to hear

When a bhikkhu is restrained of tongue, quotes wise sayings, and is peaceful, expounding both letter and spirit—his speech is good to hear (Dhammapada 363).

This, too, is clear, but I would like to point out that Buddha mentions that a worthy teacher is peaceful, he does not engage in arguments or polemics of any kind, but speaks calmly and reasonably. He teaches but never entertains. Rather, his speech is quiet and straightforward, devoid of theatrics, cuteness or cleverness.

Steadfast

With joy in the Teaching, delighting in the Teaching, and pondering over the Teaching, the bhikkhu who remembers the Teaching does not fall away from the [true] Teaching (Dhammapada 364).

Thanissaro Bhikkhu: "Dharma his dwelling, Dharma his delight, a monk pondering Dharma, calling Dharma to mind, does not fall away from true Dharma [saddhamma]."

Dharma is the total concern of the worthy monk–it occupies his thoughts and actions, filling the entire horizon of his mind and life. Such a monk is the embodiment of dharma (dharmamayi).

Envy

One should not underestimate what one has got, and one should not live envying others. A bhikkhu who envies others does not achieve stillness of mind in meditation (Dhammapada 365).

Envy is a form of identity with materiality, a poison generated by the selfish and greedy ego.

Praiseworthy

Even if he has only received a little, if a bhikkhu does not look down on what he has received, even the devas praise him, pure of life and determined as he is (Dhammapada 366).

Such a monk as this is the opposite of the one described in sutra 365.

Undefined

When a man is without self-identification with any object or idea, and does not grieve for what does not exist–that is what is called a bhikkhu (Dhammapada 367).

This sutra can be understood in a broad way and in a more defined way, both being valid.

First the broad way. It is necessary for us to cease identification with anything–body, birth, nationality, social situation, associations, and even religious identity. Sometimes when people would approach Sri Ramana Maharshi to ask his blessing to become a monk, he would reply: "Why take on another false identity?" Obviously he saw that instead of really being a monk they would egotistically pride themselves on being a monk–would only look like a monk, but not be one at all. Buddha often warned against the dangers of self-concepts based on either externals or internals (such as emotions, aspirations, personality, etc.). To define ourselves in any terms whatsoever is a grave error. Jesus said: "According to your faith be it unto you" (Matthew 9:29), meaning that however we think of ourselves, so shall it be. We are constantly limiting ourselves in this manner. So Buddha is telling us to have no self-identification with anything material or intellectual. Next he urges us to forget all about what either does not or cannot be–just as did the great Greek philosopher Epictetus. That is why the Zen Master Seung Sung often said the two profound words: "Make Nothing." It is self-torment to agitate ourselves over what is not, just as much as it is to make ourselves miserable over what is in the present, including the fear of something either coming into being or going out of being in the future. Basically, we should care about nothing except our quest for Nirvana. Then we will be worthy disciples of Buddha.

Now the narrower way. Buddha is telling us that we must never desire or reach out for any object or for the fulfillment of an aspiration. This would also include reforming society or launching a movement of any kind, however beneficial or wise it may seem to be. We need to focus on our life and let others live theirs. People censured Buddha for being standoffish and uncaring because he lived in the forest and never went around preaching and converting people. Instead he only taught those who sought him out and asked for wisdom. (On occasion he would go to places where his intuition had shown him there were worthy people, but even then he waited until they asked him for teaching.) So he followed his own counsels. This sutra also tells us to not only be indifferent to external objects or intellectual ideas, but also to not wish that something would come to exist or occur that is not presently existing. We should be detached from all things and not hope for others to come into being. Further, the loss or disappearance of something should be a matter of indifference to us. The wise person neither holds on to or reaches out toward anything. The Bhagavad Gita, too, advises us to not consider anything either desirable or undesirable. We should see things as they are and let them be as they are.

We must keep in mind that such principles as these are not being presented to everyone, only to those who have decided to seek for enlightenment. Society has its own ways, contrary to the Buddha Way, and that, too, should not matter to us. Our assurance should be the next sutra:

The bhikkhu who lives full of goodwill, with faith in the teaching of the Buddha–he will reach the place of peace, the satisfaction of stilling the functions of the mind (Dhammapada 368).

Empty the boat

Empty the boat, bhikkhu. Empty it will sail lightly for you. When you have cut away desire and aversion, you will come to nirvana as a result (Dhammapada 369).

All relative existence is known as "the ocean of samsara," and our aspiration is to cross over it and attain the permanent peace of Nirvana. Our body and mind are the "boat" in which we sail on the samsaric sea. If we do not empty it of everything, its weight will cause it to founder and sink, and we will drown–just as we have done so many lives before. The empty boat sails lightly, but any unnecessary objects will hinder its progress and ultimately sink it. Cutting away desire and aversion is the quick way to reach the other shore and end samsara forever. That is why in the Guild of the Master Jesus, the Christian mystery school of Dion Fortune, one of the prayers included the phrase: "Teach us to travel light, as do all who travel on the Path."

Crossed over

Cut away the five (lower fetters), abandon the five (remaining fetters), and then develop the five (faculties). The bhikkhu who has transcended the five fetters is said to be "crossed over the flood" (Dhammapada 370).

Everybody has their own list of possible factors listed here. Instead of giving mine, here is the translation of Harischandra Kaviratna and his comments:

"'(Of the fetters) cut off the five, renounce the five, and (of the virtues) cultivate the five. He who has gone beyond the five attachments is called a bhikkhu who has crossed the stream.'

"The five fetters that one should cut off are: self-allusion, doubt, clinging to mere rules and rituals, sensuous craving and ill will.

"The five fetters to be renounced are: craving for material existence, craving for immaterial existence, conceit, restlessness, and ignorance.

"To destroy the fetters, the vigilant monk has to cultivate the five virtues: faith, mindfulness, energy, concentration, and wisdom.

"The five attachments are: lust, hatred, delusion, pride, and false views."

Meditate, or...

Meditate, bhikkhu, do not be careless, do not let your mind take pleasure in the senses. Do not have to swallow the iron ball for being careless. Do not have to cry out, "This is terrible" as you burn (Dhammapada 371).

Harischandra Kaviratna: "Meditate, O monk! Be not heedless! Let not your mind wander among the pleasures of the senses, lest through your heedlessness you swallow the red-hot iron ball (in hell) and cry out, as you thus burn–'This is suffering.'" Thanissaro Bhikkhu: "Practice jhana, monk, and don't be heedless. Don't take your mind roaming in sensual strands. Don't swallow–heedless–the ball of iron aflame. Don't burn and complain: 'This is pain.'"

Each of these translations gives a different nuance of meaning, so I have included them. But the basics are in all three.

1) It is made clear that those who do not meditate regularly and deeply will be heedless in mind and careless in their life. It is inescapable.

2) The mind must never graze in the pasture of the senses, but be ever disciplined and restrained from wandering in their poisonous attractions and distractions. Here, too, heedlessness will be the result.

3) Those who are careless and heedless will "swallow the red-hot iron ball" of samsaric existence and inevitably suffer.

4) There is no virtue in just saying "ouch" as we burn inwardly, having swallowed the hot iron ball, just as there is no virtue in the sinner doing nothing more than admitting or confessing his sin. Instead we must expel the burning instrument of our torment, just as the

sinner must forsake his sin. Otherwise there will never be anything but suffering.

Another thing we should keep aware of is the fact that, as Buddha said, suffering has a cause. All our suffering is directly caused by us, not by "fate" or by other persons or any kind of "accident." There is no such thing as "life's lottery" or "luck" good or bad. Our misery is the reaction to our own past action. Certainly we should feel sympathy for those who suffer, but the only thing that will really help them is their learning the way to end suffering. Just being comforted by us will accomplish nothing in the long run, though sometimes that is really all we can do for those who are not evolved enough to comprehend the law of karma and live accordingly.

Meditation and wisdom

There is no meditation without wisdom, and there is no wisdom without meditation. When a man has both meditation and wisdom, he is indeed close to nirvana (Dhammapada 372).

This is as profound as it is brief, and should never be forgotten. A person can gain great intellectual facility and be a living encyclopedia of facts and philosophical theorems, but he will have no wisdom if he does not meditate, and he will not take up meditation if he has no wisdom. Obviously they are simultaneous, a matter of profound evolutionary opening. Moreover, wisdom will fade away from the mind of those that slack off in meditation, and lacking wisdom they will not realize the need to return to their former discipline and intentness on the meditative life. That is why Saint Paul wrote: "We ought to give the more earnest heed to the things which we have heard, lest at any time we should let them slip" (Hebrews 2:1). Another equally legitimate translation is: "It behooves us to attend more earnestly to the things we have heard, lest perhaps we ourselves should slip away" as so many have done before us, easily sliding down the slippery slope of carelessness and inattention.

The good news is that those who cultivate and increase their meditation and wisdom are close to Nirvana.

Alone and at peace

The bhikkhu who has retired to a lonely abode, who has calmed his mind, who perceives the dharma clearly, experiences a joy transcending that of men (Dhammapada 373–Narada Thera).

This sutra reminds me of *The Way of a Pilgrim*, when the pilgrim had the chance to live for a few months in an abandoned, half-ruined hut in an isolated forest: "Then I shut myself up in the hut. Ah! How delighted I was, how calmly happy when I crossed the threshold of that lonely retreat, or rather, that tomb! It seemed to me like a magnificent palace filled with every consolation and delight. With tears of rapture I gave thanks to God and said to myself, Here in this peace and quietude I must seriously set to work at my task [of interior cultivation] and beseech God to give me light."

So it ever is with those who wisely separate themselves from the hamster wheel of society and the hamsters that run in it all day long, getting nowhere and never knowing the truth of their situation. Turning within and bringing peace to their mind, they come to understand the real nature and purpose of dharma. Then they will have a joy inconceivable to others. The Taittiriya Upanishad attempts to convey the nature of that joy in a passage I quoted regarding sutra 27, but it will be good for us to look at it again in relation to this sutra as well:

"Consider the lot of a young man, noble, well-read, intelligent, strong, healthy, with all the wealth of the world at his command. Assume that he is happy, and measure his joy as one unit.

"One hundred times that joy is one unit of the joy of Gandharvas: but no less joy than Gandharvas has the seer to whom the Self has been revealed, and who is without craving.

"One hundred times the joy of Gandharvas is one unit of the joy of celestial Gandharvas: but no less joy than celestial Gandharvas has the sage to whom the Self has been revealed, and who is without craving.

"One hundred times the joy of celestial Gandharvas is one unit of the joy of the Pitris in their paradise: but no less joy than the Pitris in their paradise has the sage to whom the Self has been revealed, and who is without craving.

"One hundred times the joy of the Pitris in their paradise is one unit of the joy of the Devas: but no less joy than the Devas has the sage to whom the Self has been revealed, and who is without craving.

"One hundred times the joy of the Devas is one unit of the joy of the karma Devas: but no less joy than the karma Devas has the sage to whom the Self has been revealed, and who is without craving.

"One hundred times the joy of the karma Devas is one unit of the joy of the ruling Devas: but no less joy than the ruling Devas has the sage to whom the Self has been revealed, and who is without craving.

"One hundred times the joy of the ruling Devas is one unit of the joy of Indra: but no less joy than Indra has the sage to whom the Self has been revealed, and who is without craving.

"One hundred times the joy of Indra is one unit of the joy of Brihaspati: but no less joy than Brihaspati has the sage to whom the Self has been revealed, and who is without craving.

"One hundred times the joy of Brihaspati is one unit of the joy of Prajapati: but no less joy than Prajapati has the sage to whom the Self has been revealed, and who is without craving.

"One hundred times the joy of Prajapati is one unit of the joy of Brahma: but no less joy than Brahma has the seer to whom the Self has been revealed, and who is without craving" (Taittiriya Upanishad 2:8:1-4).

Who, then, would not avidly seek such a joy? Virtually the whole world does not seek it.

Joyful insight

Whenever he meditates on the rise and fall of the constituent elements of existence [the skandas], he experiences joy and rapture. It is immortality for men of discrimination (Dhammapada 374).

Foolish people grieve and complain over the impermanence of the world, but the wise rejoice, knowing that they have made the only right choice in seeking that which is eternal.

First things

Therefore in this teaching, this is what comes first for a wise bhikkhu—guarding of the senses, contentment, and discipline in accordance with the rules of the Order [patimokkha]. He should cultivate friends of good character, of pure behavior and resolute. He should be friendly in his manner, and well-behaved. As a result he will experience great joy, and put an end to suffering (Dhammapada 375, 376).

This is easy to understand, so I will only mention one thing: The only real friends of a seeker for Nirvana are those who will sustain him in his practice by doing so themselves and living up to the same ideals. It is extremely important to only cultivate the friendship of those who also devote their thought and life to achieve liberation. If such persons cannot be found, then the aspirant should live to himself, as Buddha has counseled in previous sutras.

Like the jasmine

In the same way that the jasmine drops its withered flowers, you too should discard desire and aversion, bhikkhus (Dhammapada 377).

The jasmine plant simply lets its withered flowers fall—it lets go of them. In the same way we must let go of all that incites desire and aversion in us, and then the capacity for desire and aversion should also drop away from us. This is a profound change, but it is attainable.

At peace

Peaceful of body, peaceful of speech and with his mind thoroughly stilled, the bhikkhu who has rid himself of attachment to the world—is called "at peace" (Dhammapada 378).

Vantalokamiso literally means to have spit out or vomited up all that pertains to the world. First we calm ourselves and then we purge ourselves—that is the way to peace profound. The world is like a cancer: we must rid ourselves of every little bit of it, especially its roots, if we would live.

Do it yourself

You should encourage yourself, yourself. You should restrain yourself, yourself. When you are self-protected like that, you will live happily as a bhikkhu (Dhammapada 379).

Self-sufficiency is a prime necessity for one who seeks enlightenment. Dependency in any form renders that search impossible. The seeker must be thoroughly self-reliant in all things. Those who are not self-motivated and self-directed will not persevere in their practice. We must empower ourselves and discipline ourselves. Protected by our own self, what can harm us? Then we will be able to live happily as a renouncer of ignorance.

One is one's own guard. What other guard could one have? One is one's own destiny. Therefore one should train oneself, like a merchant does a thoroughbred horse (Dhammapada 380).

We are the only guard and guide we can ever have. Since we ourselves are our only destiny, who else can possibly be involved in the matter? Buddha had to turn from all his teachers and from all the traditions he had learned and bring the truth from within his own self. So must we. We alone can discipline and perfect ourselves. This is the truth Buddha shares with us.

The worthy bhikkhu

The bhikkhu who experiences great joy, and has faith in the teaching of the Buddha, will attain the place of peace, the satisfaction of stilling the functions of the mind.

When a bhikkhu applies himself when still young to the teaching of the Buddha, he illuminates the world, like the moon breaking breaking away from a cloud (Dhammapada 381, 382).

What more need be said? We now need to start "doing."

Chapter 26

THE BRAHMIN

Simplistic statements are almost always wrong or misleading. This is especially true regarding the teachings of Buddha. Few things are sillier than saying that Buddha denied the existence of God or a creator, since he speaks about Brahma the Creator quite readily. Even more foolish is the statement that he denied the existence of an immortal, eternal Self, when he continually speaks of the need to know the Deathless and Birthless. Anatman (anatta) in the Pali language never means "no atman (self)," but "*not*-self," which is a standard expression of Advaita Vedanta. If Buddha had meant there was no self he would have used the word niratman (niratta)–which he never did at any time. Another baseless assertion is that Buddha rejected the idea of caste, which he did not, as he often refers to the castes as a reality. What he did oppose was the caste "system" of his time which was based on birth and not on personal characteristics.

His frequent use of the word "Brahmin" (Brahmana) tells us much. *A Brief Sanskrit Glossary* defines Brahmin in this way: "A knower of Brahman; a member of the highest Hindu caste consisting of priests, pandits, philosophers, and religious leaders." By using this word so much Buddha clearly indicates that Brahman, the Absolute Reality, certainly exists, and so does a caste, or class of human beings, whose dominant trait is that of nearness to the realization of such a Reality. These are the philosophers Plato said were so necessary to a true civilization. This entire section is addressed to them.

Knowing the unconditioned

Cut the stream and go across, abandon sensuality, brahmin. When you have achieved the stilling of the activities of the mind, you will know the unconditioned, brahmin (Dhammapada 383).

The stream of relative, conditioned existence must be cut off and transcended. This is done by turning from the outer senses of illusion and bringing into function the inner senses of true perception. Then the antics and creations of the lower mind must be stopped so the intelligence (buddhi) can come into dominance and further our evolution so that in time (out of time, actually) we will come to know the Unconditioned–Brahman–and thereby become a perfected Brahmana.

Freedom

When a brahmin has crossed beyond duality, then all the fetters of such a seer come to an end (Dhammapada 384).

Harischandra Kaviratna: "When the brahmin has reached the farther shore of the two states (of tranquillity [samatha] and insight [vipassana]), then all the fetters of that knowing one disappear."

Certainly we must go beyond dual consciousness, and definitely that is done by perfection in stillness of mind and heart (samatha) and direct realization (vipassana). So both translations give us a right understanding. This alone results in the dissolving of all bonds that is Nirvana.

Neither "this" nor "that"

When a man knows no "this shore," "other shore," or both—such a one, free from anxiety, liberated, that is what I call a brahmin (Dhammapada 385).

Buddha is underlining the fact that freedom from dual consciousness is the ultimate liberation.

Brahminical qualities

Meditating, free from stain, settled in mind, with work accomplished, without inflowing thoughts, and having achieved the

supreme purpose–that is what I call a brahmin (Dhammapada 386).

Here we have six basic traits of a brahmin, all of them worthy of our scrutiny.

Meditating. A brahmin is not just an occasional meditator, but is always involved in meditation, continuing the process outside of his formal meditation (which should occupy some hours each day) so it is the dominant trait of his life. That is why the Bhagavad Gita more than once speaks of the yogi who is always in meditation.

Free from stain. Purity is another major trait of the brahmin.

Settled in mind. Steadfast and intent on attaining liberation, the brahmin's mind is oriented toward Brahman just as the compass needle ever turns to the north wherever it may be and no matter how much it is moved about.

With work accomplished. This can be interpreted in two ways. 1) The brahmin's obligations to the world are totally finished and his only occupation is realization of the Real. 2) The perfect brahmin has finished his true work in the spirit and is established in Nirvana.

Without inflowing thoughts. He is no longer affected by external factors, so much so that they might as well not exist. He is totally an inward person, seeing Reality within. "Only that yogi whose joy is inward, inward his peace, and his vision inward shall come to Brahman and know Nirvana" (Bhagavad Gita 5:24).

Having achieved the supreme purpose. The supreme purpose is also the only purpose of the brahmin: Nirvana.

The shining Buddha

By day it is the sun which shines, at night the moon shines forth. A warrior shines in his armor, and a brahmin shines in meditation. But at all times, by day and by night, the Buddha shines in his glory (Dhammapada 387).

Here "brahmin" means one who is intent on and near the goal. Such a one shines in meditation–finds his glory in meditation–but a

Buddha shines at all times because he does not just experience the Light or "wear" the Light—he IS the Light.

The truth of things

A brahmin is called so by breaking with evil deeds. It is by pious behavior that a man is called a man of religion, and by casting out blemishes one is called one gone forth (Dhammapada 388).

Harischandra Kaviratna: "Because a man has discarded all evil, he is called a brahmin; because of his balanced conduct, he is called a monk (samana); because he has rid himself of all impurities, he is called a recluse (pabbajita)."

A brahmin is not just a person who decides to try for higher awareness. He is one who has cut off all evil thoughts, words, and deeds. Now we think that such a person is very advanced, but really he is only just ready to begin. This shows how little we understand the nature and extent of authentic dharma.

It is very dramatic to read of a criminal who in an instant becomes reformed and immediately takes up the monastic life, but here Buddha indicates that right behavior at all times is the prerequisite for monastic life. Finally he shows that only those who have cast off all defilements can really be called monks—for pabbajita means "one who has gone forth" in the sense of truly abandoning all lower things and taking up the higher modes of behavior, thought, and consciousness.

Buddha is also implying that a brahmin will progress from brahmin to samana to pabbajita, that all brahmins who remain in their path will in time become full-fledged monastics. Otherwise they would just be stuck back in a kind of pious hamster wheel mode of life. Growth implies change and leaving the lesser for the greater. How else could it be? As Sri Ma Anandamayi told two friends of mine: "Those who practice sadhana automatically become sadhus." So from that we can tell who really practices sadhana and who does not.

Violence, outward and inward

One should not strike a brahmin, and nor should a brahmin lose his temper. Shame on him who strikes a brahmin, and shame on him who loses his temper because of it (Dhammapada 389).

Ahimsa–non-injury and especially non-killing–is a foundational teaching of dharma, Hindu, Jain and Buddhist. Buddha is giving us an example of two forms of himsa (injury): outer action in the form of physical harm, and inner, mental violence arising in the form of anger. Both are infractions of the precept of ahimsa. One who has mental ahimsa will never act harmfully, but without it there is always the possibility of eventual wrongdoing. In the twelfth chapter of *Autobiography of a Yogi* (a text worthy of a lifetime's study) Yogananda give us this incident:

"It was the gentle hour of dusk. My guru was matchlessly interpreting the ancient texts. At his feet, I was in perfect peace. A rude mosquito entered the idyl and competed for my attention. As it dug a poisonous hypodermic needle into my thigh, I automatically raised an avenging hand. Reprieve from impending execution! An opportune memory came to me of one of Patanjali's yoga aphorisms—that on *ahimsa* (harmlessness).

"'Why didn't you finish the job?'

"'Master! Do you advocate taking life?'

"'No; but the deathblow already had been struck in your mind.'

"'I don't understand.'

"'Patanjali's meaning was the removal of *desire* to kill.' Sri Yukteswar had found my mental processes an open book. 'This world is inconveniently arranged for a literal practice of *ahimsa*. Man may be compelled to exterminate harmful creatures. He is not under similar compulsion to feel anger or animosity. All forms of life have equal right to the air of *maya*. The saint who uncovers the secret of creation will be in harmony with its countless bewildering expressions. All men may approach that understanding who curb the inner passion for destruction.'"

The root of violence is egotism. When that has been cut out and thrown away we will have no trouble with violence. Easy to say, not so easy to do, but the masters have shown us the way, having first travelled it themselves.

Restraint

Nothing is better in a brahmin than this—that he restrains his mind from pleasurable things. Suffering disappears for him to the same extent that he gets rid of thoughts of harming anyone (Dhammapada 390).

Harischandra Kaviratna: "It is no small advantage to a brahmin to restrain the mind from clinging to pleasurable things. In proportion to the degree that he abstains from wishing to injure others, to that degree will suffering cease."

When we think of it, both these undesirable factors are clinging to something, for both are like the tar baby in the Uncle Remus story: the more we touch them the more we get stuck up in them and become bound. Attraction and aversion both pull us into the whirlpool of samsara. Contented indifference is our protection and assurance of safety. Therefore:

He who does no wrong with body, speech or mind, but is restrained in all three spheres—that is what I call a brahmin (Dhammapada 391).

Worthy of homage

One should reverently pay homage to the man from whom one has learned the Truth, taught by the True Buddha, like a brahmin does to the sacrificial fire (Dhammapada 392).

Narada Thera: "If from anybody one should understand the doctrine preached by the Fully Enlightened One, devoutly should one reverence him, as a brahmin reveres the sacrificial fire."

Since the old ways are fading away with increasing rapidity in these times, there is little comprehension of how an ancient brahmin revered the sacred fire. It was literally the center of his life, and its maintenance was his supreme obligation. At least twice a day he roused the fire from its sleep in the form of banked coals and made offerings into it, understanding that the fire was the mouth of God and possessed the supernatural power to transfer over into the subtle worlds whatever he offered from the material world. Even more important, at the reciting of the requisite mantras the fire became a living, intelligent deva whose radiations literally entered into his subtle bodies and purified them.

I will never forget when sacred fire was brought to Dehra Dun from Dacca in East Bengal (Bangaladesh) where it had been kept burning for several decades at the direction of Ma Anandamayi. When it was kindled into flame for the first time, Ma motioned for me to come and stand very near and fix my attention on the fire. As I did so, I could feel the subtle radiation penetrating my whole body and the firm conviction arose in my mind that karmas were being consumed and corrections being made in my subtle bodies. When I glanced at Ma she indicated her satisfaction, so I knew I had perceived rightly. Wherever it takes place, in the daily morning kindling of the holy fire at one point the fire becomes alive and remains so.

So when Buddha says to reverence those who teach us the Dharma, he is saying a very serious thing. We should consider them living extensions of the Buddha principle, the Dharmakaya, that dwells in all things. Now if we should so regard the teachers of Dharma, how much, much more then should we revere the Dharma itself. In truth, if Buddha had not given us the Dharma, what value would he be to us? It is the constant failing in religion to value the messenger far above his message. This is a complete reversal of the right order of things.

Wrong externals

One is not a brahmin by virtue of matted hair, lineage or caste. When a man possesses both Truth and righteousness, then he is pure, then he is a brahmin. What use is your matted hair, you fool? What use is your antelope skin? You are tangled inside, and you are just making the outside pretty (Dhammapada 393, 394).

This applies to so many people in so many ways, and it certainly needs no explanation, especially not to those Buddha is calling fools.

Right externals

The man who wears robes made from rags off the dust heap, who is gaunt, with his sinews standing out all over his body, alone meditating in the forest—that is what I call a brahmin (Dhammapada 395).

This is the picture of a brahmin. One time many years ago when I was a novice, I visited the home of a dear friend. Her very outspoken daughter-in-law was there and when she was introduced to me she said in all sincerity: "Wow, this is great! Your clothes are so crummy!" Apparently she had seen enough of Christian monks in habits that looked like costumes. (At one time in the West there was the Order of Saint John the Baptist whose members wore burlap clothes, never cut their hair or shaved, wandered the countryside giving spiritual teaching to whoever would listen, and lived on alms alone, refusing money. The other orders were so shamed by their example that they clamored for the Pope to dissolve the order, which he did.)

Of course it is the solitary meditation that really makes someone a brahmin.

Non-possession

I do not call him a brahmin who is so by natural birth from his mother. He is just a supercilious person if he still has possessions of his own. He who owns nothing of his own, and is without attachment—that is what I call a brahmin (Dhammapada 396).

According to Patanjali, aparigraha (non-possessiveness and non-acquisitiveness) is a requisite for spiritual life. Buddha agreed.

More

Here are a few verses that really need little or no comment, but deserve deep pondering:

He who, having cut off all fetters, does not get himself upset, but is beyond bonds—that liberated man is what I call a brahmin.

He who has cut off both bond and strap, halter as well as bridle, who has removed the barrier, himself a Buddha—that is what I call a brahmin.

He who endures undisturbed criticism, ill-treatment and bonds, strong in patience, and that strength his power—that is what I call a brahmin.

"Without anger, devout, upright, free from craving, disciplined and in his last body—that is what I call a brahmin" (Dhammapada 397-400).

A true brahmin is one who has snapped the bonds of rebirth and will be seen no more in this world under the compulsion of birth. He may return to help others, but it is an act of total freedom and he can nevermore be bound as before. Since he will never identify with body or background he will in a sense not really be "born" at all.

Like water on a lotus leaf, like a mustard seed on the point of an pin, he who is not stuck to the senses—that is what I call a brahmin (Dhammapada 401).

Water cannot soak into a lotus leaf, and a mustard seed is so hard that it cannot be pierced by a pin. Both the water and the pin will simply slip off. In the same way a brahman cannot be affected by any external factors to any degree.

He who has experienced the end of his suffering here in this life, who has set down the burden, freed!—that is what I call a brahmin.

The sage of profound wisdom, the expert in the right and wrong road, he who has achieved the supreme purpose—that is what I call a brahmin.

Not intimate with laity or monks, wandering about with no abode, and few needs—that is what I call a brahmin (Dhammapada 402-404).

Detachment is a cardinal virtue for all sadhakas.

Abandoning violence to all living creatures moving or still, he who neither kills or causes killing—that is what I call a brahmin.

Unagitated amongst the agitated, at peace among the violent, without clinging among those who cling—that is what I call a brahmin (Dhammapada 405, 406).

To be unaffected by those around him is another primary trait of a brahman.

He from whom desire and aversion, conceit and hypocrisy have fallen away, like a mustard seed on the point of a pin—that is what I call a brahmin.

He who utters only gentle, instructive and truthful speech, criticizing no-one—that is what I call a brahmin.

He who takes nothing in the world that has not been given him, long or short, big or small, attractive or unattractive, that is what I call a brahmin.

He who has no desires in this world or the next, without longings, freed!—that is what I call a brahmin.

He who has no attachments and has been freed from uncertainty by realization, who has plunged into the deathless—that is what I call a brahmin.

He who has even here and now transcended the fetter of both good and evil, who is sorrowless, faultless and pure—that is what I call a brahmin.

The man who is stainless, pure, clear and free from impurities like the moon, the search for pleasure extinguished—that is what I call a brahmin.

He who has transcended the treacherous mire of samsara and ignorance, who has crossed over, reached the other shore, meditating, motionless of mind, free from uncertainty, and who is at peace by not clinging to anything—that is what I call a brahmin.

He who by here and now abandoning sensuality, has gone forth a homeless wanderer, the search for pleasure extinguished—that is what I call a brahmin.

He who by here and now abandoning craving, has gone forth a homeless wanderer, the search for pleasure extinguished—that is what I call a brahmin.

He who has abandoned human bonds, and transcended those of heaven, liberated from all bonds—that is what I call a brahmin.

He who has abandoned pleasure and displeasure, is cooled off and without further fuel, the hero who has conquered all worlds—that is what I call a brahmin.

He who has seen the passing away and rebirth of all beings, free of clinging, blessed, awakened—that is what I call a brahmin.

He whose path devas, spirits and men cannot know, whose inflowing thoughts are ended, a saint—that is what I call a brahmin.

He who has nothing of his own, before, after or in between, possessionless and without attachment—that is what I call a brahmin (Dhammapada 407-421).

The perfect brahmin-monk

Verses 415 and 416 speak of one who "has gone forth a homeless wanderer." This is a technical term for formal monastic life. The last two verses of the Dhammapada list the characteristics of such a one, so in conclusion we will look at them in detail.

Bull-like, noble, a hero, a great sage, and a conqueror, he who is motionless of mind, washed clean and awakened—that is what I call a brahmin.

He who has known his former lives and can see heaven and hell themselves, while he has attained the extinction of rebirth, a seer, master of transcendent knowledge, and master of all masteries—that is what I call a brahmin (Dhammapada 422, 423).

Bull-like. This was a common expression in Buddha's day to mean someone who was absolutely fearless. Fear is rooted in the human psyche, and that is why deceptive religion and politics traffic in fear, and even the news media capitalizes on the natural fear response in people. It is the conditioning of countless lifetimes—many in pre-human forms—that is manifesting. Fearfulness comes in many forms, some personal and some social, but all can coerce a person into doing wrong or neglecting the right. For those who are highly evolved, this comes in many subtle forms easy to cover up and ignore. Fear that undermines our integrity and self-respect is usually the last to go, and is very hard to detect and uproot. Yet it must be done.

It is the fearlessness necessary to gain liberation that is referred to in the book of Revelation: "They loved not their lives unto the death" (Revelation 12:11), for Nirvana is of necessity the death of all that binds–that with which we have identified for lives beyond number, so much so that we think its death will be the death of us, when in reality it will be our resurrection into Life. That is why Jesus said: "Whosoever shall seek to save his life shall lose it; and whosoever shall lose his life shall preserve it" (Luke 17:33).

Noble. In a culture where cheapness is "cool" and the order of the day, nobility is not even given a thought. Dignity and integrity are jokes in a society where "getting ahead" is the sole motivation and anyone who sacrifices personal gain or advantage to preserve them is considered a fool and arouses the indignation of those who pursue "the good life" above all. But those who seek liberation must understand and cultivate nobility of thought and life. Simply writing these words has caused a flood of memories to arise, memories of saints and masters I have known, all of whom possessed nobility of character that revealed itself in their every word and act–even their mere presence. All of them were accessible, embodiments of maitri (loving-kindness) and warm friendship. Everyone was at ease in their company, feeling a deep kinship with them. Yet their nobility was never lost sight of. They were the true royalty of humanity. I was always aware that they were living in the heights of consciousness, that they were calling me to ascend those heights as well. They were near and far away at the same time, but if I would I could join them completely. A person who is not a challenge to higher life just by being with us is of no worth to us spiritually.

A hero. Great courage is required to attain the Goal. When we look at the lives of saints of all traditions and ages, we see that they exerted tremendous will power and courage. Consider Buddha beneath the bodhi tree. Cosmic evil–Mara–itself came and threatened to destroy him. It took courage to withstand threats and attempts to overcome him with fear, and even more courage to withstand the blandishments and temptation of pleasure and material ease. It is not enough to just not be a coward: those who aspire to nirvana must be heroic in all things. Tremendous will power must be developed in order to succeed in the struggle with ignorance and evil.

A great sage. A master is not a lovable, naïve, "childlike" ignoramus. He is the embodiment of wisdom and knowledge (jnana). Yogananda used to say that stupid people do not find God. The liberated are possessed of the highest degree of intelligence, even if it is not expressed through academic intellectuality. When I met Swami Sivananda the first thing that impressed me was his incredible intelligence–it was literally awesome.

I have met saints that pretended to be fools, but they were not; their intelligence was impressive. For example, Saint John Maximovitch was thought by many to be a fool–and real fools considered him to be so–but his intellectual power was amazing. When he felt it necessary he could come to grips with the most abstruse aspects of philosophy and theology. I well remember one morning at Holy Trinity Monastery in Jordanville, New York, when nearly everyone was smiling or laughing. Seeing my puzzlement, some of the monks explained that the venerable Archbishop Averky, who lived in the monastery, had gone early in the morning to the library. There he saw many high stacks of books arranged in a circle. Curious, he stepped over the nearest stack, and stepped right on Saint John, who was sitting, asleep, in the circle of books! What a surprise! So everyone was amused by the incident. But since I knew Saint John hardly ever slept, I realized that he had gathered those books and studied them throughout the night, only dozing off momentarily. He was a great intellectual, despite his habitual, disheveled appearance and seemingly eccentric ways. If anyone ever had a mind like a steel trap, it was Saint John Maximovitch.

A conqueror. All spiritual aspirants must be fearless and ruthless warriors, even though their battles are fought inwardly–and occasionally externally, as well. The perfected ones are those that win through the strife and become conquerors. They are battle-scarred but unbowed, fearsome to Mara and his followers.

Some Russian friends of mine became disciples of a great master in Russia. He never wore clothes, saying that in his previous life he had been a naked sadhu in India and got out of the habit of clothing. He travelled throughout Russia, riding on the train without paying (as used to be done by sadhus in better days in India). The Communists were terrified of this (seemingly) defenseless, naked old man, and every few months the newspapers would claim he had died—but he kept right on living. The awakening he helped others to attain was widespread and profound. He was a mighty man of battle, a vanquisher of evil and ignorance.

He who is motionless of mind. Nevertheless, the warrior-master is ever at peace, dwelling in silence of mind and heart that is the fullness of Conscious Light—his own Self. However much his body may move around, his inner awareness remains unmoving. That is why Sri Ramana Maharshi said there was no place for him to "go" when his body would die. When Sri Ma Anandamayi visited his ashram in Tiruvannamalai some years after his mahasamadhi, his disciples begged her to stay there, and she simply replied: "I neither come nor go."

Washed clean. A liberated person has purified himself totally; purification has been a major part of his endeavor, a necessary part of his success. And it has all been accomplished by his own action.

Awakened. A Buddha is one who is all Consciousness (chinmaya). He is not merely aware: he is permanently awake. When someone met Buddha just after his enlightenment, he was astounded at his evident greatness and asked him: "Who are you?" Buddha answered: "I am awake." Nothing more could be said.

He who has known his former lives. Buddha said this was sign of enlightenment, however it is more than mere remembrance—it is understanding the present in the connotation of the past. It is seeing past and present as an organic whole—as consciousness at play.

And can see heaven and hell themselves. Literally a master is everywhere in the sense that he can see/perceive at any moment anything he wills. No matter where his body may be, he can see into all worlds and even interact there. Just as saints have been seen physically in two or more places at once, in the same way a master can be on several planes of being simultaneously. The great Master Yogananda revealed that he was working in other worlds just as much as in this one. This is the practical omnipresence and omniscience of a Buddha.

Has attained the extinction of rebirth. Even if he seems to be born in the future, his consciousness will be untouched, unchanged by the event, so that he will not be "born" in the ordinary sense. Only a body will appear and eventually disappear. To the liberated one, nothing will have really happened at all—only a simple act of will.

Seer. A Buddha "sees" all things at his will, both internally and externally, and sees the inner meaning of all outer things. Nothing is unknown to him, "knowing" being meant in the highest sense.

Master of transcendent knowledge. Dwelling in transcendent consciousness, he is a natural master of transcendent knowledge. Moreover, he can convey that knowledge more completely and perfectly than anyone else, even though some things cannot be expressed in human speech. Yet, often his mere presence enables people to intuitively comprehend those things that cannot be put into words.

Master of all masteries. A Master is a master of all aspects of life. For example, some time ago a man in Benares (Varanasi) was considered to have attained enlightenment, so some people came and tested him. They found that there was no question, either practical or philosophical, that he could not answer. Finally they gave him the needed material and told him to make a pair of shoes—and he did!

Yogananda once decided to paint a picture and produced a masterpiece depicting Krishna. When people marveled at how he could do that, he said: "Krishna came and I painted him." Once when he needed money desperately to pay the bills of the ashram, he invested in stocks and made a huge profit. For quite a while afterward people would come to the ashram and pester him to reveal his secret. He would laugh and say: "I don't know anything about the stock market." He was often visited by one of America's major mathematicians and also by a major physicist, because he was the only person in America they could speak to about their fields who would perfectly understand their ideas and discuss them profitably. One of them remarked that Yogananda must–like him–constantly read to keep up with all the developments. Yogananda smiled and quietly said: "I have not read four books in the last twenty-five years." Knowing That Which Must Be Known, he knew all.

The end of it all

So now we have come to the end of the Dhammapada–but only to the end of my limited, partial understanding. It is my hope that you will continue to read and ponder Buddha's profound wisdom and be inspired to yourself become a Buddha and be a living Dhammapada.

GLOSSARY

Ahimsa: Non-injury in thought, word, and deed; non-violence; non-killing; harmlessness.

Ajahn Fuang Jotiko: A major twentieth-century teacher in the Thai Forest Tradition.

Ananda: Bliss; happiness; joy. A fundamental attribute of Brahman, which is Satchidananda: Existence, Consciousness, Bliss.

Anandamayi Ma: One of the major spiritual figures in twentieth-century India, first made known to the West by Paramhansa Yogananda in his *Autobiography of a Yogi*.

Aparigraha: Non-possessiveness, non-greed, non-selfishness, non-acquisitiveness.

Arya(n): One who is an Arya–literally, "one who strives upward." Both Arya and Aryan are exclusively psychological terms having nothing whatsoever to do with birth, race, or nationality. In his teachings Buddha habitually referred to spiritually qualified people as "the Aryas." Although in English translations we find the expressions: "The Four Noble Truths," and "The Noble Eightfold Path," Buddha actually said: "The Four Aryan Truths," and "The Eightfold Aryan Path."

Ashram(a): A place for spiritual discipline and study, usually a monastic residence. Also a stage of life. In Hinduism life is divided ideally into four stages (ashramas): 1) the celibate student life (brahmacharya); 2) the married household life (grihasta); 3) the life of retirement (seclusion) and contemplation (vanaprastha); 4) the life of total renunciation (sannyasa).

Atma(n): The individual spirit or Self that is one with Brahman. The true nature or identity (self).

Bhagavad Gita: "The Song of God." The sacred philosophical text often called "the Hindu Bible," part of the epic Mahabharata by Vyasa; the most popular sacred text in Hinduism.

Bhikkhu (Bhikshu): One who lives on bhiksha (almsfood); a mendicant; a sannyasi; also a designation of a Buddhist monk.

Brahmacharya: Continence; self-restraint on all levels; discipline; dwelling in Brahman.

Brahman: The Absolute Reality; the Truth proclaimed in the Upanishads; the Supreme Reality that is one and indivisible, infinite, and eternal; all-pervading, changeless Existence; Existence-knowledge-bliss Absolute (Satchidananda); Absolute Consciousness; it is not only all-powerful but all-power itself; not only all-knowing and blissful but all-knowledge and all-bliss itself.

Brahmin: A knower of Brahman.

Buddha: "And awakened one;" one who has attained enlightenment (bodhi), and thereby moksha (liberation). The usual reference to Gautama (Sakyamuni) Buddha of the sixth century B.C,

Buddhi: Intellect; understanding; reason; the thinking mind; the higher mind, which is the seat of wisdom; the discriminating faculty.

Chinmaya: Full of consciousnes; formed of consciousness.

Deva: "A shining one," a god–greater or lesser in the evolutionary hierarchy; a semi-divine or celestial being with great powers, and therefore a "god." Sometimes called a demi-god. Devas are the demigods presiding over various powers of material and psychic nature. In many instances "devas" refer to the powers of the senses or the sense organs themselves.

Devaloka: The world (loka) of the gods.

Dharma: The righteous way of living, as enjoined by the sacred scriptures and the spiritually illumined; characteristics; law; lawfulness; virtue; righteousness; norm.

Dharmakaya: Reality; the Void; the Absolute; Sheath of the Law–the Embodied Law.

Eightfold Path: 1) Right View, 2) Right Intention, 3) Right Speech, 4) Right Action, 5) Right Livelihood, 6) Right Effort, 7) Right Mindfulness, 8) Right Concentration.

Four Truths: 1) There is suffering. 2) Suffering has a cause. 3) Suffering can be ended. 4) There is a way to end suffering.

Gita: Song; The Bhagavad Gita.

Jnana: Knowledge; knowledge of Reality–of Brahman, the Absolute; also denotes the process of reasoning by which the Ultimate Truth is attained. The word is generally used to denote the knowledge by which one is aware of one's identity with Brahman.

Kaivalya: Transcendental state of Absolute Independence; state of absolute freedom from conditioned existence; moksha; isolation; final beatitude; emancipation.

Kama: Desire; passion; lust.

Karma: Karma, derived from the Sanskrit root *kri*, which means to act, do, or make, means any kind of action, including thought and feeling. It also means the effects of action. Karma is both action and reaction, the metaphysical equivalent of the principle: "For every action there is an equal and opposite reaction." "Whatsoever a man soweth, that shall he also reap" (Galatians 6:7). It is karma operating through the law of cause and effect that binds the jiva or the individual soul to the wheel of birth and death. There are three forms of karma: sanchita, agami, and prarabdha. Sanchita karma is the vast store of accumulated actions done in the past, the fruits of which have not yet been reaped. Agami karma is the action that will be done by the individual in the future. Prarabdha karma is the action that has begun to fructify, the fruit of which is being reaped in this life.

Krishna: A Divine Incarnation born in India about three thousand years ago, Whose teachings to His disciple Arjuna on the eve of the Great India (Mahabharata) War comprise the Bhagavad Gita.

Krodha: Anger, wrath; fury.

Mahasamadhi: Literally "the great union [samadhi]," this refers to a realized yogi's conscious departure from the physical body at death.

Maitreya: Friendliness; friendship; love.

Manas(a): The sensory mind; the perceiving faculty that receives the messages of the senses.

Manasic: Having to do with the mind (manas).

Mara: The embodiment of the power of cosmic evil, illusion, and delusion.

Moha: Delusion–in relation to something, usually producing delusive attachment or infatuation based on a completely false perception and evaluation of the object.

Moksha: Release; liberation; the term is particularly applied to the liberation from the bondage of karma and the wheel of birth and death; Absolute Experience.

Muni: "Silent one" (one observing the vow of silence (mauna); sage; ascetic.

Nirvana: Liberation; final emancipation; the term is particularly applied to the liberation from the bondage of karma and the wheel of birth and death that comes from knowing Brahman; Absolute Experience. See Moksha.

Nityananda (Paramhansa): A great Master of the nineteenth and twentieth centuries, and the most renowned So'ham yogi of our times. His Chidakasha Gita contains some of the most profound statements on philosophy and yoga.

Pushpaka: An ancient Indian flying machine.

Ramana Maharshi: A great sage of the twentieth century who lived in Arunachala in South India. He taught the path of Self-Inquiry (Atma Vichara) wherein the person simply turns his awareness within with the unspoken question–the attitude–of "Who am I?" until the self (atma) is revealed.

Sadhaka: One who practices spiritual discipline–sadhana–particularly meditation.

Sadhana: Spiritual practice.

Samadhi: In Buddhist terminology: meditation.

Samsara: Life through repeated births and deaths; the wheel of birth and death; the process of earthly life.

Samsaric: Having to do with samsara; involved with samsara; partaking of the traits or qualities of samsara.

Samsarin: One who is subject to samsara—repeated births and deaths—and who is deluded by its appearances, immersed in ignorance.

Samskara: Impression in the mind, either conscious or subconscious, produced by previous action or experience in this or previous lives; propensities of the mental residue of impressions; subliminal activators; prenatal tendency. See Vasana.

Sanatana Dharma: "The Eternal Religion," also known as "Arya Dharma," "the religion of those who strive upward [Aryas]." Hinduism.

Sankalpa: A life-changing wish, desire, volition, resolution, will, determination, or intention—not a mere momentary aspiration, but an empowering act of will that persists until the intention is fully realized. It is an act of spiritual, divine creative will inherent in each person as a power of the Atma.

Sankhya: One of the six orthodox systems of Hindu philosophy whose originator was the sage Kapila, Sankhya is the original Vedic philosophy, endorsed by Krishna in the Bhagavad Gita (Gita 2:39; 3:3,5; 18:13,19), the second chapter of which is entitled "Sankhya Yoga." The Ramakrishna-Vedanta Wordbook says: "Sankhya postulates two ultimate realities, Purusha and Prakriti. Declaring that the cause of suffering is man's identification of Purusha with Prakriti and its products, Sankhya teaches that liberation and true knowledge are attained in the supreme consciousness, where such identification ceases and Purusha is realized as existing independently in its transcendental nature." Not surprisingly, then, Yoga is based on the Sankhya philosophy.

Sannyasa: Renunciation; monastic life. Sannyasa literally means "total [san] throwing away [as]," absolute rejection.

Sannyasi(n): A renunciate; a monk.

Santosha: Contentment; peacefulness.

Satsang(a): Literally: "company with Truth." Association with godly-minded persons. The company of saints and devotees.

Shankaracharya: The great reformer and re-establisher of Vedic Religion in India around 300 B.C. He is the unparalleled exponent of Advaita (Non-Dual) Vedanta. He also reformed the mode of monastic life and founded (or regenerated) the ancient Swami Order.

Sivananda (Swami): A great twentieth-century Master, founder of the world-wide Divine Life Society, whose books on spiritual life and religion are widely circulated in the West as well as in India.

Skanda: Aggregate; a component of which human beings are comprised, five in number.

Smriti: Memory; recollection; "that which is remembered." In this latter sense, Smriti is used to designate all scriptures except the Vedas and Upanishads (which are considered of greater authority).

Sukha(m): Happiness; ease; joy; happy; pleasant; agreeable.

Sutra: A Buddhist scripture.

Tanha: Craving; desire; thirst.

Tapasya: Austerity; practical (i.e., result-producing) spiritual discipline; spiritual force. Literally it means the generation of heat or energy, but is always used in a symbolic manner, referring to spiritual practice and its effect, especially the roasting of karmic seeds, the burning up of karma.

Trishna: Thirst; craving; desire.

Vairagya: Non-attachment; detachment; dispassion; absence of desire; disinterest; or indifference. Indifference towards and disgust for all worldly things and enjoyments.

Vak: Speech.

Vakya: Word or statement.

Vasana: A bundle or aggregate of similar samskaras. Subtle desire; a tendency created in a person by the doing of an action or by enjoyment; it induces the person to repeat the action or to seek a repetition of the enjoyment; the subtle impression in the mind capable of developing itself into action; it is the cause of birth and experience in general; the impression of actions that remains unconsciously in the mind.

Yama: Yamaraja; the Lord of Death, controller of who dies and what happens to them after death.

Yogananda (Paramhansa): The most influential yogi of the twentieth century in the West, author of *Autobiography of a Yogi* and founder of Self-Realization Fellowship in America.

DID YOU ENJOY
READING THIS BOOK?

Thank you for taking the time to read *Dhammapada for Awakening*. If you enjoyed it, please consider telling your friends or posting a short review at Amazon.com, Goodreads, or the site of your choice.

Word of mouth is an author's best friend and much appreciated.

Get your FREE Meditation Guide

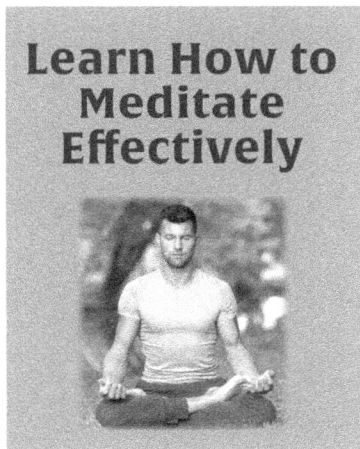

Sign up for the Light of the Spirit Newsletter and get
Learn How to Meditate Effectively.

Get free updates: newsletters, blog posts, and podcasts, plus exclusive content from Light of the Spirit Monastery.

Visit: OCOY.org/signup

About the Author

Swami Nirmalananda Giri (Abbot George Burke) is the founder and director of the Light of the Spirit Monastery (Atma Jyoti Ashram) in Cedar Crest, New Mexico, USA.

In his many pilgrimages to India, he had the opportunity of meeting some of India's greatest spiritual figures, including Swami Sivananda of Rishikesh and Anandamayi Ma. During his first trip to India he was made a member of the ancient Swami Order by Swami Vidyananda Giri, a direct disciple of Paramhansa Yogananda, who had himself been given sannyas by the Shankaracharya of Puri, Jagadguru Bharati Krishna Tirtha.

In the United States he also encountered various Christian saints, including Saint John Maximovich of San Francisco and Saint Philaret Voznesensky of New York. He was ordained in the Liberal Catholic Church (International) to the priesthood on January 25, 1974, and consecrated a bishop on August 23, 1975.

For many years Swami Nirmalananda has researched the identity of Jesus Christ and his teachings with India and Sanatana Dharma, including Yoga. It is his conclusion that Jesus lived in India for most of his life, and was a yogi and Sanatana Dharma missionary to the West. After his resurrection he returned to India and lived the rest of his life in the Himalayas.

He has written extensively on these and other topics, many of which are posted at OCOY.org.

Atma Jyoti Ashram
(Light of the Spirit Monastery)

Atma Jyoti Ashram (Light of the Spirit Monastery) is a monastic community for those men who seek direct experience of the Spirit through yoga meditation, traditional yogic discipline, Sanatana Dharma and the life of the sannyasi in the tradition of the Order of Shankara. Our lineage is in the Giri branch of the Order.

The public outreach of the monastery is through its website, OCOY.org (Original Christianity and Original Yoga). There you will find many articles on Original Christianity and Original Yoga, including he Christ of India. *Foundations of Yoga* and *How to Be a Yogi* are practical guides for anyone seri-ously interested in living the Yoga Life.

You will also discover many other articles on leading an effective spiritual life, including *Soham Yoga: he Yoga of the Self* and *Spiritual Benefits of a Vegetarian Diet*, as well as the "Dharma for Awakening" series—in-depth commentaries on these spiritual classics: the Bhagavad Gita, the Upanishads, the Dhammapada, the Tao Teh King and more.

You can listen to podcasts by Swami Nirmalananda on meditation, the Yoga Life, and remarkable spiritual people he has met in India and elsewhere, at http://ocoy.org/podcasts/

READING FOR AWAKENING

Light of the Spirit Press presents books on spiritual wisdom and Original Christianity and Original Yoga. From our "Dharma for Awakening" series (practical commentaries on the world's scriptures) to books on how to meditate and live a successful spiritual life, you will find books that are informative, helpful, and even entertaining.

Light of the Spirit Press is the publishing house of Light of the Spirit Monastery (Atma Jyoti Ashram) in Cedar Crest, New Mexico, USA. Our books feature the writings of the founder and director of the monastery, Swami Nirmalananda Giri (Abbot George Burke) which are also found on the monastery's website, OCOY.org.

We invite you to explore our publications in the following pages.

Find out more about our publications at
lightofthespiritpress.com

BOOKS ON MEDITATION

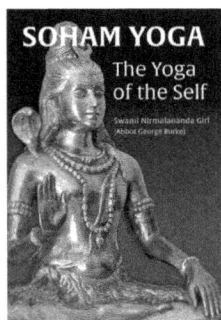

Soham Yoga
The Yoga of the Self

A complete and in-depth guide to effective meditation and the life that supports it, this important book explains with clarity and insight what real yoga is, and why and how to practice Soham Yoga meditation.

Discovered centuries ago by the Nath yogis, this simple and classic approach to self-realization has no "secrets," requires no "initiation," and is easily accessible to the serious modern yogi.

Includes helpful, practical advice on leading an effective spiritual life and many Illuminating quotes on Soham from Indian scriptures and great yogis.

"This book is a complete spiritual path." –Arnold Van Wie

Light of Soham
The Life and Teachings of Sri Gajanana Maharaj of Nashik

Gajanan Murlidhar Gupte, later known as Gajanana Maharaj, led an unassuming life, to all appearances a normal unmarried man of contemporary society. Crediting his personal transformation to the practice of the Soham mantra, he freely shared this practice with a small number of disciples, whom he simply called his friends. Strictly avoiding the trap of gurudom, he insisted that his friends be self-reliant and not be dependent on him for their spiritual progress. Yet he was uniquely able to assist them in their inner development.

The Inspired Wisdom of Gajanana Maharaj
A Practical Commentary on Leading an Effectual Spiritual Life

Presents the teachings and sayings of the great twentieth-century Soham yogi Gajanana Maharaj, with a commentary by Swami Nirmalananda.

The author writes: "In reading about Gajanana Maharaj I encountered a holy personality that eclipsed all others for me. In his words I found a unique wisdom that altered my perspective on what yoga, yogis, and gurus should be.

"But I realized that through no fault of their own, many Western readers need a clarification and expansion of Maharaj's meaning to get the right understanding of his words. This commentary is meant to help my friends who, like me have found his words 'a light in the darkness.'"

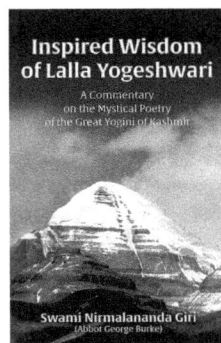

Inspired Wisdom of Lalla Yogeshwari
A Commentary on the Mystical Poetry of the Great Yogini of Kashmir

Lalla Yogeshwari was a great fourteenth-century yogini and wandering ascetic of Kashmir, whose mystic poetry were the earliest compositions in the Kashmiri language. She was in the tradition of the Nath Yogi Sampradaya whose meditation practice is that of Soham Sadhana: the joining of the mental repetition of Soham Mantra with the natural breath.

Swami Nirmalananda's commentary mines the treasures of Lalleshwari's mystic poems and presents his reflections in an easily intelligible fashion for those wishing to put these priceless teachings on the path of yogic self-transformation into practice.

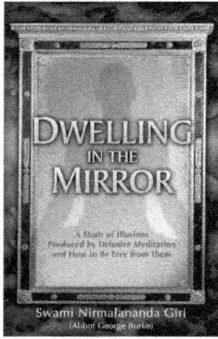

Dwelling in the Mirror

A Study of Illusions Produced By Delusive Meditation
And How to Be Free from Them

Swami Nirmalananda says of this book:

"Over and over people have mistaken trivial and pathological conditions for enlightenment, written books, given seminars and gained a devoted following.

"Most of these unfortunate people were completely unreachable with reason. Yet there are those who can have an experience and realize that it really cannot be real, but a vagary of their mind. Some may not understand that on their own, but can be shown by others the truth about it. For them and those that may one day be in danger of meditation-produced delusions I have written this brief study."

BOOKS ON YOGA & SPIRITUAL LIFE

Satsang with the Abbot

Questions and Answers about Life, Spiritual Liberty,
and the Pursuit of Ultimate Happiness

The questions in this book range from the most sublime to the most practical. "How can I attain samadhi?" "I am married with children. How can I lead a spiritual life?" "What is Self-realization?" "How important is belief in karma and reincarnation?"

In Swami Nirmalananda's replies to these questions the reader will discover common sense, helpful information, and a guiding light for their journey through and beyond the forest of cliches, contradictions, and confusion of yoga, Hinduism, Christianity, and metaphysical thought.

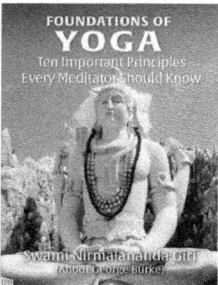

Foundations of Yoga

Ten Important Principles Every Meditator Should Know

An introduction to the important foundation principles of Patanjali's Yoga: Yama and Niyama

Yama and Niyama are often called the Ten Commandments of Yoga, but they have nothing to do with the ideas of sin and virtue or good and evil as dictated by some cosmic potentate. Rather they are determined by a thoroughly practical, pragmatic basis: that which strengthens and facilitates our yoga practice should be observed and that which weakens or hinders it should be avoided.

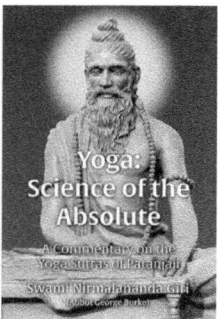

Yoga: Science of the Absolute

A Commentary on the Yoga Sutras of Patanjali

The Yoga Sutras of Patanjali is the most authoritative text on Yoga as a practice. It is also known as the Yoga Darshana because it is the fundamental text of Yoga as a philosophy.

In this commentary, Swami Nirmalananda draws on the age-long tradition regarding this essential text, including the commentaries of Vyasa and Shankara, the most highly regarded writers on Indian philosophy and practice, as well as I. K. Taimni and other authoritative commentators, and adds his own ideas based on half a century of study and practice. Serious students of yoga will find this an essential addition to their spiritual studies.

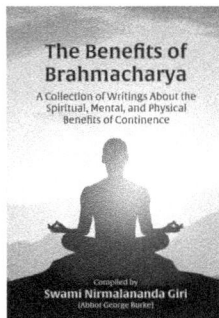

The Benefits of Brahmacharya
A Collection of Writings About the Spiritual, Mental, and Physical Benefits of Continence

"Brahmacharya is the basis for morality. It is the basis for eternal life. It is a spring flower that exhales immortality from its petals." Swami Sivananda

This collection of articles from a variety of authorities including Mahatma Gandhi, Sri Ramakrishna, Swami Vivekananda, Swamis Sivananda and Chidananda of the Divine Life Society, Swami Nirmalananda, and medical experts, presents many facets of brahmacharya and will prove of immense value to all who wish to grow spiritually.

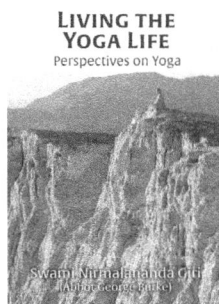

Living the Yoga Life
Perspectives on Yoga

"Dive deep; otherwise you cannot get the gems at the bottom of the ocean. You cannot pick up the gems if you only float on the surface." Sri Ramakrishna

In *Living the Yoga Life* Swami Nirmalananda shares the gems he has found from a lifetime of "diving deep." This collection of reflections and short essays addresses the key concepts of yoga philosophy that are so easy to take for granted. Never content with the accepted cliches about yoga sadhana, the yoga life, the place of a guru, the nature of Brahman and our unity with It, Swami Nirmalananda's insights on these and other facets of the yoga life will inspire, provoke, enlighten, and even entertain.

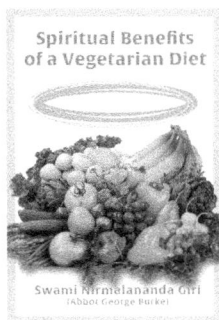

Spiritual Benefits of a Vegetarian Diet

The health benefits of a vegetarian diet are well known, as are the ethical aspects. But the spiritual advantages should be studied by anyone involved in meditation, yoga, or any type of spiritual practice.

Diet is a crucial aspect of emotional, intellectual, and spiritual development as well. For diet and consciousness are interrelated, and purity of diet is an effective aid to purity and clarity of consciousness.

The major thing to keep in mind when considering the subject of vegetarianism is its relevancy in relation to our explorations of consciousness. We need only ask: Does it facilitate my spiritual growth—the development and expansion of my consciousness? The answer is Yes.

BOOKS ON THE SACRED SCRIPTURES OF INDIA

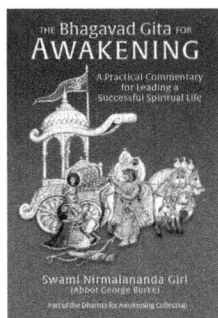

The Bhagavad Gita for Awakening
A Practical Commentary for Leading a Successful Spiritual Life

Drawing from the teachings of Sri Ramakrishna, Jesus, Paramhansa Yogananda, Ramana Maharshi, Swami Vivekananda, Swami Sivananda of Rishikesh, Papa Ramdas, and other spiritual masters and teachers, as well as his own experiences, Swami Nirmalananda illustrates the teachings of the Gita with stories which make the teachings of Krishna in the Gita vibrant and living.

From *Publisher's Weekly*: "[The author] enthusiastically explores the story as a means for knowing oneself, the cosmos, and one's calling within it. His plainspoken insights often distill complex lessons with simplicity and sagacity. Those with a deep interest in the Gita will find much wisdom here."

The Upanishads for Awakening
A Practical Commentary on India's Classical Scriptures

The sacred scriptures of India are vast. Yet they are only different ways of seeing the same thing, the One Thing which makes them both valid and ultimately harmonious. That unifying subject is Brahman: God the Absolute, beyond and besides whom there is no "other" whatsoever. The thirteen major Upanishads are the fountainhead of all expositions of Brahman.

Swami Nirmalananda illumines the Upanishads' practical value for spiritual seekers from the unique perspective of a lifetime of study and practice of both Eastern and Western spirituality.

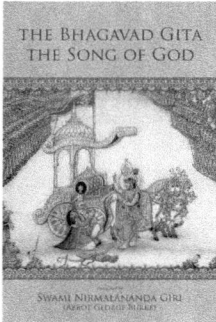

The Bhagavad Gita–The Song of God

Often called the "Bible" of Hinduism, the Bhagavad Gita is found in households throughout India and has been translated into every major language of the world. Literally billions of copies have been handwritten or printed.

The clarity of this translation by Swami Nirmalananda makes for easy reading, while the rich content makes this the ideal "study" Gita. As the original Sanskrit language is so rich, often there are several accurate translations for the same word, which are noted in the text, giving the spiritual student the needed understanding of the fullness of the Gita.

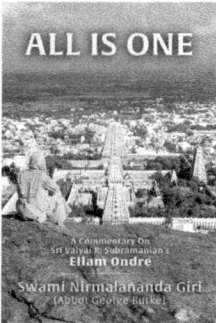

All Is One
A Commentary On Sri Vaiyai R. Subramanian's Ellam Ondre

"I you want moksha, read and practice the instructions in Ellam Ondre." –Ramana Maharshi

Swami Nirmalananda's insightful commentary brings even further light to Ellam Ondre's refreshing perspective on what Unity signifies, and the path to its realization.

Written in the colorful and well-informed style typical of his other commentaries, it is a timely and important contribution to Advaitic literature that explains Unity as the fruit of yoga sadhana, rather than mere wishful thinking or some vague intellectual gymnastic, as is so commonly taught by the modern "Advaita gurus."

A Brief Sanskrit Glossary
A Spiritual Student's Guide to Essential Sanskrit Terms

This Sanskrit glossary contains full translations and explanations of hundreds of the most commonly used spiritual Sanskrit terms, and will help students of the Bhagavad Gita, the Upanishads, the Yoga Sutras of Patanjali, and other Indian scriptures and philosophical works to expand their vocabularies to include the Sanskrit terms contained in these, and gain a fuller understanding in their studies.

BOOKS ON ORIGINAL CHRISTIANITY

The Christ of India
The Story of Original Christianity

"Original Christianity" is the teaching of both Jesus and his Apostle Saint Thomas in India. Although it was new to the Mediterranean world, it was really the classical, traditional teachings of the rishis of India that even today comprise the Eternal Dharma, that goes far beyond religion into realization.

In *The Christ of India* Swami Nirmalananda presents what those ancient teachings are, as well as the growing evidence that Jesus spent much of his "Lost Years" in India and Tibet. This is also the story of how the original teachings of Jesus and Saint Thomas thrived in India for centuries before the coming of the European colonialists.

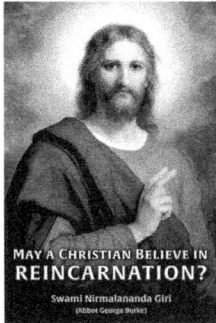

May a Christian Believe in Reincarnation?

Discover the real and surprising history of reincarnation and Christianity.

A growing number of people are open to the subject of past lives, and the belief in rebirth–reincarnation, metempsychosis, or transmigration–is commonplace. It often thought that belief in reincarnation and Christianity are incompatible. But is this really true? May a Christian believe in reincarnation? The answer may surprise you.

"Those needing evidence that a belief in reincarnation is in accordance with teachings of the Christ need look no further: Plainly laid out and explained in an intelligent manner from one who has spent his life on a Christ-like path of renunciation and prayer/ meditation."—Christopher T. Cook

The Unknown Lives of Jesus and Mary
Compiled from Ancient Records and Mystical Revelations

"There are also many other things which Jesus did, the which, if they should be written every one, I suppose that even the world itself could not contain the books that should be written." (Gospel of Saint John, final verse)

You can discover much of those "many other things" in this unique compilation of ancient records and mystical revelations, which includes historical records of the lives of Jesus Christ and his Mother Mary that have been accepted and used by the Church since apostolic times. This treasury of little-known stories of Jesus' life will broaden the reader's understanding of what Christianity really was in its original form.

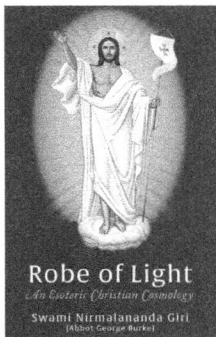

Robe of Light
An Esoteric Christian Cosmology

In *Robe of Light* Swami Nirmalananda explores the whys and wherefores of the mystery of creation. From the emanation of the worlds from the very Being of God, to the evolution of the souls to their ultimate destiny as perfected Sons of God, the ideal progression of creation is described. Since the rebellion of Lucifer and the fall of Adam and Eve from Paradise flawed the normal plan of evolution, a restoration was necessary. How this came about is the prime subject of this insightful study.

Moreover, what this means to aspirants for spiritual perfection is expounded, with a compelling knowledge of the scriptures and of the mystical traditions of East and West.

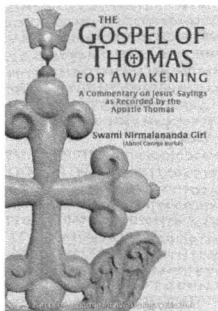

The Gospel of Thomas for Awakening
A Commentary on Jesus' Sayings as Recorded by the Apostle Thomas

When the Apostles dispersed to the various area of the world, Thomas travelled to India, where evidence shows Jesus spent his Lost Years, and which had been the source of the wisdom which he had brought to the "West."

The Christ that Saint Thomas quotes in this ancient text is quite different than the Christ presented by popular Christianity. Through his unique experience and study with both Christianity and Indian religion, Swami Nirmalananda clarifies the sometimes enigmatic sayings of Jesus in an informative and inspiring way.

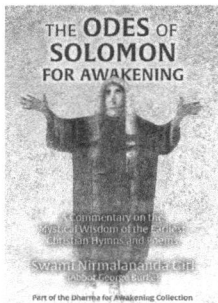

The Odes of Solomon for Awakening
A Commentary on the Mystical Wisdom of the Earliest Christian Hymns and Poems

The Odes of Solomon is the earliest Christian hymn-book, and therefore one of the most important early Christian documents. Since they are mystical and esoteric, they teach and express the classical and universal mystical truths of Christianity, revealing a Christian perspective quite different than that of "Churchianity," and present the path of Christhood that all Christians are called to.

"Fresh and soothing, these 41 poems and hymns are beyond delightful! I deeply appreciate Abbot George Burke's useful and illuminating insight and find myself spiritually re-animated." –John Lawhn

The Aquarian Gospel for Awakening (2 Volumes)
A Practical Commentary on Levi Dowling's Classic Life of Jesus Christ

Written in 1908 by the American mystic Levi Dowling, The Aquarian Gospel of Jesus the Christ answers many questions about Jesus' life that the Bible doesn't address. Dowling presents a universal message found at the heart of all valid religions, a broad vision of love and wisdom that will ring true with Christians who are attracted to Christ but put off by the narrow views of the tradition that has been given his name.

Swami Nirmalananda's commentary is a treasure-house of knowledge and insight that even further expands Dowling's vision of the true Christ and his message.

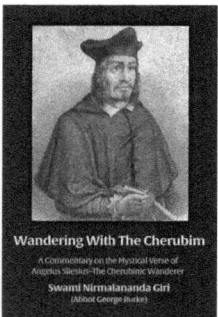

Wandering With The Cherubim
A Commentary on the Mystical Verse of Angelus Silesius–The Cherubinic Wanderer"

Johannes Scheffler, who wrote under the name Angelus Silesius, was a mystic and a poet. In his most famous book, "The Cherubinic Wanderer," he expressed his mystical vision.

Swami Nirmalananda reveals the timelessness of his mystical teachings and The Cherubinic Wanderer's practical value for spiritual seekers. He does this in an easily intelligible fashion for those wishing to put those priceless teachings into practice.

"Set yourself on the journey of this mystical poetry made accessible through this very beautifully commentated text. It is text that submerges one in the philosophical context of the Advaita notion of Non Duality. Swami Nirmalananda's commentary is indispensable in understanding higher philosophical ideas, for Swami's language, while readily approachable, is rich in deep essence of the teachings."–Savitri

BOOKS ON BUDDHISM & TAOISM

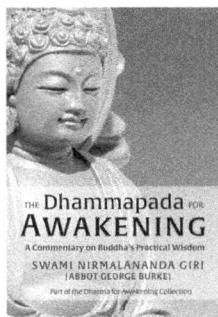

The Dhammapada for Awakening
A Commentary on Buddha's Practical Wisdom

Swami Nirmalananda's commentary on this classic Buddhist scripture explores the Buddha's answers to the urgent questions, such as "How can I find find lasting peace, happiness and fulfillment that seems so elusive?" and "What can I do to avoid many of the miseries big and small that afflict all of us?" Drawing on his personal experience and on parallels in Hinduism and Christianity, the author sheds new light on the Buddha's eternal wisdom.

"Swami Nirmalananda's commentary is well crafted and stacked with anecdotes, humor, literary references and beautiful quotes from the Buddha. I found it to be entertaining as well as illuminating, and have come to consider it a guide to daily living."
–Rev. Gerry Nangle

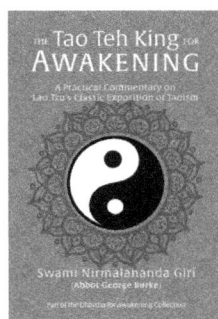

The Tao Teh King for Awakening
A Practical Commentary on Lao Tzu's Classic Exposition of Taoism

"The Tao does all things, yet our interior disposition determines our success or failure in coming to knowledge of the unknowable Tao."

Lao Tzu's classic writing, the Tao Teh King, has fascinated scholars and seekers for centuries. His presentation of the Tao which is the Eternal Reality, and the Way of the Sage that is the path to the realization of and dwelling in this Reality is illuminating, but its deeper meanings and practical applications remain obscure to many, especially in the West.

Swami Nirmalananda offers a commentary that makes the treasures of Lao Tzu's teachings accessible and applicable for the sincere seeker.

More Titles

The Four Gospels for Awakening

Light on the Path for Awakening

How to Read the Tarot

Light from Eternal Lamps

Vivekachudamani: The Crest Jewel of Discrimination for Awakening

Magnetic Therapy: Healing in Your Hands

Sanatana Dharma: The Eternal Religion